FEDERAL MANAGEMENT REFORM IN A WORLD OF CONTRADICTIONS

FEDERAL MANAGEMENT REFORM IN A WORLD OF CONTRADICTIONS

Beryl A. Radin

Georgetown University Press
WASHINGTON, DC

Georgetown University Press, Washington, D.C. www.press.georgetown.edu

Library of Congress Cataloging-in-Publication Data

Radin, Beryl.
  Federal management reform in a world of contradictions / Beryl A. Radin.
      p. cm.—(Public management and change series)
  Includes bibliographical references and index.
  ISBN 978-1-58901-892-1 (pbk. : alk. paper)
1. Civil service reform—United States.   2. Public administration—United States.
3. Administrative agencies—United States—Management.   I. Title.
  JK692.R33 2012
  352.3'670973—dc23   2011036097

⊗ This book is printed on acid-free paper meeting the requirements of the American National Standard for Permanence in Paper for Printed Library Materials.

15 14 13 12   9 8 7 6 5 4 3 2 First printing

Printed in the United States of America

CONTENTS

LIST OF FIGURES AND TABLES

Figures

Tables

PREFACE

FOR MOST AUTHORS THE PROCESS OF WRITING A BOOK PROVIDES AN INTER-esting story. But this book had unusual origins and a path that was often bittersweet.

The idea for this work began in synagogue on Yom Kippur 2009. One of the congregation members gave what is called "the drash"—something like a sermon that is meant to provide the congregants with ideas that put the ritual in an inspirational framework.

Thus I heard Dennis Kirschbaum talk about one of his favorite films, *Groundhog Day,* and suggest the message that it provided was relevant to the Day of Atonement. He noted, "Yom Kippur represents an opportunity, a unique space in time when, if we do what we need to do, we can go forward into this new year and be different." He quoted Rabbi Sharon Brous, who writes that the reason we "choose not to change, is because we believe that we are already finished. That who we are now is who we must be. That we are so entrenched that there is no way to start anew."

This was an unusual challenge. At first I responded to it as an individual, thinking about family, friends, and personal issues. But then I began to think about this message as a call to think about the world of federal management reform—the topic that has largely preoccupied me over forty years as a scholar and sometimes practitioner.

As I thought about the range of reforms that I had studied over the years—reorganization, performance measurement, budgeting, personnel, federalism, and contracting out—I had the sense that my colleagues and the public management community were trapped in a dynamic very much like that experienced by the "hero" of the movie. We seemed to be repeating the same behavior and the same prescriptions time and time again and yet very little changed. Our goals were commendable but our means did not accomplish those goals.

I was sitting in the synagogue with one of my closest and longtime friends, Carla Cohen, the founder of the incredible Washington bookstore, Politics and Prose. We were both struck by Kirschbaum's remarks and they became the basis for conversations that lasted over a year and often involved Carla's husband, David.

But as the months progressed and the book took form in my mind, Carla had to deal with a rare form of cancer that eventually overpowered her in

October 2010. She received the diagnosis of bile duct cancer in November. It was only in the last month or so of her life that she was unable to engage in the energetic exchange of ideas that so characterized her incredibly vital life. Soon after she died my writing was interrupted by my own health scare.

Thus this book is dedicated to Carla Furstenberg Cohen. I had looked forward to launching the book at Politics and Prose with Carla at the helm (like I had done with four other books). Perhaps that launch will occur. But it will not be the same without her.

During the development of this argument I received advice from a number of colleagues and friends. These included Robert Agranoff, Susannah Ali, Howell Baum, Ann Bowman, David Cohen, George Frederickson, John Hart, Stephanie Newbold, Paul Posner, Norma Riccucci, Colin Talbot, John Uhr, Bill West, and several anonymous reviewers. And I continue to appreciate the advice of Don Jacobs of Georgetown University Press.

INTRODUCTION

THIS IS A BOOK THAT IS LIKELY TO STIR HEATED DEBATE IN SOME PARTS OF the public management community in terms of both substance and methodological approach. It emphasizes problems and limitations that have emerged from a path and agenda that represent some core beliefs of the public administration/public management field. The book's approach emerged because I have attempted to sort out the differences between the reforms that come from those core beliefs and the acknowledgment that there are issues that cannot be resolved in a way that satisfies many scholars and practitioners. So I begin this volume in the spirit of Plato, who advised that "the only true wisdom is in knowing you know nothing" and that "an unexamined life is not worth living."

Clearly there are instances of success in specific areas of management reform. And certainly there is a need for reform in many areas and processes within the federal government. But examining the efforts over the past fifty years does not provide an optimistic picture of the reform agenda.[1] When we look at the time and energy expended in the reform process, it appears that we have not learned much from the analyses of problems experienced with implementation of the reforms. Rather, we seem to repeat similar strategies without making the changes that these analyses suggest should be made the next time that proposals are advanced for change.

This generates a sense of running in place. It is not a case of incremental decision making but of repetition of similar approaches that have limited success. The result is the absence of improvements in the situations that stimulated the desire for reform. It seems to me that federal management reformers have not even achieved the changes that Charles Lindblom envisioned in his work "Muddling Through" as he offered an alternative to what he called the "synoptic" or comprehensive model of decision making.[2] Lindblom would expect there to be gradual learning. In that sense, what I have found is more depressing than acknowledging the limits of incrementalism; it is difficult to identify even marginal improvements in the management reform efforts.[3]

Many of the comments that are made in this volume rest on earlier work that I have completed on a number of the issues examined in this book.[4] My past work on reorganization, performance measurement, and federalism especially circled around the contradictions that I have identified within the US system, and my summary comments about these reforms (and the others) rest on that quite detailed work.

There are several themes drawn from this past work that are emphasized in this volume. First is the tendency in the public administration field to avoid politics and the role of the political institutions within the United

States as reform agendas are devised and implemented. The second theme revolves around the analytic methodologies used to examine the reform experience. And the third focuses on the interaction (or lack of interaction) between academic perspectives on reform and the multiple players within the world of practice.

Despite the rhetoric in the academy that the politics-administration dichotomy is dead, I have found that my colleagues are very uncomfortable about raising issues dealing with politics.[5] This is particularly true in confronting the role and structure of Congress in nearly every federal management reform effort. The contemporary reality of complexity, conflict, and partisanship in Congress makes dealing with this set of players difficult but, given the US structure, inevitable. This book does provide some examples of efforts involving Congress but most often those efforts are rejected by the executive branch.

Methodologically this volume is also vulnerable to criticism by some academics. As Norma Riccucci has noted, because the public administration field "lacks a paradigm, it cannot be treated as a normal science in the Kuhnian sense. Instead, public administration is a postnormal science, one that is driven by multiple norms and traditions, and hence can be studied through a variety of epistemic and ontological lenses."[6]

Unlike research that seeks to prove or disprove an existing theory, the methodology that is used in this volume employs a combination of and variation on grounded theory and meta-analysis of extant analytical work as it seeks to generate new theories. Grounded theory, conceived by Barney Glaser and Anselm Strauss, has been described as almost the reverse of the scientific method.[7] It does not begin by researching and developing a hypothesis but uses data collection through a variety of methods to generate new theories.

Thus the six different reform areas discussed in this book are examined using a variety of information sources. The specific works cited do not represent new analyses; this is not a book that attempts to create new sources of information. Rather, it is an attempt to use existing analyses of the specific reform efforts and look at them through a different lens—the contradictions that characterize the US system. The volume focuses on the ways that all six of the reforms appear to shy away from dealing with three critical contradictions that are a part of the American political and social fabric—structural dimensions of the system of shared powers, multiple values and approaches, and political and administrative attributes of the US public sector. Each of the chapters draws on both academic and practice examples to illustrate the general problem with the strategies employed.

While this approach is not the usual pathway taken by public management scholars, it has received attention from some quarters both in the academy and in the world of practice. John Fenwick and Janice McMillan's collection of essays dealing with public management in what they call the postmodern era provides ways of thinking about the field as it confronts an era of constant change.[8] A variation on this approach is also found in what has been described as "a new breed of consultants" working with private-sector companies. As reported in the *New York Times,* this approach indicates that "much of corporate America has gone meta—it has started thinking about thinking."[9] The article highlights a California consulting group called JUMP that focuses on new ways to frame issues and to find opportunities to generate new ideas, unlearn existing beliefs and practices, and tune in and tune out possibilities.

Both of these examples combine the world of the academy and that of practitioners. This is important because academic reality is not always reflected in the world of practice and, conversely, academics do not always pay attention to the practitioner world. A field such as public administration has to keep its eye on both settings. Thus this book has been written for a range of players from both worlds who are involved in the federal management reform process. It is my hope that decision makers in both legislative and executive-branch settings will be interested in this argument. I am concerned about the ways that advisers to decision makers (both practitioners and academics) base their advice on assumptions that are inappropriate or at least limited in their application within the US system. It is my hope that these issues can become a part of the mind-set of students in programs of public administration and management.[10]

This book does not provide a map to a clear alternative pathway. That is likely to be problematic for readers who want a clear GPS system on which to base their advice. Rather, this book is a call for modesty and reality in the way that we frame management reform efforts and define the participants in those initiatives. It is my hope that this book provides a way for academics and practitioners to think about federal management reform in new ways. I seek to open the door to new queries about past approaches. It is time to at least consider departing from the same conceptual and strategic road along which we have already traveled.[11]

The Structure of This Book

Chapter 1 provides a historical and conceptual background for the volume that follows. Chapters 2 and 3 of the volume relate the source of the reforms to two constant debates within the public administration field. The first is the debate about the level of differences between the public and private sectors and the increasing tendency within the discipline to use private-sector assumptions, values, and vocabulary to describe changes for public organizations. The second debate involves the differences between structures/forms of democratic government, particularly the presidential, parliamentary, and shared power systems as well as structures of federalism. These two debates are particularly relevant because a number of the reforms began either in the private sector or in parliamentary systems.

Chapters 4 through 9 examine each of the categories of reform efforts separately, describing the initiatives that have been proposed and debated within each topic area and the way that those initiatives have dealt with the three areas of contradictions. Each chapter identifies both literatures and initiatives that are illustrative of past efforts and approaches. The discussions will indicate whether the reforms acknowledged the contradictions, sought to create trade-offs between those contradictory elements, or rested on one or another of the elements.

Chapter 4 focuses on contracting out, particularly the effort within the federal government through the Office of Management and Budget (OMB) circular A-76 (and its amendments) to find a way to differentiate between what are known as inherently governmental functions and those functions that can be contracted out.

Chapter 5 examines efforts related to personnel policy reform, particularly the ideas that began with the Civil Service Reform Act of 1978 and subsequent proposals.

Chapter 6 focuses on reorganization efforts. It highlights assumptions about the authority base for reorganization as well as the arguments that have been used to justify reorganizations. These will be contrasted with the results of several reorganization decisions.

Chapter 7 looks at the various budget reform efforts that have been proposed over the years, their relationship to earlier efforts (such as the Planning, Programming, and Budgeting System), and the sources of their concepts.

Chapter 8 analyzes the efforts to deal with policies and procedures relating to federalism and intergovernmental relations. It highlights the assumptions that were used to justify these approaches.

Chapter 9 deals with performance measurement, focusing on the Government Performance and Results Act as well as the Bush administration's Program Assessment Rating Tool. It examines the conflicts that have emerged as these requirements have been implemented. It is discussed last because performance measurement intersects with a number of the other reform areas.

The final chapter will describe patterns of behavior across the six reform areas. It will focus on the possibility of devising alternative strategies to achieve management reform. It will also offer suggestions about posing these alternatives in new ways, highlighting practitioner as well as theoretical choices. The conclusion will draw lessons from the academic literature as well as practices that support other approaches.

Notes

1. There are a number of issues that can be confronted in a reform agenda. For the purposes of this book, they include contracting out, personnel policy, reorganization, budgeting, federalism, and performance measurement.
2. See the special issue of *Policy and Society* 30, no. 1 (February 2011), especially Allison and Saint-Martin, "Half a Century of 'Muddling.'"
3. There continue to be groups and individuals involved with public management reform who emphasize positive aspects of various efforts. For example, a report titled "Securing the Future: Management Lessons of 9/11," issued by the Partnership for Public Service and Booz Allen Hamilton in August 2011, commented that "the majority of people we interviewed felt the creation of the department [of Homeland Security] was the right decision and well worth the effort" (p. 1).
4. Specific citations to this work are found in the pages that follow.
5. I cannot count the number of times I have sat in meetings of the National Academy of Public Administration and raised issues about the role of Congress in the public administration world. My colleagues at these meetings always seem to look at me as if I am describing some unnatural behaviors.
6. Riccucci, *Public Administration*, 4.
7. See Glaser and Strauss, *Discovery of Grounded Theory.*
8. See Fenwick and McMillan, *Public Management.*
9. See David Segal, "Corporate America Wants Help Coming Up with Fresh Ideas," *New York Times Magazine*, December 19, 2010.
10. My own career has involved movement between the university and the world of practice and I have found that this gives me a perspective on classic public administration issues that is different from views that are generated only from the formal academic literature.
11. In 1946 a young Herbert Simon published "The Proverbs of Administration." In that post–World War II environment he found that the public administration field was "rationalizing behavior that has already taken place or justifying action that has already been decided upon" (p. 53). He pointed to the use of proverbs as a way to find "equally plausible and acceptable contradictory principles." One could say that the field has moved away from proverbs to rules.

1

THE BACKGROUND

Do I contradict myself?
Very well then I contradict myself,
(I am large, I contain multitudes.)

Walt Whitman

The gods had condemned Sisyphus to ceaselessly rolling a rock up to the top of a
mountain, whence the stone would fall back of its own weight. They had thought
with some reason that there is no more dreadful punishment than this futile and
hopeless labor.

Albert Camus, *The Myth of Sisyphus and Other Essays*

If you listen to the people who are working with the problem, oftentimes they also
have the solution. They just don't have the confidence in their solution. Sometimes
they don't believe that somebody's going to hear them. They just kind of keep it
to themselves. So a mistake oftentimes made by managers and leaders is to bring
solutions from outside without engaging the people who are really involved.

Rajiv Jain, US Department of Veterans Affairs,
quoted in Partnership for Public Service and Hay
Group, "Leading Innovation in Government"

IT IS NOT SURPRISING THAT THE US PUBLIC ADMINISTRATION FIELD DURING
the twentieth and now the twenty-first centuries has emerged with a strong
interest in management reform. Growth in the role of government in the
American society during this period has provoked attention to the way that
the public sector operates. At the same time, major shifts in the US economy
have challenged the assumption that the United States will continue to expand and grow. This has occurred at all levels of government, illustrated by
efforts in state, local, and federal jurisdictions.

It is not an exaggeration, however, to characterize the totality of these
reform efforts as "lots of reform, little accomplished, and not much learning
about why the problems occurred."[1] Or, as another put it, "In hindsight, we
might conclude that whilst the goals of a reform were usually desirable, the
mechanisms themselves were often far from perfect. The promised benefits
of the reform were theoretical—the actual implementation impacts were
not."[2] A more recent overview of the government-wide reform efforts in the
United States noted that they "might have helped on the margins, but the
keys to successful turnarounds are found within the individual agencies."[3]

Despite the many changes that have occurred in the society during these
years (and the use of a marginally different vocabulary to describe the

reforms), one cannot help but be struck by the repetition that occurs in the assumptions used in conceptualizing the changes as well as the similarity in techniques that are devised.

There are several relatively recent developments in the field that have had an impact on the contours of management reform initiatives found both in the United States and abroad. While these efforts can be clustered under the concept of "new public management" they did have different pathways toward influence. The 1992 publication of David Osborne and Ted Gaebler's book *Reinventing Government* in the United States occurred about the same time that a movement titled new public management (NPM) emerged in the United Kingdom and New Zealand.[4] Both of these efforts relied on the belief that public management should look to practices in the private sector for prescriptions to achieve change. While many scholars have focused on the expectations associated with this movement, others agree with Larry Lynn who (over a decade ago) argued that "New Public Management is an ephemeral theme likely to fade." He wrote that this is likely to occur for four reasons: the impact of political succession, awareness of differences across countries, the term "new" seems out of date, and political debate requires a "fresh theme."[5]

Christopher Hood has characterized the rise of NPM as confronting the problem of "administrative limits—in the sense of constraints or bounds on what can be achieved by the activity of administration in general and public administration in particular." He distinguishes between administrative limits (dealing with the politics over contested issues) and technical limits ("what is feasibly taxable and how far or how quickly complex public service systems can be reprogrammed").[6] Some of these issues transcend political structures and systems and others stem from different cultural or ideological biases.

Hood also has linked NPM to four other "administrative 'megatrends'": attempts to slow down or reverse government growth, privatization and quasi privatization, automation, and the development of a more international agenda. He also notes that "there is no single accepted explanation or interpretation of why NPM coalesced or why it 'caught on.'"[7] Hood offers several possible explanations for this—the fashion interpretation, the response to economic and social conditions, the debates within the theoretical framework of public administration. But he seems to be particularly struck by what he calls the view of NPM as a "cargo cult" phenomenon—"the endless rebirth, in spite of repeated failures, of the idea that substantive success ('cargo') can be gained by the practice of particular kinds of (managerial) ritual."[8]

The American Experience

We can look to the recent efforts to understand the management reform agenda across the globe but the American experience in this area has its own particular story. Thus it is important to place these approaches in a broader context of US history. The American experience does have unique qualities since unlike the European tradition it did not have a traditional administrative apparatus that was linked to the authority of the royal court or the church. Until the development of industrialization after the Civil War, a public administration agenda (or even a vocabulary) was not a part of the American context.

Thus stepping back to earlier decades, we see the appearance of a number of themes that deal with theories of government, theories of management, and impact of the political system (both in partisan terms and also in terms of structures of government). From the publication of *The Federalist Papers* onward, it was clear that those who designed the US system envisioned a governmental structure that encompassed multiple and often conflicting values. The voices of Alexander Hamilton and James Madison in that volume clearly represented divergent views about governance, and neither really focused on the role of administrative systems in any detail.

While this book looks at specific initiatives related to federal-level management reform, it is important to link these developments to the general intellectual history of public administration in the United States. One can emphasize the nuts and bolts of management reform proposals, but it is relevant to place those proposals in the context of the identity of the American institutional structure as well as the public administration field itself. The substance of this attention reflects classic American tendencies: optimism about change and possibilities for improvement and, at the same time, skepticism about the scope and scale of those changes. It illustrates the American dualism that seems to have set the context for what has been termed "American exceptionalism": development of goals that search for perfection yet are assumed to operate in a pragmatic and realistic fashion.[9] And "realism" in this context includes fear of concentrated power, be it defined by a colonial power or found in the institutions of the United States.

Much of the literature of American public administration has emphasized the optimistic approach. It places the actual development of the field in the context of the Progressive movement and the presence of what is often described as the good government movement. Progressivism spoke to the values of industrialization and a growing middle-class urban population and was based on goals that emphasized efficiency, value neutrality, and the separation of politics and administration. Frederick Mosher's description of the profession illustrates this; he defined the field as containing "a fundamental optimism that mankind could direct and control its environment and destiny for the better."[10]

Yet another piece of the literature on American exceptionalism moves further back in US history and cites the comments of Alexis de Tocqueville about the country that he observed as a result of his travels. He wrote in the 1830s:

> The position of the Americans is therefore quite exceptional, and it may be believed that no democratic people will ever be placed in a similar one. Their strictly Puritanical origin, their exclusively commercial habits, even the country they inhabit, which seems to divert their minds from the pursuit of science, literature, and the arts, the proximity of Europe, which allows them to neglect these pursuits without relapsing into barbarism, a thousand special causes, of which I have only been able to point out the most important, have singularly concurred to fix the mind of the American upon purely practical objects. His passions, his wants, his education, and everything about him seem to unite in drawing the native of the United States earthward; his religion alone bids him turn, from time to time, a transient and distracted glance to heaven.[11]

The behaviors that de Tocqueville described actually spawned a philosophical movement—pragmatism—that is often linked to American exceptionalism.[12]

As Stephen Skowronek has noted, Tocqueville observed that government in the United States functioned as an "invisible machine" where the distinction between state and society was blurred. Tocqueville wrote:

> [In the United States] society governs itself for itself. All power centers in its bosom, and scarcely an individual is to be met with who would venture to conceive or, still less, to express the idea of seeking it elsewhere. The nation participates in the making of its laws by the choice of its legislators, and the execution of them by the choice of agents of the executive government; it may also be said to govern itself, so feeble and so restricted is the share left to the administrators, so little do the authorities forget their popular origin and the power from which they emanate. The people reign in the American political world as the Deity does in the universe.[13]

The Progressive Era

Tocqueville's observations seem to have been forgotten as the United States moved into the twentieth century. Perhaps the clearest expression of the impact of the values of industrialization and urbanization was found in what Barry Bozeman called "the quintessential scientific management statement in public administration": Luther Gulick and Lyndall Urwick's *Papers on the Science of Administration*.[14] This work provided the field with the awkward acronym POSDCORB—a reference to the seven principles of public administration: planning, organization, staffing, directing, coordinating, reporting, and budgeting. These are generic functions that structure the work of most types of organizations and thus apply to private-sector, nonprofit, as well as public organizations.

The governance processes that emerged from the Progressives shaped the contours of the public administration field. Donald Kettl has commented that "the Progressives worked to develop a model of American politics and policy, with hierarchical control of an enclosed service system." Further, as they worried about the rise of monopolies and the quality of citizens' lives, the Progressives "sought to expand government power as a counterbalance, but they faced again the challenge of the founders: how to expand government's power without risking tyranny."[15] The Progressives borrowed "the best" management technologies from other countries and from the private sector, most of which built on hierarchy.

While the public administration field has emphasized its link to the Progressive movement, that was not the only social movement that was found in the American society of the turn of the twentieth century. The Progressives represented the growing middle class, its emphasis on education and professional training, and a tendency to look to Europe for ideas. By contrast, the movement called Populism grew out of agrarian populations who feared urbanization, industrialization, the wave of new immigrants, and the powers of Wall Street. Progressivism's strength was mainly on the East and West Coasts with Populism found in both the South and much of the Midwest. For at least some of the Populists, the professionalization of the public sector represented further problems.

Skowronek's study of national administrative capacities from 1877 to 1920 sets the historical context for the situation that we find today. He points to the nineteenth-century role of the federal government as providing promotional and support services for state government and what he terms the "rather innocuous role played by central authority in the government of the nation."[16] He describes the centerpiece role of Congress and the conflicts between the Senate and the House as well as other federal institutions over what they viewed as their constitutional prerogatives.[17]

Skowronek's influential analysis highlights the struggles that took place within the federal government during an era of industrialization, corporatization, and urbanization. The creation of the regulatory commissions of that period also indicated an approach that combined powers of both legislative and judicial institutions. The battles for control between the branches of government and the emergence of a significant bureaucracy during that period were substantively unique to that era but provide an important perspective for an analysis of public management reform today.[18]

Trapped in Progressivism?

Indeed, with few exceptions, the field of public administration has written its history as a story within the Progressive Era framework and the executive branch. With few exceptions (particularly those that emerged during the

New Deal), as the field developed it moved along two separate tracks—one attached to experience of practitioners and one attached to more traditional academic settings accentuating theory rather than practice.

As Harold Seidman noted, orthodox theory created certain assumptions about the nature and purpose of organization and administration. "The starting point is a rigid interpretation of the constitutional doctrine of separation of powers. Public administration is viewed as being concerned almost exclusively with the executive branch, 'where the work of government is done,' with only grudging recognition given to the roles of the legislative branch in the administrative process. Preoccupation with the executive branch is coupled with an ill-concealed distrust of politics and politicians as the natural enemies of efficiency."[19] David Rosenbloom's *Building a Legislative-Centered Public Administration* is one of the very few works that has sought to define the appropriate role for a national legislature in a separation-of-powers system.[20]

Most depictions of the field's history have highlighted the possibilities of change that can occur within the confines of the bureaucracy and largely ignored the constraints that flow from the American system of shared powers involving Congress and the courts. Despite the complex system that emerged from the Constitution where each branch of the government has the ability to stop or at least constrain another branch (e.g., involving what many view as intrinsically administrative matters such as selection of top officials, budget decisions, and hiring and firing), public administration students often proceed as if the American bureaucracy can operate in ways that are similar to the private sector or to parliamentary political systems. The fragmentation that characterizes the US system not only emerges from the shared powers between the executive, legislative, and judicial branches but also from other aspects of the system. Foremost are the tensions in our federal system between authorities located in the national government, states, and localities as well as conflict that stems from the multiple players found in Congress (the fragmentation that occurs because of a strong bicameral system and separate Senate and House authorizing and appropriating committees).[21]

By the end of World War II, public administration theorists sought to find a way to characterize the state of the field, dealing with the growth of the federal government that accompanied both the Depression and the war. Michael Harmon noted that this search had several components: first, attempting to identify the meaning, role, and limitations of thinking about administrative study as a science; second, defining the distinctions between values and facts as well as policy and administration; third, defining the nature of responsible administration; and fourth, examining the relevance of constitutional democratic theory for the study of public administration.[22]

The Simon-Waldo Inheritance

The fourth topic became the main subject for the 1952 debate between Herbert Simon and Dwight Waldo, published in the *American Political Science Review*.[23] That debate revolved around several subjects: efficiency as a value-neutral concept; the relationship among science, moral principles, and public administration reform; and the relationship between administration and policy.

While the published debate seemed to some to have exaggerated the differences between Simon and Waldo in several areas, these two perspectives became the intellectual framework for several generations of scholars, continuing into the twenty-first century.[24] At least four different camps seem to have emerged from that debate, representing both academicians as well as practitioners who sought to change management practices largely at the federal government level. One camp emphasized Waldo's perspective, pointing to the normative aspects of public administration and the difficulty of avoiding value decisions in the administrative process. Another camp rooted its arguments in Simon's search for ways to separate facts and values, emphasizing linkages between economic reasoning and administrative determinations. A third camp jumped ahead and looked explicitly at ways to apply principles of efficiency and the logic of the private market to the public sector.[25] And a fourth camp shared Herbert Kaufman's characterization of developments in the field as "generating discord more profound and far-reaching than any that has ever hitherto divided students of public administration" and sought other pathways to understand the field.[26]

It is not surprising that the debates that have continued about this set of issues have not produced coherent perspectives. Some of the original controversy took place within political science journals (the Simon, Waldo, and Kaufman comments were in those journals). As the years progressed, other perspectives were voiced in the growing list of public administration journals. These originally included both theoretical and practitioner perspectives, but as time went on fewer practitioner perspectives found their way to the academy. Advocates of various management reforms emerged from still other areas, including views and approaches developed in the private sector and generic management views as well as the growing public policy field.[27]

This later development represented a shift in the conceptual frameworks that some scholars brought to the field. First of all, it shifted the language used to describe the field; a number of both scholars and practitioners began to call the field "public management" rather than "public administration."[28] Second, it represented an implicit criticism of the way that traditional public administration emphasized processes rather than substantive outcomes of public-sector action.[29] Political science was not the only discipline that influenced the policy field; economics took the preeminent intellectual role in many policy as well as public administration academic programs. Third, it coincided with the development of a global skepticism about the powers of the public sector. As a result, European scholars as well as American scholars thought about ways to decrease those powers (arguing that they had not been effective or concentrated too much power in the hands of officials) and, instead, emphasized the lessons that could be transferred from management schools to the public sector. The concept of the market began to receive more attention as these developments became closely aligned with what was called New Public Management (NPM).[30]

The literature of public administration found ways to absorb some of these newer ideas. Judith Gruber's classic work, *Controlling Bureaucracies: Dilemmas in Democratic Governance,* provides an analysis of the complex and difficult choices involved in assuring democratic control of bureaucracy. She wrote that "the road to successful control lies in understanding both the democratic and bureaucratic sides of the problem and carefully crafting efforts so that neither democratic norms nor bureaucratic fact are denied."[31] John Burke has noted in his work on bureaucratic responsibility that there are very separate expectations imposed on bureaucrats from external sources versus expectations from internal sources.[32] Barbara Romzek and Melvin Dubnick's framework for assessing accountability expectations provides a similar perspective; they separate accountability expectations that emerge from internal sources (hierarchical and professional) from those that emerge from external sources (legal and political).[33]

Despite this differentiation, there has been limited attention to the impact of the structure of shared powers outlined in the US Constitution on the way that we think about bureaucracy. When discussed, it is usually posed as the source of difficulty for bureaucrats. Robert Gilmour and Alexis Halley termed the relationship "co-management" but noted that there are at least five styles of congressional co-management that emerged from their analysis of ten different case studies. These are

- strategic leadership
- consultative partner
- superintendent
- combative opponent
- passive observer[34]

They note that co-management emerges from such critical events as institutional policy differences, institutional distrust, chronic executive program difficulties, human tragedy or other crisis, desire for more coherent policy, and constituency concerns.[35] Although these authors begin their analysis by highlighting Madison's "auxiliary precautions" that led to the system of checks and balances, they argue that the precautions taken by Congress to check the executive have "led to great concern about the government's institutional capacity to govern."[36]

The issues that have been summarized here have surfaced in many ways over the more than 220 years since the US Constitution was adopted. For the purposes of this volume, I am focusing on a range of management reform efforts that have been developed in the United States from the Johnson administration to contemporary times. This book argues that these efforts have been less than effective and tend to repeat the same problems over and over again. While others have come to a similar conclusion about the lack of effectiveness of these reform efforts, they have emphasized different reasons for that result. Three works have come to the conclusion that reform efforts have not been effective, but the authors differ in the way they pose those problems. They are Paul Light's *Tides of Reform,* George Downs and Patrick Larkey's *Search for Government Efficiency,* and Christopher Pollitt and Geert Bouckaert's *Public Management Reform.*

Light's study of a wide range of reform efforts between 1945 and 1995 opens with the following sentence: "This book is based on the notion that there is not too little management reform in government, but too much."[37] His extremely useful analysis highlights the variety of reforms that have emerged over the years. The four tides that he examines represent quite different reform philosophies: what he terms scientific management, war on waste, watchful eye, and liberation management. He argues that these reforms create problems because they are piled up on one another, that they are defined in comprehensive statutes, that they are often at cross purposes, and that they are emerging more frequently than they did in the past.[38] This work provides an important compilation of a wide range of reform efforts.

Downs and Larkey concentrate on the relationship between governments and businesses and find "that many reform strategies have been tried again and again with no success and that there are more promising lines of reform."[39] They focus on seven areas. First, "governments are probably not as poorly managed and businesses are certainly not as well managed as is generally believed." Second, "running a government bureaucracy is not the same as running a business." Third, "attempts to reform government are almost never informed sufficiently by past attempts at reform." Fourth, "there are probably inherent limitations on how efficiently any large organization can operate." Fifth, "politics and administration are inextricably intertwined." Sixth, "performance appraisal is a treacherous business." And seventh, "grandiose strategies for improving government efficiency . . . contain the seeds of their own destruction."[40]

The third work, by Pollitt and Bouckaert, is based on a comparative analysis of management reform in ten countries across three continents. They note that "if management reform really does produce cheaper, more efficient government with higher-quality services and more effective programs, and if it will simultaneously enhance political control, free managers to manage, make government more transparent and boost the images of those ministers and mandarins most involved, then it is little wonder that it has been widely trumpeted." They also note that "there is a good deal of evidence to show that management reforms can go wrong."[41] The range of examples that are included in this analysis clearly illustrates the complexity of this topic.

Two Contrasting Approaches

Although the history of American administrative action is lined with multiple initiatives, there are two broad efforts that provide a picture of attempts to change the federal structure: the Brownlow Committee of the 1930s and the National Performance Review (NPR) of the 1990s.[42] John DiIulio found that the President's Committee on Administrative Management (usually called the Brownlow Committee) "left indelible organizational marks on the federal government and were treasured moments in the golden age of American public administration. But no previous government or private commission on the federal service . . . captured public attention in quite the way the NPR did."[43]

Both of these initiatives threw out wide nets that encompassed multiple approaches and topics, a number of which are included in this volume. According to Light, both of these efforts pay their respects to the aims of scientific management; "Efficiency is rarely far from the first droplet of reform."[44]

But each of these efforts operated in a very different fashion. The Brownlow staff was relatively small and made up of individuals who were not really known outside of the administrative community. It seemed to function in a way that exemplified its own advice that public servants should have "a passion for anonymity."[45] The report it delivered to the president was quite short—only fifty-three pages long—and included efforts to establish new procedures for accountability and control (especially involving reorganization, personnel issues, and budget processes). Interestingly, however, the committee spent much of its time during the summer of 1936 out of the United States. In his account of the Brownlow Committee after fifty years, James Fesler recounted the atmosphere during those months. "We and the Committee had met for two days in May, but during the summer the Committee members were little in evidence. Louis Brownlow and Charles Merriam spent most of that period in Europe, attending meetings of international public administration organizations and looking at European administrative practices."[46]

By contrast, not only was the National Performance Review announced by the vice president, Al Gore, but he did so in a highly public fashion, appearing on a network television talk show to describe its goals. The strategy employed was a cross between a public relations approach and a political campaign. While the Brownlow effort emphasized administrative specialists, the NPR was fast, intense, and controlled by generalists. Individual staff members were drawn from all parts of the federal government establishment; the program operated out of the vice president's office, but many members were assigned to work in agencies, programs, and policies other than their home base.

The agenda for change was broad; it included efforts at substantive policy change, reorganization, budget reductions, empowering line managers, improving customer service, and changing decision systems (including federalism).[47] Multiple reports were issued over the several years of the initiative, presented in colorful and glossy formats. According to Donald Kettl, in order to "get the NPR moving, the reinventers made short-term tactical decisions to get quick wins. . . . It has shown great potential, but the risk is that the NPR will become just a short-term political tactic instead of a lasting reform."[48]

A Different Framework

This work attempts to add still another organizing framework to the exploration of this set of issues but draws on the work of a number of other scholars. Over the years I have studied a wide range of management reforms proposed and sometimes adopted by the various institutions within the US federal government, especially reorganization authority, the National Performance Review, and performance measurement (the Government Performance and Results Act and the Program Assessment Rating Tool). I began to see some of the same obstacles repeatedly emerge in these reform attempts. As others have noted, these obstacles were neither anticipated by the proponents of the change nor were they dealt with once the problems surfaced.[49]

While the impact of this pattern is quite depressing, it has generated a set of experiences that illustrate the difficulty faced by advocates of change in US management practices. It is not surprising that a society with the political, social, and economic complexity of the United States must constantly deal with a range of contradictions that makes reform extremely challenging. It is not only poets who must deal with those contradictions.

David Rosenbloom has described the field of public administration as one that is extremely difficult to characterize because it draws on at least three intellectual traditions, each of which "emphasizes different values, promotes different types of organizational structure, and views individuals in markedly distinct terms." He labels these three the managerial, political, and legal approaches and notes that they have influenced one another over the years. He characterizes them as following the pattern of the constitutional separation of powers, and thus "it is unlikely that the three approaches can be synthesized without violating values deeply ingrained in the United States political culture."[50]

Paul Light has also noted that one of the problems dealing with reform efforts is that the four tides that he discusses "have different goals, inputs, products, participants, and champions, as well as very different defining moments, statutes and patron saints."[51] He argues that the tides of reform (scientific management, war on waste, watchful eye, and liberation management) are driven by the institutional sponsor of reform.

This book draws on both the Rosenbloom and Light analyses but frames the argument in a somewhat different way. It is organized around a number of contradictions found both in the past and in the present. These contradictions are found in the heritage of the US system in general and public administration in particular. They make up the political landscape that surrounds the management reform agenda. Rarely have the management reformers who have designed a variety of initiatives from within the Executive Office of the President acknowledged these contradictions; instead, they have devised initiatives that seek to respond to just one perspective or approach. These contradictions involve structural dimensions of the US system, predominant values that determine approaches, and attributes of the public sector. They are presented here as separate dynamics but the very complexity of the system means that they are interwoven and interrelated. One of the main problems dealing with these contradictions is that the players involved in reform efforts often use the same terms but define them in different ways (see table 1.1).

Contradictions in the US System

Structural Dimensions: Shared versus Separate Powers

As Tocqueville and succeeding writers have observed, the US system of shared powers created a governmental system that was very unusual. There are two main aspects of this system—the establishment of three branches of the national government with separate but overlapping powers and the system of federalism involving national, state, and local players. Unlike the European systems that emerged from centralized authority (either the church or royalty), the US system of checks and balances makes it difficult for a single branch to move clearly and cleanly in a particular direction. This framework became the structure for American democracy. At the same time, each player in the system has a set of responsibilities that it attempts

TABLE 1.1: Contradictions Affecting Federal Management Reform

Issue	Examples
Structural dimensions	Shared powers: executive, legislative, and judiciary Federal role vs. states
Predominant values and approaches	Optimism vs. pessimism Multiple values: efficiency, effectiveness, equity
Attributes of the public sector	Separation of politics and administration Government-wide action vs. program/policy/agency-specific action

to carry out within that complex system. Although we view the national bureaucracy as a part of the executive branch, the Constitution sets relatively explicit limits on the authority of the president to move without action by both the legislative and judicial branches. Even within branches, the structure sets up tension between elements. For example, the two branches of Congress could be viewed as separate rather than overlapping systems.

Similarly, the federal structure sends out what are often viewed as contradictory messages. Over two centuries of US history the role of the national government has increased vis-à-vis state authority but often in a direction that adds to already unclear responsibilities. It is not clear whether the national government is expected to be the preeminent player in the system, to have limited relationships with states (and sometimes localities), or to have overlapping responsibilities with states and localities.[52]

Predominant Values and Approaches

The multiple elements of the governmental structure provide the framework for the articulation of a range of values and conceptual approaches that have the ability to impact the development of management reform efforts. As has been noted, US history provides examples of very different approaches to government. Throughout this history we see both optimism about the government's ability to shape the future as well as skepticism about the scope of activity that is appropriate for the public sector. Efforts have been devised that accentuate one or another of the two approaches; rarely do they acknowledge that both are a part of the American tradition. At the same time, some players in the system search for solutions that are simple and clear while others focus on the components of what they describe as a complex system.[53]

But perhaps the most important element in this process involves the conflict between the three traditional values that comprise the goals of public-sector action: efficiency, effectiveness, and equity.[54] From the Progressive Era onward, efficiency values and the concept of a market have been the predominant values for public administrators.[55] While there is some acknowledgment that effectiveness and sometimes equity are important, rarely do the reform efforts find a way to establish venues and processes that provide for trade-offs between these elements.[56] Aaron Wildavsky noted that the person who values "efficiency most dearly, may discover that the most efficient means for accomplishing his ends cannot be secured without altering the machinery for making decisions. He not only alters means and ends (resources and objectives) simultaneously but makes them dependent on changes in political relationships."[57]

Attributes of the Public Sector

The third source of contradictions that has an impact on management reform stems from different interpretations of the attributes of the public sector. Despite the structure of the US system (separation of powers) and the values built into the system, there has been a dispute over the elements of the public sector that should be included in administrative decision making. From the turn of the twentieth century onward, there has been dispute about the level of interdependence between policy and administration. Woodrow Wilson's 1887 *Study of Administration* called for a clear separation between politics and administration and seemed to move toward a sorting out of the institutions with responsibility for each set of functions.[58] It fed into an emphasis on internal strategies for change, either avoiding or downplaying the importance of issues and players who were a part of public organizations' external structure.[59] In addition, the separation also led to a belief that establishment of policy and program goals could take place without concern about the details of implementing those goals.

Closely related was the way that advocates of change conceptualized the level of analysis that generated initiatives. Some strategies conceptualized change as a government-wide effort, covering all aspects of the federal government and looking to institutions that sought agendas that included all aspects of the large and diverse government structure. This approach emerged from the management side of the Office of Management and Budget as well as the other federal overhead agencies (the General Services Administration and the Office of Personnel Management). This government-wide mind-set also was found within the congressional government reform committees that generated the legislative face of management reform.

By contrast, focusing on the fragmented nature of the US federal system leads to a conceptualization of the change agenda as a case-by-case, program-by-program strategy. This set of assumptions mirrors the structure of decision authority in both the executive and legislative branches. Proposals are generated by staff in individual departments and agencies, individual budget examiners, and congressional committees and subcommittees charged with both authorizing and appropriating authority.

This book examines an array of federal management reforms by looking at the way that they deal with the three sets of contradictions just described: the structural dimensions of the US system, predominant values that determine approaches, and attributes of the public sector. These reforms include contracting out, personnel management reforms, reorganization reforms, budget reforms, federalism and intergovernmental relations, and performance measurement. The discussion about these reforms also illustrates the four quite conflicting approaches that have emerged from the Simon-Waldo debate; these include an emphasis on normative and value issues, an emphasis on economic reasoning and administrative determinations, a search for ways to apply principles of efficiency and the market, and a sense of frustration about these issues.

Notes

1. I thank Ann Bowman for her characterization of this problem (personal communication with author).
2. Hodge, *Privatization,* 5.
3. Brian Friel, "Management Matters," *Government Executive,* August 4, 2010.
4. Osborne and Gaebler's book became the bible for the Clinton administration's National Performance Review.
5. Lynn, "New Public Management," 232.
6. Hood, "Can We?" 527, 528.
7. Hood, "Public Management for All Seasons?" 3, 6.
8. Ibid., 7.
9. See, e.g., Marone, *Democratic Wish.* Exceptionalism has at least two quite different meanings. One of the definitions provides an opportunity for Americans to argue that they are better than others. The other definition focuses on differences between the US system and those in other countries and does not attempt to assert which is better. This discussion focuses on the latter definition. It is particularly relevant today because the discussion of American exceptionalism has moved from academic discussions to the partisan world of politics during the Obama administration. As a *Washington Post* reporter put it, "The word 'exceptional' or 'exceptionalism' lately has become a litmus test for patriotism" (Kathleen Parker, "President Obama and That 'Exceptional' Thing," *Washington Post,* January 30, 2011).
10. Mosher, "American Setting," 3.
11. Tocqueville, *Democracy in America,* pt. 2, chap. 9, 36.
12. The emphasis on pragmatism is a theme that is echoed in the work of Dwight Waldo.
13. Quoted in Skowronek, *Building a New American State,* 6. From Tocqueville, *Democracy in America,* 59.
14. Bozeman, *Management and Policy Analysis,* 33.
15. Kettl, *Next Government,* 107.
16. Skowronek, *Building a New American State,* 23.
17. Ibid.
18. The emergence of the Tea Party movement in 2010 has a number of attributes that are similar to those of the Populist movement of the turn of the twentieth century.
19. Seidman, *Politics, Position, and Power,* 5–6.
20. One would also look to Goodnow's 1905 book on administrative law as well as Wilson's *Congressional Government.*
21. Much of the work on federalism and intergovernmental relationships is viewed as a separate area of study, and there has been little attention to the interplay between public administration theory and theories of federalism.
22. Harmon, "Simon/Waldo Debate," 437.
23. Simon, Drucker, and Waldo, "Development of Theory."
24. See Harmon, "Simon/Waldo Debate."
25. See discussion in chapter 2.
26. Kaufman, "Emerging Conflicts," 1057.
27. See, e.g., Lynn, *Public Management.*

28. See Perry and Kraemer, *Public Management*, x. Their introduction to the book defines public management as "a merger of the normative orientation of traditional public administration and the instrumental orientation of general management."
29. See Elmore, "Graduate Education in Public Management," for a description of this process.
30. NPM is very difficult to define. There is a range of definitions that include a diverse array of attributes. In addition, experiences vary from country to country and over time. See Hood and Peters, "Middle Aging," for one interesting view.
31. Gruber, *Controlling Bureaucracies*, 214.
32. Burke, *Bureaucratic Responsibility.*
33. Romzek and Dubnick, "Accountability in the Public Sector."
34. Gilmour and Halley, "Co-managing," chap. 12.
35. Ibid., 337.
36. Ibid., v.
37. Light, *Tides of Reform*, 1.
38. Ibid., intro. In many ways, Light's book provides an important starting point for many of the issues that are considered in this volume.
39. Downs and Larkey, *Search for Government Efficiency*, v.
40. Ibid., 2–4.
41. Pollitt and Bouckaert, *Public Management Reform*, 6.
42. There are other examples as well, but these two efforts provide a useful way to contrast developments in different eras.
43. He also included the two Commissions on Organization of the Executive Branch (known as the Hoover Commissions) as earlier efforts. DiIulio, "Works Better and Costs Less?" 3.
44. Light, *Tides of Reform*, 21.
45. See Fesler, "Brownlow Committee."
46. Ibid., 291.
47. See Radin, "Varieties of Reinvention."
48. Kettl, *Reinventing Government?* v.
49. E.g., Hood and Peters, "Middle Aging."
50. Rosenbloom, "Public Administrative Theory," 219.
51. Light, *Tides of Reform*, 221.
52. See Wright, *Understanding Intergovernmental Relations.*
53. This contrast is captured by H. L. Mencken's maxim: "Explanations exist: they have existed for all times, for there is always an easy solution to every problem—neat, plausible and wrong."
54. See Okun, *Equality and Efficiency.*
55. See Bozeman, *Public Values and Public Interest.*
56. These three values are also represented by analyses such as that by Rosenbloom in "Public Administrative Theory."
57. Wildavsky, "Political Economy of Efficiency," 292.
58. Wilson's work also called for comparisons between public and private organizations as well as an emphasis on efficiency values.
59. See Riccucci, *How Management Matters*, for an example of a policy area in which implementation issues were separated from policy goals.

2

PUBLIC/PRIVATE
MANAGEMENT RELATIONSHIPS

For people who are concerned about the quality of public service and attention to issues of social injustice, fairness in governmental action, environmental protection, and so on, something about running government like a business does not feel right. It seems to degrade the commitment to public service, reducing it to technical-instrumental market functions not unlike the manufacture and marketing of a consumer product.

Richard C. Box, "Running Government Like a Business"

ONE OF THE CONSTANT THEMES IN THE PUBLIC ADMINISTRATION LITERA-ture revolves around the debate about the relationship between public management and private management.[1] This topic is found throughout the history of the academic public administration field, and the debate about similarities and differences between the two sectors is chronicled in a wide range of journals and books. The exchange takes many different forms, a number of which relate to or have an impact on the topic of federal management reform. Despite its constancy as a topic, the pendulum of opinion has swung back and forth over the years, emphasizing either similarities or differences between the two sectors, responding to developments within the society that emphasize skepticism about one or the other perspective. But the debate goes on and the question has not been resolved. Perhaps the most familiar quip about the topic came from Wallace Sayre, a professor at Columbia University, who coined the oft-quoted aphorism, "Public and private management are fundamentally alike in all unimportant respects."[2]

While there is a rich literature around this topic, scholars have empha-sized very different aspects of the issue in their work. As a result, there is not clear evidence nor an accepted perspective about the issue. As Michael A. Murray wrote, the two different institutional approaches to management science have "not gone unchallenged."[3] He notes that despite the movement to conceptualize the field as one best served by a generic approach that in-cludes both sectors, there are a number of reasons why there has been resis-tance to this development. He describes the "traditional mistrust or misunderstanding between the public and private practitioner," the threat to schools of business and public administration, and "little specific com-parative analysis that is discussion of points where public and private man-agement converge or diverge."[4] Indeed, the more that hierarchy became the norm for the government, the easier it appeared to be to look to the private sector for models and strategies.

This chapter reviews a range of perspectives and views on this topic because the colloquy on the issue sets the backdrop for much of the discussion on various approaches to public management reform. Each of these perspectives begins with a set of assumptions about the two fields. As Murray put it, the debate centers around two idealized types. "The key substantive issue is whether there is an inherent conflict between the rational, private management model with its criteria of economic efficiency, and the political public management model with its criteria of consensus and compromise."[5] This chapter discusses attempts to sort out differences between the two sectors, questions that deal with perspectives on efficiency and the concept of "the public interest," dimensions of generic administration, and alternative conceptualizations of the topic. It also includes discussion of efforts to base policies and initiatives on assumptions about the similarities between the two sectors.

A Review of the Public/Private Literature

Barry Bozeman and Stuart Bretschneider offer a macro framework for conceptualizing the topic, differentiating between two approaches to what they call "the publicness puzzle."[6] They note that most students of public organizations have been drawn to what they call the "core approach," the distinction between public and private organizations based on legal type. The alternative approach, what they call the "dimensional approach," begins with the assumption that publicness is not a discrete attribute but that "organizations are more or less public depending on the extent to which externally imposed political authority affects them."[7]

Much of the literature that is related to this topic focuses on behaviors defined by traditional hierarchical relationships and clarity about responsibilities for administration of programs and policies. It is relevant, thus, to acknowledge that this literature does not often capture the changing and increasing interest in the public management field about networks and partnerships. Networks and partnerships have increasingly encouraged processes and structures that include both public and private players.[8] These developments have made the sorting out of responsibilities between the two sectors even more difficult.

It is also relevant to note that much of the literature on this topic has emerged from English-speaking countries. In France, for example, the legal framework for public-private relationships is clearly defined and reinforced by statistical classifications. Yet Celine Desmarais and Emmanuel Abord de Chatillon note that there is still an ongoing debate about the two sectors. They comment that "because of differences in how the public and private sectors are defined, evidence from surveys . . . show [*sic*] a general consensus that any differences between public and private management and organizations are relatively insignificant in terms of management practices."[9]

Attempts to Sort Out Attributes of the Two Sectors

As Bozeman and Bretschneider suggested, much of the literature around this topic represents the "core approach"; that is, attempts to sort out differences between the two sectors. Those who seek to document those differences often find themselves faced with data that, upon analysis, suggest that the two worlds are not as different as the researcher seems to have suggested. While there are a number of reasons for these findings, perhaps the most common attribute that leads to this is the way that the problem is framed. If one focuses on the way that the organization deals with general management functions that occur inside almost all organizations, it is not surprising that—to paraphrase Gertrude Stein—an organization is an organization is an organization.

Yet, as Paul Appleby commented, "It is exceedingly difficult clearly to identify the factors which make government different from every other activity in society. Yet this difference is a fact and I believe it to be so big a difference that the dissimilarity between government and all other forms of social action is greater than any dissimilarity among those other forms themselves."[10] He found that three aspects differentiate government from all other institutions and activities: breadth of scope, impact, and consideration; public accountability; and political character.

The definition of the internal functions that is most familiar to students of public administration draws from Luther Gulick's contribution of POSDCORB—planning, organizing, staffing, directing, coordinating, reporting, and budgeting.[11] As is obvious, this list focuses exclusively on the internal activities within an organization and ignores the external context in which it operates.

Others, however, have attempted to capture the external context in their typology. Hal Rainey, Robert Backoff, and Charles Levine (partially in response to Murray's argument about the blurring of the two sectors) surveyed the extant literature in the mid-1970s and broadened the framework to include three sets of factors: environmental factors, organization-environment transactions, and internal structures and processes.[12] In another work, John T. Dunlop drew on his personal experience in government to list ten areas of contrast:

1. time perspective
2. duration
3. measurement of performance
4. personnel constraints
5. equity and efficiency

6. public processes versus private processes
7. role of press and media
8. persuasion and direction
9. legislative and judicial impact
10. bottom line[13]

Another framework was offered by Richard E. Neustadt as a result of his analysis of six major differences between presidents of the United States and chief executive officers of major corporations; these include time horizon, authority over the enterprise, career-system, media relations, performance measurement, and implementation.[14] Still another comparison of public and private management is offered in table 2.1.

All of these depictions represent the urge within the academic field of public administration to clearly sort out the differences between the two sectors. One conjures up a picture of someone with a deck of cards who is sorting out the cards by suits; in that case, it is clear what is a heart, a spade, a club, and a diamond. This sorting-out task of separating the public and private sectors would not be so difficult if we had the clarity and agreed-upon boundaries found in a deck of cards. Yet those scholars who are attempting to test the various hypotheses that emerge from the public/private debate

TABLE 2.1: Differences between Public and Private Management

Item	Public	Private
Time perspective	Short term	Long term
Budget process	Complex, multiple players	Hierarchical
Duration	Political short term, career long term	As required
Measurement of performance	Multiple goals	Profit
Authority over work	Shared authority	Control over work
Control over structure	Legislative involvement	Internal control over structure
Personnel constraints	Civil service systems	Internal control
Equity and efficiency	Need for trade-offs	Efficiency major
Processes	Open	Closed
Role of press and media	Open access	Closed access
Persuasion and direction	Multiple authorities	Straight-line authority
Coerciveness	Mandatory, formal	Informal
Implementation	Complex by design	Move to simplify
Complexity of objectives	Multiple and overlapping	Move to simplify
Bottom line	Not clear	Profit

Source: This list was developed by the author from multiple sources and conversations with students.

have found it important to establish some level of clarity about what is public and what is private before quantitative analyses can be performed, whether or not others agree with their decisions. In addition, this approach to research is dependent on the availability of data sets that can be used to test these hypotheses. Indeed, in the 1970s, much of the conversation about this topic took place within the pages of the *Public Administration Review*'s "Developments in Research" section.

The differentiation between attributes of the two sectors has served as an organizing concept for a number of research efforts about specific topics in the public administration field. Some sought to compare sectors to show similarities while others attempted to document differences. For example, Hal Rainey, Sanjay Pandey, and Barry Bozeman examined public and private managers' perceptions of red tape and, using data collected by the National Administrative Studies Project, found a mixed picture of these perceptions.[15] Peter Robertson and Sonal Seneviratne's study of planned organizational change in the public sector compared that experience to the one in the private sector and found that generally organizational change interventions were equally successful in both sectors.[16] Nancy Kurland and Terri Egan studied formalization, outcomes, and perceptions of justice among public- and private-sector employees; while the two groups were similar on the formalization and outcomes results, they differed in terms of justice perceptions.[17] And Mak Khojasteh examined the motivation of private- versus public-sector managers and found that there were differences between the two in terms of reward systems.[18]

Scholars from private/sector perspectives have also used the public/ private framework to examine management issues raised in both settings. For example, Ram Lachman focused on perceptions of role environments among CEOs from public and private organizations and found "that the public/private distinction may not be a very useful conceptual framework for explaining differences in organization-environment interactions."[19] The definition of "environment" that was used in this study, however, seemed to focus on the task environment rather than the decision-making environment.

George Boyne sought to examine the NPM criticism of transfer of business practices to the public sector through a meta-analysis of thirty-four empirical studies of differences between public agencies and private firms. He concluded that the range of studies suggests that the findings are unclear and "most of the statistical evidence is derived from studies that use narrow measures of publicness and fail to control for other relevant explanatory variables."[20]

Despite attempts to establish clear demarcations between public and private organizations through formal quantitative methods, it appears that the scholars who embark on this work cannot escape from establishing caveats to their findings. These caveats appear over and over again in those works as well as other analytical approaches. For example, the reality of the blurring of boundaries between the two systems is echoed in advice from Herbert Simon: "There are no simple formulas for choosing between markets and organizations, or between governmental and private organizations, in a modern society. A great variety of patterns can be seen in the world today without clear choice among them."[21]

And it is relatively rare for scholars to link the differentiation between public and private to substantive policy outcomes even though these policy decisions are often linked to values and ideologies. Andrew Stark reminds us that policy debates such as those over welfare and workfare are instructive in attempting to think about drawing the line between the two sectors. He comments that these debates "are typically portrayed as conflicts between one side championing the values of the public sphere, whether civic equality, communal obligation, or secular neutrality, and the other those of the private realm, whether market, family or religion." He suggests that each side of the debate relies on both sets of values but "applies them in inverse or opposing ways."[22] He finds that the debate is not about the characteristics of the two sectors but on the values that motivate particular actors concerned about the decision. This complex set of views is particularly difficult when it not only involves value conflicts but does so in policy situations where public action has the effect of constraining private behavior.

The research that has been undertaken on private/public differentiation draws on experience in different levels of government as well as different types of organizations. It is not clear how these differences impact the attempt to draw clear lines between the sectors. Intuitively one thinks that it may be very relevant to differentiate between government agencies in federal (or national), state, and local settings. Indeed, the literature on intergovernmental relationships suggests that responsibilities and roles at different jurisdictional levels of government make some difference. This is particularly important since increasingly federal government officials do not actually deliver services; as Joseph Califano once commented about the Department of Health, Education, and Welfare, "We don't deliver services; we deliver dollars and regulations." And while researchers often attempt to define the terms that they use in a way that avoids definitional conflict it is not always clear that public- and private-sector respondents actually mean the same thing even though they use the same terms.

However, researchers are often at the mercy of the availability of data and the data sets may focus on one specific setting (e.g., public and private organizations in upstate New York).[23] Similarly, researchers might focus on a national association's membership that draws on both public and private sources (e.g., a telecommunications trade association).[24] In addition, the scholarship represents different levels of analysis; some of the research on public/private differentiation focuses on the organization itself while other elements examine the behavior of individual managers within the organization. Rarely, however, do the researchers have data available that allows them to make finer differentiations between organizations or to focus on diverse approaches to the level of analysis of the research. And in even rarer circumstances is the data available on a longitudinal basis. Despite this, in many cases the urge to generalize about findings is quite strong, and it is unusual to confront these different approaches with more than a caveat when reporting findings and making recommendations.

On the private-sector side, even those scholars who might be skeptical about the significance of differences between the public and private sectors often do acknowledge that it is important to focus on the kind of organization it takes to deal with different situations. For example, Paul Lawrence and Jay Lorsch's classic work on organizations and environment moved the focus away from determining "*the one best way to organize in all situations*" to answering the question, "What kind of organization does it take to deal with different environmental conditions?"[25] They write:

> Managers must find answers to such questions as: What type of organization will best coordinate our sales effort? How much control and direction should we give our research scientists? Can improvements in our organization help us to develop more new products? What can we do to achieve better coordination between sales and plant personnel on delivery schedules? Will changes in our financial reward or control systems improve the effectiveness of our managers? . . . Too often in the past these decisions have been made with no systematic analysis, or on the basis of generalizations about "the best way" to organize, or simply in imitation of a competitor who has adopted a particular organizational practice.[26]

Others, such as Stephen Osborne, have been critical of the public management field because it draws from that part of the private-sector literature that focuses on the experience of the manufacturing sector rather than the services sector. He notes that "this is a fatal flaw in the theoretical basis of our discipline and has persisted despite the existence of a substantive theory of services management."[27]

Not Just an Academic Issue

As this book will demonstrate, issues related to the definition and attributes of the two sectors have been at play in the world of practice. But perhaps no initiative more dramatically illustrated a view that the public sector must learn from the private sector than the President's Private Sector Survey on Cost Control (PSSCC), commonly known as the Grace Commission because it was headed by the then shipping company head J. Peter Grace. This effort was requested by President Ronald Reagan in his first term and issued forty-one separate reports at the end of 1983. The group was made up of private-sector officials who were charged with investigating waste and inefficiency in the US federal government. Individuals were assigned to focus on each of the federal departments and to bring their private-sector expertise to the task. They described their experience in terms of the role of a board of directors and, in one of their reports, commented:

> In our experience, the greater a Board of Directors or a top level management's involvement with day-to-day decisions, the less effective and productive the operating management becomes, especially when over time operating management is thereby prevented from adjusting to the inevitable changes in its environment. . . . Successful private sector corporations are generally guided by the following basic tenets of management:

- tell those with executive program responsibility what to accomplish, not how to do the job;
- give management the tools and sufficient authority to accomplish this mission;
- give management the flexibility to employ as they see best the personnel and other resources allocated to them to accomplish their mission; and
- monitor senior management executives to see if they are accomplishing the stated mission, but do not saddle them with an outside presence that tells them how to do their job and constantly meddles in even the smallest details of their operation.[28]

Worrying about Efficiency

Among the most contentious issues within the public/private debate is the role of efficiency values in the two systems. First of all, the term "efficiency" has a number of meanings even before it is placed in the context of the debate about differences or similarities between the public and private sectors. The specific definition depends on many factors; the views of an economist may differ from those of a political scientist or someone from another field. And some of the definitions focus on microlevel behaviors where actors seek to minimize the expenditure of resources in organizing their work. That could involve money, staff, time, and other appropriate resources. Because this approach to efficiency often seeks to quantify the ratio between inputs and outputs or outcomes, the resources that are usually emphasized involve items that can be expressed in numerical forms. This can lead to a liberal use of indicators (rather than direct measures) of outcomes and performance that do not always capture the qualitative nature of the activity, particularly the quality of services.

Others, however, attach efficiency concepts to broader economic frameworks and assumptions. From this perspective, efficiency is embedded in views about the market; indeed, creating or using a market is viewed as the best way to achieve efficient results. While one could devise a market that is internal to the public sector, it is usually assumed that efficiency is achieved almost automatically through markets within the private sector. Since Adam Smith, markets are believed to operate through the behavior of individuals who make choices about options.[29] Some scholars have attempted to conceptualize political institutions as players in the market, but there is not a comfortable fit between the collective action of political institutions and individual actions of separate citizens.

George Downs and Patrick Larkey have differentiated between two types of efficiency: managerial efficiency and economic efficiency. They argue that managerial efficiency is a ratio between outputs and inputs and that it does not question the outputs' benefit. They find that economic efficiency is more abstract than managerial efficiency and rests on the Pareto criterion that calls for action that does not make anyone worse off as a result of the change. They also find that "because the economic efficiency criteria are defined with respect to individuals, they do not suffer from the same potential moral insensitivity as the managerial efficiency criteria. . . . The economic efficiency criteria . . . endorse the status quo regardless of its moral standing."[30]

Efficiency is also closely linked to the measurement of performance (e.g., the ratio between inputs and results). The private sector's bottom-line assessment of performance rests on the results determined by the profit margin. There is not an easy analogue to this within the public sector. Scholars have found it difficult to create frameworks that provide a way to compare apples and oranges since many public-sector programs involve multiple and conflicting goals rather than a single goal analogous to the profit margin. This has troubled a number of scholars; for example, Robertson and Seneviratne's study of organizational development techniques confronted that problem.[31] A similar problem was faced by Nutt and Backoff in their study of strategic management in both public and private organizations.[32]

The Concept of Customers

In recent years many elements within the public sector have been intrigued by the concept of "the customer." In both theory and practice viewing citizens as customers is evidence of applying business (read private-sector) principles to government. It is most evident in the work of the National Performance Review, the Clinton administration's effort to set customer service standards and benchmark federal government standards against the best in business.[33]

While a number of commentators about these efforts could agree with the need to improve federal government activity, there was strong disagreement about the assumptions behind these efforts. H. George Frederickson posed the problem in several commentaries:

> The fundamental difference between the two movements in both assumptions and philosophy regarding responsiveness has to do with the role of citizens versus customers. Much of the new public administration literature is tied to an elevated conception of citizenship, a vision of the informed, active citizen participating "beyond the ballot box" in a range of public activities with both elected and appointed public servants. . . . It assumes that citizens have much more than individual and self-serving interests in government and public administration. The use of the customer metaphor in the reinventing government perspective borrows heavily from utilitarian logic, the public choice model, and the modern application of market economics to government. In this model, the empowered customer makes individual (or family) choices in a competitive market, thus breaking the bureaucratic service monopoly.[34]

John Alford, also a critic of the Clinton customer service activity, highlights two sets of differences between private-sector customers and the "publics" of government organizations. "The first has to do with *who performs* the primary functions . . . —expressing preferences and receiving goods or services—while the second concerns the *nature* of those functions."[35]

In the private sector the customer is clearly defined and considered directly; the public sector, on the other hand, can have layers of separation. For example, the public expects that the government is regulating and inspecting food-processing facilities. However, it is rare that the general public gets involved in what those regulations entail or how frequently facilities are or are not inspected. The true customer of food safety regulations (everyone living within the United States) does not deal directly with regulating agencies. At the same time, regulators frequently interact with the regulated industry and advocacy groups. This puts the agencies in a position of needing to be responsive to those who are regulated as well as advocacy groups while keeping their customer (the general public) safe. One can look at customers in two quite different ways: they can be examined in terms of the public's view of the government but also how the government views the public.

It is also confusing to define the customer in policies and programs that apply sanctions. For example, who is the customer in the criminal justice prison system; is it the victim, the general public, or the incarcerated individual? These are questions that the private sector does not need to confront.

As a contrast, consider services provided by government where the relationship to the customer is quite similar to that of the private sector. Medicare, for example, serves the same function for millions of Americans as private-sector health insurers. A Medicare recipient deals directly with the government when facing questions about claims and benefits.

Thus relying on the concept of the market—one of the strongest attributes of the private sector—has limited ability to provide advice to the varied and multiple programs and policies within the federal government.

The Dilemma of Defining the Public Interest

In many ways, attempting to differentiate the public from the private sector is like a "tell," an archeological dig in which layers of cultures are built on one another but it is not always clear where one culture begins and another ends. In the same way that public/private differentiations are closely linked to concepts of efficiency, both of these notions are embedded in views of "the public interest." It is not easy to differentiate between the public and the private when one has difficulty determining what the public sector actually does.

Barry Bozeman's *Public Values and Public Interest: Counterbalancing Economic Individualism* provides a rich analysis of these issues, placing the concept of the public interest in both a conceptual as well as a historical framework. He notes that "the harshest critics of public interest theory rail loudest about its ambiguities and a seeming inability to determine when and if public interest theory has progressed." He argues that quantitative and behavioral approaches to political science made discussions of the public interest seems passé and, worse, "metaphysical and unscientific. . . . Ironically, the success of some modern governments may have contributed to a diminished interest in deliberations about the public interest. Whereas in past centuries the idea of the public interest was set against despotic governments and tyrants, many modern nations have managed to develop governments that more often act as a bulwark against tyranny than as a perpetrator."[36]

Bozeman contrasts public interest theory with economic individualism, which emphasizes individual liberty and each person's role as a producer and consumer.[37] He notes that "in an era increasingly influenced by a philosophy of economic individualism, public leaders and the public at large oftentimes look first to markets for solutions and then to government and nonmarket institutions only in those instances where market approaches seem unworkable." He writes that market efficiency acts as a rationale in several ways: as a rationale for delivery of goods and services as well as a "cry for businesslike, entrepreneurial, or market savvy government."[38]

Bozeman's analysis rests on the conception of "dimensional publicness," a view that "*publicness* is best defined not on the basis of the legal status of institutions or their ownership (ie., government or business) but according to the degree of political authority constraints and endowments affecting the institution. Similarly, an institution's 'privateness' may be viewed according to the degree of *market* authority constraints and endowments affecting the institution." He defines "public values" as follows:

> A society's "public values" are those providing normative consensus about (a) the rights, benefits, and prerogatives to which citizens should (and

should not) be entitled; (b) the obligations of citizens to society, the state, and one another; and (c) the principles on which governments and policies should be based.[39]

He draws on John Dewey's view that "the public interest is an ideal that is given shape, on a case-by-case basis, by a public motivated to secure its common interests as a public." Bozeman builds on this approach and notes that concepts involving "economic individualism affect not only the design and analysis of public policy but also its management and implementation."[40]

For some, this set of interrelated definitions is counterintuitive since their differentiation between public and private is only about the two sectors' differences in terms of legal status. Thus it makes little sense to them that some public agencies may be "more private" than "public" while some private agencies may be "more public" than some "private" organizations. In addition, rarely is there acknowledgment that a complex society such as the United States is likely to contain multiple interests with competing views that might make it difficult to define a single public interest and a clear view of a "common well-being" or "general welfare."[41]

The Blurring of the Sectors

As this discussion indicates, it is not easy to draw lines around the boundaries of the two sectors. More than thirty years ago Rainey, Backoff, and Levine argued that it was impossible to clearly define public and private but, nonetheless, that scholars have attempted to specify the range of variation among and within the sector.[42] They noted that the "blurring" or convergence of the sectors involves two sets of activities: The first is "an intermingling of governmental and nongovernmental activities, which is observable in government regulation of various activities and in various 'mixed' undertakings." The second is "an increasing similarity of function, context, or role of the organizations. . . . This 'blurring' certainly complicates the delineation of the sectors, but the real question is how much to make of it."[43]

Despite this, both scholars and practitioners have dealt with the blurring in different ways. Some have decided that there is enough similarity in the functions and reality of organizations—be they public or private—that it is appropriate to think about them as a single family unit. This has led to the creation of generic schools of administration where both public- and private-sector subcategories are located.[44] On the practitioner side, there is a group of individuals and organizations who believe it is possible to bring approaches and techniques from the private sector directly to the public sphere.[45] This is most likely to occur in those policy areas that could be defined as hybrids, such as health policy, where the public and private sectors intersect on a day-to-day basis and thus practitioners are likely to interact with one another.

The idea of homogenizing all organizations has been roundly criticized by Herbert Simon. He wrote, "The idea that there is one form of organization—specifically, the private corporation—that has a unique capacity for efficient action is simply a myth that ignores both the motivations at work in organizational behavior and the limits on our capacities for measuring consequences and converting them into costs and demand prices."[46]

But there are players in both the public and private sectors who continue to see the two areas as clear and distinct. Indeed, depending on their values, they seek to differentiate themselves from each other and view the relationship as an adversarial one that does not call for balancing conflicting imperatives.[47] Each set of players spends significant time criticizing the other.

Shifting Involvements

This review of the public-private dynamic would be limited if it did not include discussion of Albert Hirschman's work, *Shifting Involvements: Private Interest and Public Action*. Once again Hirschman takes a familiar issue and conceptualizes it in a very creative and innovative fashion. He introduces the work by reminding his readers that he was in Paris in 1978, where people were celebrating the anniversary of the 1968 uprising—a time when people had "a sudden and overwhelming concern with public issues—of war and peace, of greater equality, of participating in decision-making." He notes that by the late 1970s people returned to their concerns about their private interests. That made him "raise the question whether our societies are in some way predisposed toward oscillations between periods of intense preoccupation with public issues and of almost total concentration on individual improvement and private welfare goals."[48]

Hirschman's analysis suggests a very different way of looking at the public/private differentiation. Rather than searching for some way of sorting out the differences and similarities between the two sectors, he introduces a differentiation not as a sorting out but as a dynamic process. This process involves swings related to changes in the environment or changes because of technological, social, or economic conditions that evoke swings in the cycles of collective behavior. He argues that in the case of changes in the public/private dimension "outside events can generally be credited with much of the responsibility."

Hirschman "aims at correcting the exogenous bias of previous accounts and at giving an enhanced role to people's critical appraisals of their own experiences and choices as important determinants of new and different choices."[49] His focus on shifts in individual perceptions opens up a view of the public and the private that is quite different from many others. He sees public action as action in the political realm and as involvement of the citizen in civic or community affairs but finds it more problematic to define the antonym of public. He suggests that there are "*two varieties of active life:* one is the traditional *vita activa* which is wholly concerned with public affairs;

and the other is *vita contemplativa* which focuses on the pursuit of a better life for oneself and one's family."[50]

Hirschman highlights the concept of "disappointment" to explain the swing back and forth from one variety to another. He argues that when individuals find that their expectations have not been met, they exhibit a sense of disappointment about their situation and "large groups of people will on occasion move together from the pursuit of one kind of happiness to that of another."[51] Yet, he notes, there is no assurance that similar movements of disappointment or revulsion will not occur again.

He finds that certain external events (e.g., wars, revolutions, etc.) play an important role in the changes and particularly the swing toward the public side. "Such events may in part be caused by the disappointments of the previous private phase, but once they take place they draw in all kinds of people and thus compel a synchronization of public concerns and therefore of the public-private cycle. The same is true for periods of rapid economic growth—such growth similarly induces large groups of people to concentrate for a while on their private affairs, with the result that they will go together through any disappointment experiences that may unfold during that phase."[52]

Hirschman's analysis is extremely useful for several reasons. First, whether or not one agrees with his cyclical argument, his perspective reminds us that issues related to the construct of the public and private sectors take place in a turbulent, ever-changing environment. Clear and constant classification of attributes does not fit comfortably within that environment. Second, his perspective on disappointment and changing expectations from individual citizens moves the discussion from an abstract argument to a process of thinking about individual action. This shifts the discussion to acknowledge that individuals play some role in the process, often reflected in political and economic behavior. And third, the Hirschman conceptualization links shifting views to political decision making.

What Do We Do?

A review of the literature on public/private differentiation actually raises more questions than it answers. Despite some protestations to the contrary, the literature indicates that one should be skeptical about assumptions held by either practitioners or scholars that one can proceed to either act or study public/private differentiation assuming that a single agreed-upon perspective has emerged. This is what Hal Rainey and Barry Bozeman describe as a priori views about the public/private distinction in organizational and managerial research. They note that "a priori refers to untested assertions and foregone conclusions about this distinction."[53] While they urge scholars to continue to sort out similarities and differences between the sectors, they acknowledge that there has been limited attention to the context in which differentiation occurs or the decision-making processes that attempt to use defined similarities involving efficiency and the market.

Rainey and Bozeman note that this inquiry has implications beyond the academic borders. These implications include "privatization of public services; allocation of functions and tasks among sectors; the nature of the sectors themselves; the dimensions that define the sectors, including their complex overlapping and blurring with the third and nonprofit sectors; administrative reforms and organizational change; and the theoretical and practical analysis of major administrative topics, such as organizational goals, structure and individual motivation and work attitudes."[54]

It is clear to me that this topic does not lend itself to clarity and certainty. Indeed, the discussion in this chapter indicates that the topic actually illustrates a set of behaviors and problems that are consistent with the argument that the US society and its institutions are constructed to generate contradictions. We want an effective public sector but fear that it might overshoot its authority base and overly constrain the private sector. We want efficiency but aren't clear what that means or what has to be traded off against that value. And we believe that government should express something like a public interest but aren't sure how it can be determined or how it can be conceptualized in a society with multiple interests.

Once we move away from the classic internal functions described through POSDCORB, the world becomes even fuzzier.[55] We must confront the nature of the environment in which these interactions occur. That not only includes the structural issues associated with the formal political system in the United States (e.g., shared powers and federalism), but also quite dramatic differences between organizations that deal with specific policy issues. We often think about cultures of organizations but forget about cultures of policies. All of these elements make it extremely difficult to devise a grand theoretical framework that serves as a road map for change. Movements such as NPM do proceed with a set of assumptions that seem to illustrate an a priori belief that the two sectors—as a whole—have much in common with each other and, as a result, the private sector's views about efficiency and outcomes can be transferred effectively to the public sphere.

This set of issues, while fascinating in itself, has significant consequences for the topic of federal management reform because the debate about the dimensions of the public and private sectors undergirds many of the management reform initiatives in the federal government. Most of the initiatives that are discussed in this book are constructed on assumptions about the relationship between the two sectors—their differences and similarities—and, perhaps most importantly, the appropriateness of using private-sector strategies as the basis for government-wide approaches to change. It is important to recognize that the borrowing process seems to work in just one direction; I am not aware of any instances in which the private sector borrowed techniques from the public sector. The private sector appears to be happy if the relationship is limited to the financial transfer of public funds to private sources. The various approaches that will be discussed in this volume are drawn from a range of experiences and illustrate the important role of structure, values, functions, and ways of defining attributes of the public sector. Public/private differences and similarities are a subject that becomes more complex as one digs into them and, as a result, are not well sorted out.

Notes

1. For more than thirty years, nonprofit management has been added to this comparison as developments in the nonprofit world and in the spread of contracts from both the public and private sectors have contributed to the growth of that sector. For the purposes of this discussion, however, I am focusing on the two original sectors.
2. Quoted in Allison, "Public and Private Management."
3. Murray, "Comparing," 364.
4. Ibid.
5. Ibid.
6. Bozeman and Bretschneider, "Publicness Puzzle."
7. Ibid., 202.
8. See, e.g., Radin et al., *New Governance.*
9. Desmarais and Abord de Chatillon, "Are There Still Differences," 128.
10. Appleby, *Big Democracy,* 7.
11. Gulick and Urwick, *Papers.*
12. Rainey, Backoff, and Levine, "Comparing."
13. Dunlop, list quoted in Allison, "Public and Private Management," from personal communication to Allison. Some find this list somewhat oversimplified.
14. Neustadt, list quoted in Allison, "Public and Private Management."
15. Rainey, Pandey, and Bozeman, "Research Note."
16. Robertson and Seneviratne, "Outcomes."
17. Kurland and Egan, "Public v. Private Perceptions."
18. Khojasteh, "Motivating."
19. Lachman, "Public and Private Sector Differences," 678.
20. Boyne, "Public and Private Management," 98.
21. Simon, "Why Public Administration?" 10.
22. Stark, *Drawing the Line,* 10.
23. See Rainey, Pandey, and Bozeman, "Research Note."
24. See Kurland and Egan, "Public v. Private Perceptions."
25. Lawrence and Lorsch, *Organization and Environment,* 3. Italics found in the original.
26. Ibid.
27. Osborne, "Delivering Public Services," 1.
28. President's Private Sector Survey on Cost Control, *Management Office Selected Issues,* vol. 8, *The Cost of Congressional Encroachment,* report submitted to the subcommittee for consideration at its meeting on January 15, 1984, i–ii.

29. The economic framework has been used to describe other aspects of public action. E.g., Downs, *Economic View of Democracy.*
30. Downs and Larkey, *Search for Government Efficiency,* 6–7.
31. Robertson and Seneviratne, "Outcomes of Planned Organizational Change," 548.
32. Nutt and Backoff, "Organizational Publicness."
33. See Clinton and Gore, *Putting Customers First '95.*
34. Frederickson, "Comparing," 265.
35. Alford, "Defining the Client," 338.
36. Bozeman, *Public Values,* 2.
37. Ibid., 3.
38. Ibid., 5, 6.
39. Ibid., 7–8, 13.
40. Ibid., 68. His work sets the stage for a number of issues that will appear later in this volume, such as those reform efforts associated with the NPM movement.
41. Skepticism about using the concept of customers has appeared in other countries as well. For example, the British Liberal Party issued a discussion document titled "Citizens Not Customers" that argued that a customer focus rather than a citizen focus will both increase institutional costs and disable individuals and communities from doing things for themselves.
42. Rainey, Backoff, and Levine, "Comparing," 234.
43. Ibid.
44. These generic schools are likely to favor private-sector concepts and approaches over public-sector views. Some of this occurs because of the accreditation process through which they must jump.
45. Private-sector consulting practices have been drawn to the public sector in this process and are sometimes the transmitters of those ideas.
46. Simon, "Why Public Administration?" 10.
47. A contemporary example of this is found in the positions of Libertarians who oppose civil rights legislation because various aspects of requirements limit the autonomy of the private sector.
48. Hirschman, *Shifting Involvements,* 3.
49. Ibid., 4, 6.
50. Ibid., 7.
51. Ibid., 14.
52. Ibid., 15.
53. Rainey and Bozeman, "Comparing," 448.
54. Ibid., 450.
55. Despite the belief among some academics that the POSDCORB model is no longer relevant, it continues to be alive to a significant number of practitioners.

3

POLITICAL STRUCTURES MATTER

Thus, although we locate elite decision making at the centre of the process of reform, and although we would maintain that intentional acts of institutional design have been crucial to the story we have to tell, this should not be read as an elevation of organizational elites into God-like designers who are routinely able to realize bold and broad schemes of improvement. On the contrary, we envisage their schemes as frequently vulnerable to cognitive limitations, cross-cutting actions, politico-administrative roadblocks and unforeseen developments of a wide variety of kinds.

Christopher Pollitt and Geert Bouckaert, *Public Management Reform*

AN ACKNOWLEDGMENT OF GLOBALIZATION IS ONE OF THE DISTINCT changes that has occurred in the public administration/management field over the past two decades. Developments in technology and travel opportunities over these years have almost erased the boundary lines between domestic American administrative scholarship and what has traditionally been termed "comparative administration."[1]

Even the Government Accountability Office (which usually focuses only on behaviors and issues within the United States) has found it useful to draw on examples across the globe as it examined a number of administrative reform efforts within the federal government.[2] Evidence of globalization is found in the programs of research organizations that historically focused only on US issues. Books such as Pollitt and Bouckaert's *Public Management Reform* seek to sort out the several ways in which the subject might be developed; they differentiate between activity, structures, and processes of executive government and the systematic study of either activities or structures and processes.[3]

But despite the interest in globalization and acknowledgment of shared problems across the globe, there has been limited attention to the origins of the US system. Frank Goodnow observed that the system of administration originally established in this country, while based on that of England, differed from the English system in several respects. He noted that the characteristics of the parliamentary system with the powers of the Crown greater than those of the Parliament were "abandoned by the framers of the new governments on this side of the Atlantic. They made a complete break with the formal institutions of the past, and based their new governments on the principle of popular control."[4]

By contrast, however, Daniel Carpenter has observed that "much as the American Revolution was energized by a revolt against executive power, Americans quickly came to reembrace executive and bureaucratic institutions in the early Republic. In doing so, they both knowingly and unknowingly embraced and inherited organizational forms that they had attacked just decades earlier."[5]

The result of opportunities for exchange of experiences and comparison of methods has generated two rather distinct approaches to comparative analysis of different systems. One approach searches for patterns that transcend national boundaries and emphasize shared or similar functions, problems, and opportunities. I call this the search for similarities. The other approach acknowledges these patterns but emphasizes the importance of differences between systems that emerge from their histories, cultures, and structures.[6] I call this the search for differences. The second debate often involves attention to the differences between structures/forms of democratic government, particularly the presidential, parliamentary, and shared-power systems and structures dealing with federalism. It thus attempts to develop an understanding of the forces that lead to the actions of different governance systems.

These two perspectives are useful as one attempts to describe the literature and approaches to management reform both in the United States and in many countries across the globe. There is a range of scholars who have searched for similarities in almost all the subject areas discussed in this volume. Their work is found in accepted scholarly settings; these include a number of journals, the conference programs of international organizations, and books and articles. They tend to focus on several issues. First, they comment on the shared problems that have emerged in quite diverse settings and tend to use the same English words to describe them. These words are often drawn from the technical aspects of reform, relate to administrative functions, and largely avoid attention to the external environment of the organizations and the context of the change desired. In that sense, they avoid dealing explicitly with political actors and their agendas as well as other players (such as interest groups) who vie with the managers for attention and changes. Even if the management reform agenda in some situations has emerged from ideological or political concerns, the language that is used to describe the activity minimizes attention to those concerns.

Second, in an era where most nations are facing fiscal scarcity, they focus on efficiency issues, the costs of public spending, taxation, and concern about citizen support for expenditures. Thus a number of the reform efforts are either directly or indirectly related to the government's budget process.

And third, given these two tendencies, management reformers find it helpful to draw on private-sector models. They do not emphasize politics but accentuate the importance of efficiency and generally differentiate between facts and values. Arguments based on "the facts" are common, and advocates of this approach seek to make their cases dealing with what they describe as straightforward issues that can generate value-free and neutral information. It is not surprising that this approach fails to produce interest in distributional or redistributional questions but rather tends to stay at assessments at the aggregate level. In particular it fails to produce information that determines what element of the citizenry needs or benefits from programs.

But it is the second approach—the search for differences—that is of interest to me and this book. It is my argument that too many US public management scholars and practitioners have failed to appreciate the importance of structure in determining how management reform efforts play out. In a sense we are expressing a residue of our colonial past. We rest on assumptions drawn from the British parliamentary system that are difficult to fit into the US structure of shared powers and federalism. Since there are more parliamentary systems around the world, globalization has made Americans more conscious of efforts of those within parliamentary systems. Although each parliamentary system around the globe has its own distinct characteristics, the scope of the British Empire and the use of the British government system as a model in many parts of the world seem to me to justify attention to the Westminster system.[7]

This chapter explores this set of issues by contrasting the characteristics of the US and British systems and examining how these differences help to understand the management reform agendas that have been devised in those two countries over the years. While I acknowledge that both systems produce similar agendas and devise similar initiatives, they have quite different meanings because of the structures that define them. At the same time, they often share some problems dealing with the concerns of management reformers. This chapter discusses the general characteristics of the two systems and then contrasts the way they operate in two areas: performance measurement and relationships between central government and state/local governments.[8]

Characteristics of the British System

Colin Talbot has described the United Kingdom as one of the most centralized systems in the developed world. He notes that although the vast majority of the public services in the United Kingdom are not formally part of the central government and the civil service, the central government actually holds and uses great powers over how these services operate. Further, "Central government in Westminster holds great legal power in that it authorizes all lower tiers of government and public services—none of which have any constitutional standing. Even the devolved governments in Scotland, Wales, and Northern Ireland exist only on the basis of Acts of Parliament, which could in theory be amended or even evoked at any time. Local governments likewise only exist by permission of the central Parliament and can be reorganized or even abolished by it."[9]

The contemporary approach within the United Kingdom to management reform largely emerged during the past three decades and is built on the Northcote-Trevelyan report of 1854, which became the blueprint of the modern British civil service.[10] That report established the elite and independent public service that was pictured in the two BBC television series *Yes Minister* and *Yes, Prime Minister.*[11]

During the era of Prime Minister Margaret Thatcher, a range of actions were taken that actually became the basis for management reform issues undertaken by the Blair government in its New Labour approach.[12] It began by the abolishment of the Civil Service Department and a transfer of control to the Prime Minister's Office and the Cabinet Office. A report titled "Improving Management in Government: The Next Steps" was issued in 1988 and provided the blueprint for subsequent change. According to Hogwood, "The implication was that the structure of government would move from an old pattern of monolithic departments with no clear separation of policy and executive functions, and with ministers responsible for all activities, however detailed, to a new standard pattern of small policy cores with nearly all executive activities carried out by agencies within departments and with ministers not responsible for day-to-day operational decisions."[13]

Talbot lists four characteristics of the British system that are particularly important. First, "the executive branch of government (Cabinet and civil service) has strong discretionary and administrative powers quite unlike many other advanced democracies." Second, the parliamentary branch of government is relatively weak on a number of issues such as authorizing and scrutinizing expenditures. Third, the UK government "has systematically created, or enhanced, and then delegated to, third-party auditors and inspectors" for monitoring purposes. And fourth, "the judicial branch of British government is reluctant to interfere with administrative decisions and whilst this has been changing in recent years, levels of judicial intervention are still relatively low."[14]

Given the centralization of power in the British structure, it is not surprising that attention is given to the "core executive"—three entities made up of the Prime Minister's Office (often known as No. 10), the Cabinet Office, and the Treasury Department (called Her Majesty's [HM] Treasury). According to Talbot, No. 10 and the Cabinet Office have blurred relationships; the Strategy Unit was created in 2001 to look at issues that cut across departmental boundaries and thus pose long-term challenges.[15] And the Prime Minister's Delivery Unit was originally created as a part of No. 10/the Cabinet Office but was transferred to Treasury in 2002.

Historically Treasury has occupied a relatively strong position in the British government. Talbot commented on its recent role: "Treasury has always had some influence over the policy-options of spending Ministries through the Budget process. It can agree, or veto, various spending plans and thereby affect policy-choices. By making these spending decisions more medium-term, and adding the formal requirement to report what was achieved for the spending . . . and as well as what was spent, Treasury markedly increased its influence [relative to the spending ministries]. . . . [Its] hand had clearly been strengthened by the additional levers available to it under the new system."[16]

Because of this structure, decisions that relate to the issues discussed in this volume begin and usually end inside No. 10, the Cabinet Office, and Treasury. Two tensions do emerge from this system but they have not really eroded the core executive control. The first, according to Richard Whitaker, involves "suggestions for reform of parliamentary procedure aimed at improving parliament's ability to scrutinize legislation and build up expertise and information independently of the executive. . . . A common criticism of standing committees at Westminster is that while they provide an opportunity for line-by-line scrutiny of legislative proposals, amendments put forward in committee by anyone other than the government are rarely accepted and governments are very infrequently defeated."[17] It is somewhat ironic that the Westminster parliamentary structure produced a system in which the executive (once chosen by the party in power) has effectively eroded its role in many areas, particularly those that are of concern to management agendas.

The second involves tension between the specialized cabinet departments and the core executive. This occurred both between the units created by No. 10 and the Cabinet Office and the substantive departments as well as between Treasury and the departments, largely over budget decisions.

Characteristics of the US System

Whereas there are some elements of the British system that seem familiar to an American, the authority structure of the US system is clearly quite different from that in Britain.[18] Unlike the United Kingdom, the US system is designed both to avoid concentrated power and to fragment decision making in a way that makes it difficult to establish clear goals, values, and approaches. And unlike the British civil service system (usually defined as an elite system), the US federal bureaucracy is a mixture of individuals who are drawn from a range of socioeconomic sectors of the society and who are largely specialists (rather than management generalists) in particular policy areas.

Where the British system makes it possible for players to assume the predominant role of the executive, the US system's structure of shared powers between the executive, the legislature, and the judiciary has produced a predictable system of conflict between the players. While the original designers of the system (especially Madison) viewed Congress as the first branch of government, the post–Civil War expansion of government, urbanization, and industrialization made the executive branch more important than it had been in the past to those concerned about management. And this clearly continued as the government grew in size, functions, and complexity.

The structure, however, defined areas of conflict between the legislature and the executive in ways that were unknown both to those in Westminster systems and those in the private sector.[19] Unlike the prime minister and the treasury minister in a parliamentary system, the president does not have authority to determine the budget; rather the president produces a budget that Congress can change and must approve. Party identification is not a firm predictor of what will occur. Similarly, the president can propose legislation that can be ignored by Congress. And vice versa, Congress must deal with the potential of a veto by the president for both the budget and legislation. In addition, the Senate has the ability to reject top appointments to important positions within the executive branch and to play an oversight role as it holds the executive branch accountable for the implementation of programs and policies approved by Congress and the president. And unlike the Westminster system, the bicameral structure of Congress makes it difficult to know what "the Congress" actually wants.

Even the structure of the budget side of the Office of Management and Budget (OMB) mirrors the fragmentation found in the congressional committees and subcommittees that deal with appropriation and authorizing authorities separately. Despite attempts to develop cross-cutting and government-wide decision processes in both Congress and the White House, those processes make it extremely difficult to determine what it means to have decisions made by "the government" in the United States. Is it what comes from the White House or from the multiple committees and subcommittees of Congress?

While the system created multiple centers of authority, it is not always clear which branch of government comes out ahead and is ascendant at a given time. Even when both branches of Congress and the White House are controlled by the same political party, party discipline does not always lead to agreement. Indeed, institutional conflict between the branches often seems more important than shared political party affiliation. Unlike a parliamentary system, ignoring political party discipline does not cause a government to fall.

The fragmentation of the US system also creates a complex set of interactions that define the relationships between the Executive Office of the President and the programmatic departments. Like the UK Treasury, OMB within the Executive Office seeks to play a controlling role vis-à-vis the budget and in terms of limiting the policy discretion of the cabinet officials.[20] But the US system limits those desires since cabinet secretaries know that it is Congress that has the ability to determine budget allocation amounts and also to influence the substantive focus of programs. And Congress (no matter which party is in control of the two houses) is attentive to the wishes and influence of a range of external actors within the interest group community.

In addition, the United States has rarely experienced the discipline or even the structure of cabinet government. The recent attempts to create what have been termed "policy czars" are moves to place a trusted White House staff person in a position of coordinating or even attempting to control the discretion of the cabinet officials.[21]

All of this creates a system that demands negotiations and bargaining behavior between the multiple players in Congress and the Office of the President if any decision will actually be made. It also sets up situations in which games are played between the various actors within both branches of government. The language that OMB and the Executive Office of the President use sounds very similar to that employed by the British core executive. But rather than communicating authority and formal power, the US system encourages symbolic policy positions and bluffing behavior.

The OMB management staff is limited in size and scope and has minimal ability to follow through on implementation of management policies. If departments and agencies do not fully comply with directives, it may be because they receive conflicting directives from some element in Congress and thus have to find ways to live with both sets of expectations.

Performance Measurement in the United Kingdom

Colin Talbot has observed that performance measurement in Britain started "in piece-meal ways in local services and the National Health Service . . . in the early 1980s, gradually spread into central government in the late 1980s and early 1990s, and then culminated in the late 1990s in the establishment of a virtually universal system across all public activities—including government departments and ministries by the end of that decade." The gradual process that he described "was so pervasive that by mid-1990s there were few public services delivery bodies that did not have some form of performance reporting requirement."[22]

These efforts began during the Thatcher years and became the basis for the Public Service Agreements (PSAs) developed during the Labour government beginning in 1998. Those agreements have been described as a "double contract." They were contracts between Treasury and the ministries and, at the same time, were described as contracts between the government and the people and Parliament about what services the government would deliver as a result of the resources used to provide them.[23]

The government presented its targets through the agreements as serving four purposes:

1. Providing a clear sense of direction and ambition.
2. Providing departments with a focus for delivering results.
3. Providing a basis for monitoring what is and isn't working.
4. Providing better public accountability. [24]

Talbot characterized these agreements as clearly not contracts in the legal sense. "Although they both stated government intensions neither were approved by Parliament—actual spending decisions continue to be enacted through annual Budgets legislation and PSAs had no legal standing at all. Nevertheless, despite these caveats, PSAs had substantial political and administrative energy behind them."[25]

By 2007, following the abolition of Service Delivery Agreements, two moves shifted the approach. First, there was a focus on reducing the number of measures devised by ministries and other bodies and an emphasis on reporting achievement of outcomes. At the same time, there was a second move—the development of what Talbot called "a major efficiency programme"; this was an attempt to save money and an emphasis that flowed from increased centralization in the core executive functions.[26] These were called Departmental Strategic Objectives (DSOs).

Talbot described the impact of the shift as follows: "The nature of PSAs, as such, had clearly changed dramatically. Previous sets of (mainly) Departmental PSAs were primarily a quasi-contract between HM Treasury and the spending Ministry, linking resources to reform and delivery. But PSAs in 2007 had shifted to being mainly a statement of collective government targets. The function that PSAs had played previously between HM Treasury and individual departments was relegated to the DSOs. This was a major shift."[27]

As of this writing, evidence about performance measurement in the United Kingdom can be summarized as a complex process that seems to move toward the following:[28]

- a fairly comprehensive system that embraces everything from central government ministries down to front-line services;
- an increasing focus on outcomes;
- a largely top-down system, one in which lower-tier organizations are mandated either legally or administratively to produce data;
- use of third-party audit and inspection bodies;
- a mixed picture of both positive and negative impacts;
- shifting political priorities and time frames;
- difficulty by Parliament to adapt itself to the system;
- uncertainty about how much impact this process has had in the general population.

Performance Measurement in the United States

The major formal activity in the US federal government that focused on performance measurement came in 1993 with the passage of the Government Performance and Results Act (GPRA).[29] Unlike a number of other management reform efforts within the federal government that emerged only from the executive branch, this initiative became formalized through congressional legislative action.

The involvement of Congress in the decision process was greeted with anticipation by some scholars and management reform observers. For example, David Rosenbloom called the legislation "a powerful solution" to historical problems that dealt with difficulty determining congressional intent as well as the tendency for congressional oversight to be quite late in the process (what he called "after-the-fact"). Rosenbloom welcomed the legislation and noted that it would provide "a proactive dimension [that] would strengthen Congress's ability to steer agencies toward the realization of its objectives."[30]

GPRA required all federal agencies to develop strategic plans, annual performance plans, and performance reports. These stipulations were implemented within the constraints and realities of the annual budget process. All of these requirements were supposed to elicit a focus on the outcomes that had been achieved in the use of federal resources and to justify requests for dollars in terms of both promised and actual outcomes. Although the legislation was passed by Congress in the first year of the Democratic Clinton administration, the idea for the legislation actually began in Congress and was originally introduced and supported by Republicans in the Senate.[31]

On its face, the GPRA legislation seemed quite straightforward—indeed, almost innocuous. It clearly followed the tradition of past reform efforts within the federal government. In a report on the historical antecedents of the performance budgeting movement, the General Accounting Office concluded that GPRA "can be seen as melding the best features of its predecessors. . . . Nonetheless, many of the challenges which confronted earlier efforts remain unresolved and will likely affect early GPRA implementation efforts."[32]

At the same time, there were differences between GPRA and earlier efforts. Its enactment as legislation (rather than as executive orders) built in a role for Congress that was relatively unusual in government reform efforts. In addition, GPRA's inclusion of pilot projects and provision of a number of years for start-up are not the usual way for reform efforts to be conceptualized. Most programs are enacted and expected to be implemented within less than a year. Although GPRA was enacted in 1993, its real requirements did not take effect until 1997. This four-year period was expected to provide time for agencies to prepare their submissions. However, many agencies did not use that time and waited until the 1997 date approached to think seriously about the process.[33]

Despite what seemed to be bipartisan support for GPRA, its implementation did not avoid political partisanship. The concept of GPRA came from Congress (which was controlled by the Republicans) and was accepted by the Clinton White House. The Republican leadership in Congress focused on the first "deliverables" required by GPRA (especially departmental strategic plans) and used those submissions as a way to criticize the Democratic White House.

Although some believed that the passage of GPRA in 1993 established an approach to management reform that both involved Congress as well as the White House and was bipartisan in nature, the Bush administration created its own approach to performance management within the executive branch. This approach was implemented by the Office of Management and Budget alongside the GPRA requirements. It was not always clear how the two efforts meshed with one another.[34] It was called the Program Assessment Rating Tool (PART) and viewed as a part of the Bush management agenda—the effort to integrate the budget and performance assessments. The effort has been described as including four purposes: (1) to measure and diagnose program performance, (2) to evaluate programs in a systematic, consistent, and transparent manner, (3) to inform agency and OMB decisions for management, legislative, or regulatory improvements and budget decisions, and (4) to focus program improvements and measure progress compared with prior-year ratings.[35]

PART started as a small-scale effort and reported information on sixty-seven programs as a part of the FY 2003 presidential budget. Following that, it expanded the process to include 20 percent of all federal programs within the FY 2004 budget document (231 programs). The process was expanded to include 20 percent more federal programs for the FY 2005 budget and subsequent years. Some changes were made in the requirements but the general format remained fairly consistent. The OMB budget examiner for each program played the major role in evaluating the assessments. Each of the programs included in a special volume of the budget documents was rated along four dimensions: program purpose and design (weighted at 20 percent); strategic planning (10 percent); program management (20 percent); and program results (50 percent).

Despite the use of the same vocabulary and seemingly similar agendas in both GPRA and PART, people who are concerned about performance operate within quite different contexts. Although individuals use the same words, the meanings that they give to these terms are not always the same. One of the reasons for this is that there is not a single motivation for concern about performance. There are at least three agendas at play:

- A negative agenda that seeks to eliminate programs and tends to blame those running the programs for problems. In the public sector it blames the bureaucrat for problems and seeks to cut back on the responsibilities of government.

- A neutral agenda that focuses on a concern about change. Individuals who work from this agenda argue that what worked in the past does not always make sense in the current or future environment.
- A positive agenda whose advocates believe that performance information will allow them to make a case for their programs and respond effectively with that data to those to whom they are accountable.

Some analysts (including this author) have characterized the US experience as one that fails to fit easily into the institutional structures, functions, and political realities of the American system.[36] GPRA and PART repeat the tendency of architects of management reform (mainly practitioners) to focus on what have turned out to be fairly ineffective approaches. They are a prime example of the difficulty of dealing with federal management as a government-wide strategy and set of generic activities and requirements. Rhetoric has emerged from the executive branch through those concerned about management in OMB, from the legislative branch through the government operations and affairs committees of the two houses of Congress, and from influential public management organizations.

There are a number of aspects of the American institutional setting that have an impact on the implementation of efforts such as GPRA and PART. These include the institutional conflict between the legislative and executive branches, the fragmentation of responsibilities within the legislative branch, intergovernmental relationships, tension between OMB and departments and agencies, and differentiated responsibilities and roles inside agencies and departments.[37]

This experience with both programs identified several issues:

- The PART effort focused only on the president's budget and was thus limited to an executive-branch perspective. Agency officials found themselves in the midst of a PART assessment that differed from what was expected in the congressional appropriations process.
- The OMB staff assessment of program purpose and design was viewed by some critics as an attempt to preempt the role of Congress. These critics believe that it is not appropriate for OMB to second-guess Congress in terms of such assessment.
- Both GPRA and PART were characterized by their proponents as value-free enterprises that could "simply" rate achievement of program goals. Yet program goals often include several purposes and multiple values.
- In order to satisfy both the GPRA and PART requirements, agencies would need to collect new data; however, agencies are frequently constrained by both the mandates of the Paperwork Reduction Act and budget limitations.[38]

When one compares the US experience with that of the United Kingdom, there appears to be a combination of both differences and similarities. The United States tried to devise a comprehensive system that was outcome focused and top down (as in the United Kingdom), but that was extremely difficult to implement in the US government structure. It did not really use third-party audit and inspection bodies (other than the Government Accountability Office [GAO]). But it shared the UK experience of a mixture of both positive and negative impacts, and difficulty in getting the legislative branch to adapt itself to the system. It certainly shared the British view that it was uncertain about how much impact this process had in the general population.

Relationships between the British Central Government and Local Governments

The second area of contrast between the US and British systems deals with the relationship between the central (or national) government and the local (and, in the case of the United States, also state) governments. The United Kingdom is often described as a unitary state in which the central government substantially directs most government activity. The earlier discussion focused on the centralization that is found in the UK parliamentary system in terms of the relationship between the executive and legislative branches of government. This section of the chapter deals with another form of centralization—geographic centralization in which the national government effectively controls or limits the powers of local government.[39]

Beginning with the Middle Ages, diversity in local government was an important part of the political structure in Britain. As the years elapsed, however, that diversity was eroded. Enactment of the Local Government Act of 1972 moved to make local government more uniform to simplify its structure. Consolidation of local governments occurred as a result. In 1982 the Local Government Finance Act established the Audit Commission, a national body that was charged with assessing local government activity throughout the country; it was described as "an independent watchdog, driving economy, efficiency and effectiveness in local public services to deliver better outcomes for everyone."[40]

By 2000 another Local Government Act required local councils to move to a similar executive-based system, again minimizing the differences among the local structures. The changes that occurred limited the traditional autonomy of local governments to levy taxes and to move independently of the agenda of the central government.[41] At the same time that the Labour government moved along the unitary path, it shifted the focus of the Audit Commission away from inspecting local government compliance with national direction and targets to a process that highlighted outcomes and provided more opportunities for local governments to respond to local circumstances.[42] It sought to devise joint reviews of local government activities that would continue to determine the level of outcome performance by individual localities. Local authorities were classified along four quadrants of performance; this information was used to "name and shame" authorities who did not meet performance expectations.

When the coalition government headed by David Cameron came into power in 2010, Eric Pickles, the communities and local government secretary, announced plans to disband the Audit Commission.[43] He called for measures that would

> refocus audit on helping local people hold councils and local public bodies to account for local spending decisions. The changes will pass power down to people, replace bureaucratic accountability with democratic accountability and save the taxpayer 50 million pounds a year....
>
> The Audit Commission's responsibilities for overseeing and delivering local audit and inspections will stop; the Commission's research activities will end; audit functions will be moved to the private sector; councils will be free to appoint their own independent external auditors from a more competitive and open market; and there will be a new audit framework for local health bodies....
>
> Ministers believe that the work of the Commission has increasingly become less focused on accountability to citizens and more on reporting upwards to Government, judging services largely against top down Government imposed targets....
>
> The aim is for such a system to be in place from the 2012/13 financial year, with the necessary legislation being sought in this Parliamentary session.[44]

As of this writing, it is not clear how this will play out. In February 2001, Martin Evans (the managing director for audit policy of the Audit Commission) sought to keep some of the functions related to the role of the commission alive even though the inspection activities were likely to stop.[45] While it is expected to collect a set of standardized performance data from local authorities it is not clear what it will do with that information. Even if the Audit Commission is disbanded, the general pattern of relationships in the United Kingdom emphasizes the power of the central government and its ability to structure expectations for the use of central government grants.[46]

Relationships between the US Federal Government and States and Localities

The second element of this analysis deals with the tension between the US federal government and states (and sometimes localities). Just as conflict is built into the US system through the sharing of powers between the three branches of government, the federal structure of the US government also builds in predictable conflict and tension within the intergovernmental system. Both structural elements were designed to limit the centralized power of the US government. Indeed, the original structure of the United States in the Articles of Confederation could not be agreed upon until the thirteen original states ratified the document. Thus, agreement depended on the individual votes of each of the states, not on an aggregate vote of the states combined.

The tension between the authority of the nation as a whole (as envisioned originally by Alexander Hamilton) and the individual states has continued since the early days of the nation. While the adoption of the Constitution provided more power for the nation, the advent of the Civil War indicated that the conflict between the states and the federal government continued. That conflict combined with racial issues to create very different views about federalism in the United States due not only to differences between the federal and state perspectives but also to the significant differences between and among states.

Urbanization further complicated this set of relationships. Local government was the legal creature of the states, and immigration patterns meant that many states were faced with very different populations within their borders as the overall population increased. During the twentieth century the federal government found ways to deal with new problems but often did so indirectly, frequently providing funds with limited requirements.

By the twenty-first century, the structural stress between states and the federal government led to a new form of conflict. On one hand, the federal government moved to hold grant recipients accountable to national goals and priorities while state (and often local) governments tried to meet their self-determined needs and priorities. This led to tension that resulted from mutual dependence between the two sets of actors and inevitable conflict between them.[47] As a consequence of this tension, concern about the proper role of the federal government was embedded in a variety of policy and management debates.[48]

During the past few decades, this set of concerns was attached to attention to the devolution of responsibilities for the implementation of programs that are supported with federal dollars. Fewer and fewer federal domestic programs are entirely implemented by the federal government and, instead, responsibilities for allocating funds and delivering services have been delegated to state and local governments and other third-party organizations.[49]

As a result, federal management reform initiatives that deal with accountability for the use of federal dollars may move toward application to state and local government settings. "Because so many of the federal programs involve intricate intergovernmental relationships, federal agencies have struggled with ways to structure these relationships. Federal agencies are balancing two competing imperatives. On one hand, they are attempting to hold third parties accountable for the use of the federal monies but, on the other hand, they are constrained by the political and legal realities that provide significant discretion and leeway to the third parties for the use of these federal dollars."[50]

Often the issues involved in these debates relate to political agendas and specific attributes of a policy issue. But because of the structural relationship between the federal government and the states, these federalism issues (and the role of the states) reflect important differences between the central government and states (and localities).

Conclusion

This chapter focuses on elements of political structure that make a difference in the way that different countries deal with management reform. Globalism has convinced many observers that significant elements seem to be the same. Yet an examination of two countries—the United Kingdom and the United States—indicates that despite similar initiatives and the use of similar arguments, the structures of the nations' systems provide very different contexts for these activities.

As a unitary structure, the UK government is able to approach management reform with assumptions that revolve around a unified, executive-based system in which history has carved out a predominant role for the central government. This does not mean that there is always agreement in such a system. Political shifts, contentiousness, constant change, and economic problems do cause changes to occur. But these involve battles around the margins of the system and do not hark back to basic attributes of the political system. At any given time there may be more or less attention paid to the role of the parliament, the level of discretion given to individual cabinet members, or the amount of control that is imposed on local authorities.

By contrast, US management reform constantly has to deal with issues that emerge from the complexity and fragmentation of the US political structure. When initiatives are advanced that work most effectively if the executive branch can control them, one can assume that the other two branches—especially Congress—are likely to find a way to minimize that control. The very structure of decision making erodes the ability of the Office of the President (and especially the Office of Management and Budget) to implement those initiatives without dealing with other factors. Indeed, there are explicit points of entrance in that process that provide a way for others to raise different concerns, operate with other values, and involve players (such as interest groups and state and local government) outside the federal government system.

At the most basic level, it is difficult to devise government management reform when it is not at all clear what player is "the government." It is clear what body is the government in the United Kingdom: it is the prime minister chosen by the parliamentary party (or coalition) with a majority of seats. The House of Lords has limited powers, and the local authorities can be regulated or not by the central government. By contrast, the US system's fragmentation creates constant change and conflict that emerges from the very structure of the system. There is no clear entity that is "the government."

Notes

1. See Lijphart, *Patterns of Democracy.* However, there is little in that literature that focuses on the relationship between the structures of governments and management reform issues.
2. GAO, *Results-Oriented Cultures.*
3. Pollitt and Bouckaert, *Public Management Reform,* 2nd ed., 13.
4. Goodnow, *Politics and Administration,* 100. This was an observation that appeared to be ignored by the Brownlow Committee as it looked to Europe for ideas for management reform.
5. Carpenter, "Revolution of National Bureaucracy," 43.
6. This was the approach developed in Simeon and Radin, "Reflections on Comparing Federalism."
7. See, e.g., Rhodes, Wanna, and Weller, *Comparing Westminster.*
8. I am indebted to Colin Talbot for his work on the United Kingdom, which has provided me with the basis for this comparison. See esp. *Theories of Performance* and "Performance in Government." Both of these sources describe the situation during the Labour government era, not during the more recent coalition government.
9. Talbot, "Performance in Government," 2.
10. See Cline, "Modernisation of British Government," 148.
11. The two main figures in the program were the top career public servant who was an Oxbridge graduate and knighted and the cabinet politician who graduated from a less prestigious institution and was less confident of himself.
12. See Hogwood, "Machinery of Government."
13. Ibid., 705.
14. Talbot, "Performance in Government," 16, 17.
15. Ibid. See also Bevir, "Westminster Model." Bevir finds that the reforms adopted by New Labour "are an example of politicians handing more power and decisions to judges and courts in an attempt to address problems of effectiveness and accountability" (560).
16. Talbot, "Performance in Government," 18.
17. See Whitaker, "Parliament and Government," 695–96. Indeed, Geoffrey Smith wrote a short volume in 1979 titled *Westminster Reform* that drew on congressional experience for suggestions.
18. As James Fesler observed, the Brownlow Committee did not appear to acknowledge the differences between the parliamentary and shared-powers systems. See Fesler, "Brownlow Committee."

19. See discussion in chapters 1 and 2.
20. See Tomkin, *Inside OMB*, for an analysis of the changes that have occurred in OMB over time.
21. See Jennifer Rubin, "Czar Legislation," *Washington Post*, January 7, 2011, http://voices.washingtonpost.com/right-turn/2011/01/czar_legislation.html.
22. Talbot, *Theories of Performance*, 2, 5.
23. Ibid., 7.
24. Excerpt from memorandum submitted by the Government to the Public Administration Select Committee in Parliament, 2003, quoted in Talbot, *Theories of Performance*, 8.
25. Ibid., 7.
26. Ibid., 10.
27. Ibid., 11.
28. This is drawn from Talbot's summary of what he called "evidence and analyses from multiple sources." Ibid., 29–30.
29. While PPBS was an important development during the Johnson administration, it did not emphasize the production of data as much as GPRA.
30. Rosenbloom, *Building*, 81, 82.
31. This discussion draws on Radin, *Challenging the Performance Movement;* see esp. chap. 6. There were earlier efforts to require agencies to develop performance measures in specific programs, particularly those in the Employment Training Administration in the Department of Labor.
32. GAO, *Performance Budgeting* (1997), 7.
33. Much of this discussion is drawn from Radin, "Government Performance and Results Act."
34. Gueorguieva et al., "Program Assessment Rating Tool," 39.
35. See OMB, "Performance and Management Assessments."
36. A similar argument was made in a January 2004 GAO report. See GAO, *Performance Budgeting* (2004).
37. See Radin, *Challenging the Performance Movement*.
38. See an extensive discussion of these issues ibid.
39. Not all parliamentary systems are unitary states. Australia, Canada, and India have combined parliamentary structures with federalism, creating an interesting mixture of both centralization of executive powers and decentralization (to some degree) to states.
40. See "About the Audit Commission," Audit Commission website, accessed December 31, 2010, www.audit-commission.gov.uk/aboutus/Pages/default.aspx.
41. This discussion focuses on the local bodies in England, not on moves to provide more autonomy to Northern Ireland, Scotland, and Wales.
42. See the Right Honourable Ruth Kelly MP, Secretary of State for Communities and Local Government, "Strong and Prosperous Communities: The Local Government White Paper," October 2006.
43. There appeared to be a pattern of low performance ratings for local authorities from rural areas in which the Labour Party was not in power.
44. See "Eric Pickles to Disband Audit Commission in a New Era of Town Hall Transparency," Department of Communities and Local Government, August 13, 2010, accessed January 1, 2011, www.communities.gov.uk/news/newsroom/1688111.

45. Letter from Martin Evans, managing director for audit policy, to Colin Talbot, February 9, 2011, re "CLG Select Committee Inquiry into 'The Audit and Inspection of Local Authorities.'"
46. Local councils are funded by a combination of sources including central government money, local taxes, business rates, and fees from local services.
47. See Buntz and Radin, "Managing Intergovernmental Conflict," 403.
48. Radin, *Challenging the Performance Movement*, chap. 7.
49. Ibid., 155.
50. Ibid.

4

CONTRACTING OUT: A-76

When an apparent miracle happened, it proved divine mission to the credulous,
and proved a contract with the devil to the skeptical.

George Bernard Shaw

THE FEDERAL MANAGEMENT REFORM EFFORT THAT DEALS MOST DIRECTLY
with the relationship between the public and private sectors is found in
circular A-76, issued originally as an executive order by President Lyndon
Johnson in 1966. While this is the official pronouncement that has served as
the basis for subsequent changes, it was not the first time that competition
between the federal government and the private sector was on the policy
agenda.[1]

Indeed, the outlines for what can be called "the contract state" date back
to the Revolutionary War and stimulated attention by the framers of the
Constitution. Phillip Cooper has noted that considerable effort was made to
provide "a solid foundation for American economic as well as political development." From 1792 onward, it "was becoming clear that contractors
were quite willing to gouge the taxpayer and did not always live up to their
promises about the level and quality of service." Cooper has observed that
contracting experience during the Civil War generated "the pervasiveness of
corruption and the damage that it produced that brought about an era of
reform, which, in turn, fostered the development of modern public administration."[2] Most of the early activity took place at the state and local government level and moved to the federal level during World War I and
subsequently during the World War II era.

This chapter reviews the development of federal contracting-out policy
and focuses on defense contracting as a current example of questions and
concerns that have been raised about these efforts. It discusses the ways in
which these reform policies deal with the contradictions in the US system.
It includes some attention to the economic problems faced by the federal
government that stimulated increased use of the practice (e.g., hiring freezes
and controls on hiring). It concludes with an analysis of the problems experienced in the federal contracting areas and some alternative ways to think
about these issues.

The earliest activity on federal contracting-out policy actually emerged
from Congress, first from the House of Representatives in the 1930s and
subsequently from the Intergovernmental Relations Subcommittee of the
House Committee on Government Operations in the 1950s.[3] It also was a
topic in both Hoover Commission reports, and between 1953 and 1960 the

Senate Select Committee on Small Business held hearings on government activities that competed with business.

White House activity surfaced during the Eisenhower administration when the Bureau of the Budget, the predecessor of OMB, issued a bulletin that stated, "It is the general policy of the administration that the Federal Government will not start or carry on any commercial activity to provide a service or product for its own use if such product or service can be procured from private enterprise through ordinary business channels."[4]

Yet Eisenhower's farewell speech on January 17, 1961, conveyed a different message. In what has become a classic pronouncement, Eisenhower gave the citizenry a warning about what he called a threat to democratic government. He termed that threat "the military-industrial complex," the relationship between legislators, the military, and the industrial sector that supports them.[5]

According to a Congressional Research Service (CRS) report providing a history of the development of the effort, the policy enunciated by President Johnson in the first version of A-76 emerged because "government policymakers' interest in reducing competition between government and the private sector might have been tempered somewhat . . . by contracting related problems or issues that surfaced in the 1960s." Further,

> the problems or issues included concern for how government employees were affected by the contracting out of government functions; a study of contract personnel at an Air Force base that revealed the contract was more costly than using government employees; an opinion from the general counsel of the Civil Service Commission [the predecessor of the Office of Personnel Management] that stated it was illegal for government employees to directly supervise contract employees; and a Department of Defense (DOD) study that found "that many service contracts were in conflict with Civil Service laws and were also more costly than in-house performance."[6]

The OMB activity paralleled congressional questions about contract operations that were raised in the 1960s. Phillip Cooper notes that as early as the mid-1960s Congressman Chet Holifield (D-CA) responded to GAO studies and its auditing process and called for a major study of federal contracting processes.[7] Legislation was finally passed in 1969 to create the bipartisan Federal Procurement Commission, which issued a report in late 1972. The commission identified 450 contracting problems and specified almost 150 recommendations for change. Among its recommendations was the creation of an Office of Federal Procurement Policy, enacted by legislation in 1974. It was given responsibility for the supervision of federal contracting policy across the executive branch, working with the already existing A-76 circular.[8]

The policy framework put into place by the original promulgation of A-76 has been described by CRS as relatively stable. Despite multiple revisions over the years, CRS characterized the requirements as "a policy statement, a requirement for agencies to submit inventories of their commercial activities to OMB, and guidance for determining who—government agency or private business—will perform commercial activities."[9] Over the years, both Republican and Democratic presidents and members of Congress bought into the rhetorical framing of the issue.

Johnson's implementing memorandum to departments and agencies noted that uniform guidelines and principles were needed "to conduct the affairs of the Government on an orderly basis; to limit budgetary costs; and to maintain the Government's policy of reliance upon private enterprise." A newspaper account of the document reported that "business spokesmen have long contended that the Federal Government, taking advantage of its tax-free, non-profit status, competes unfairly with private enterprise in many areas."[10]

The 1979 revision of the circular restated the policy. "In a democratic free enterprise economic system, the Government should not compete with its citizens. The private enterprise system, characterized by individual freedom and initiative, is the primary source of national economic strength. In recognition of this principle, it has been and continues to be the general policy of the Government to rely on competitive private enterprise to supply the products and services it needs."[11]

A submission in the *Federal Register* in 1978 noted that the draft revision expanded the ongoing policy "to recognize that 'governmental functions' must be performed by Government personnel, and that the taxpayer is entitled to economy in Government, which requires appropriate emphasis on comparative cost." By 1979 the revisions of the circular stated the following: "It is the policy of the United States Government to: *achieve economy and enhance productivity, retain governmental functions in-house, and rely on the commercial sector.*"[12]

Allison Stanger argues that these processes are an expression of core American values and describes the belief attached to them that the private sector is "us." She notes, "Yet the outsourcing of oversight and the lack of transparency that has accompanied its rise undermine those very values." She portrays the demands that emerged in the post–World War II economy as a "drive to harness private sector power to the public good."[13]

A-76 Moves to Statutory Form

The implementation of A-76 from 1966 onward circled around a number of issues that troubled some of the players in the system. The original instructions from the Bureau of the Budget (which became OMB) required agencies to develop an inventory of commercial or industrial activities costing $50,000 or more or a capital investment of $25,000 or more. While it did not require agencies to conduct cost comparisons, it did provide a competitive process to decide who would supply commercial goods and services. Subsequent presidents (Ronald Reagan and George W. Bush) did take steps to require agencies to conduct cost-comparison studies.[14] Overall, however, there appeared to be discretion for agency heads and managers to decide how to define cost-comparison studies.

According to the CRS history, "Circular A-76 generated both praise and concerns. Some have applauded the program for its chief feature, competition, which promises to yield increased efficiency, cost savings, better quality products, and more innovation."[15] Brian Friel of *Government Executive* wrote in 1999 that "many contractors have complained that the A-76 process gives public workers an advantage, while federal unions have complained that the process tilts the playing field in favor of the private sector."[16]

Evaluations of the process by GAO and by OMB itself found that implementation was frequently inconsistent and inequitable. Agency participation in the program was variable. Conflicting signals were also given by members of Congress, and legislation was sponsored to restrict the application of circular A-76. A 1995 GAO report documented agency problems;[17] the congressional monitoring office found the program to be "time-consuming, difficult to implement, disruptive, and threatening to both managers and employees."[18] Further, GAO found that agencies were not able to accurately calculate the cost of functions and to verify the savings.

These conflicting views were a part of the backdrop for the congressional debate over the Federal Activities Inventory Reform Act (known as FAIR), which was devised as a way to give A-76 a statutory foundation. The first version of the legislation was introduced in 1997 by Senator Craig Thomas (R-WY) as the Freedom from Government Competition Act. That version would have significantly limited the ability of government agencies (with few exceptions such as national security) to undertake activities that could be viewed as available in the private sector.

However, the bill that finally emerged from both houses of Congress did not mandate contracting out but did include provisions that required changes in A-76 requirements. The Clinton administration supported the 1998 legislation. Indeed, it appeared to be consistent with the agenda of Vice President Gore's National Performance Review, which called for increased use of contracting and other means to increase private-sector delivery of public goods and services or to end public involvement.[19]

According to the CRS history, FAIR required a number of changes in A-76. These included mandating the competitive process that agency heads must use, based on annual inventories of commercial activities performed by their employees. This analysis would be sent to OMB but also made available to Congress and the public. It also reinforced the concept of "inherently governmental" activities and established changes involving appeals and challenges of decisions, as well as limiting the application of A-76 to agencies with fewer than one hundred employees.[20]

What Does "Inherently Governmental" Actually Mean?

In September 1992, OMB sent a policy letter to the heads of executive departments and establishments, providing them with White House expectations about inherently governmental functions related to the Federal Procurement Policy Act.[21] It began by noting that "contractors, when properly used, provide a wide variety of useful services that play an important part in helping agencies to accomplish their missions. Agencies use service contracts to acquire special knowledge and skills not available in the Government, obtain cost effective services, or obtain temporary or intermittent services, among other reasons."[22] It continued:

> Not all functions may be performed by contractors, however. Just as it is clear that certain functions, such as the command of combat troops, may not be contracted, it is also clear that other functions, such as building maintenance and food services, may be contracted. The difficulty is in determining which of these services that fall between these extremes may be acquired by contract. Agencies have occasionally relied on contractors to perform certain functions in such a way as to raise questions about whether Government policy is being created by private persons. Also, from time to time questions have arisen regarding the extent to which de facto control over contract performance has been transferred to contractors.
>
> As a matter of policy, an "inherently governmental function" is a function that is so intimately related to the public interest as to mandate performance by Government employees. These functions include those activities that require either the exercise of discretion in applying Government authority or the making of value judgments in making decisions for the Government. Governmental functions normally fall into two categories: (1) the act of governing, i.e., the discretionary exercise of Government authority, and (2) monetary transactions and entitlements.

Further, the OMB letter sought to explicate the dimensions of such functions:

> An inherently governmental function involves, among other things, the interpretation and execution of the laws of the United States so as to:
> (a) bind the United States to take or not to take some action by contract, policy, regulation, authorization, order, or otherwise;
> (b) determine, protect, and advance its economic, political, territorial, property, or other interests by military or diplomatic action, civil or criminal judicial proceedings, contract management, or otherwise;
> (c) significantly affect the life, liberty, or property of private persons;
> (d) commission, appoint, direct, or control officers or employees of the United States; or
> (e) exert ultimate control over the acquisition, uses or disposition of the property, real or personal, tangible or intangible, of the United States, including the collection, control, or disbursement of appropriated and other Federal funds.

Inherently governmental functions do not normally include gathering information for or providing advice, opinions, recommendations, or ideas to Government officials. They also do not include functions that are primarily ministerial and internal in nature, such as building security; mail operations; operation of cafeterias; housekeeping; facilities operations and maintenance, warehouse operations, motor vehicle fleet management and operations, or other routine electrical or mechanical services.

Specific examples of both types of functions were provided in appendixes to the letter.[23]

Despite the detail that is found in A-76, some observers of the process have viewed the OMB role as an encouragement of contracting out. Phillip Cooper, for example, has noted that "in an era in which functions such as the operation of prisons and the management of government contracts have been contracted out, it is becoming increasingly unclear just where the line can be drawn as to what is an inherently governmental function such that the government could not hire a contractor to deliver a particular service."[24] By the change of administration in 2001, the Bush administration extended the reach of reliance on contracting through the President's Management Agenda. One of the five government-wide initiatives was on competitive sourcing. The document detailing the agenda described the Bush approach to this issue:

> Nearly half of all federal employees perform tasks that are readily available in the commercial marketplace—tasks like data collection, administrative support, and payroll services. Historically, the government has realized cost savings in a range of 20 to 50 percent when federal and private sector service providers compete to perform these functions. Unfortunately, competition between public and private sources remains an unfulfilled management promise. By rarely subjecting commercial tasks performed by the government to competition, agencies have insulated themselves from the pressures that produce quality service at reasonable cost.[25]

This action stimulated new interest in Congress. It directed GAO to create a panel to study Circular A-76 and to report its findings to Congress no later than May 1, 2002. The panel was chaired by the comptroller general himself and included representatives from the Defense Department, private industry, federal labor organizations, and OMB.[26] Its recommendations seemed to emphasize the perspectives of career civil servants (particularly concerns about protecting civil service jobs) and those who advocated increased contracting out. It did not focus on members who were emphasizing the role and function of government and the public sector in a way that might limit how extensive contracting decisions might proceed. It did, however, identify a number of principles for the process, including one that would "establish a process that, for activities that may be performed by either the public or the private sector, would permit public and private sources to participate in competitions for work currently performed in-house, work currently contracted to the private sector, and new work."[27]

Allan Burman, former administrator for federal procurement policy in OMB (and the author of the policy letter released in 1992), commented on the inherently governmental policy in a 2008 article in *The Public Manager*. He noted that the concern about the current policy

> shows the limitation of the policy in that it states these issues as important to consider but provides no bright-line test of allowability. In other words ... a decision needs to be made on the basis of the "totality of the circumstances" to determine the appropriateness of contracting something out to the private sector. Although some activities, such as providing maintenance support on a military base, are easy to address, others, such as the kinds of politically sensitive actions many are concerned about today (intelligence gathering or security services in Iraq, for example) are not. The policy demands a case-by-case determination. Moreover, this middle area is broad, decidedly gray, and subject to considerable debate.[28]

The Development of Increased Skepticism about Contracting Out: Contracting in Iraq

During the first decade of the twenty-first century, a series of actions by the federal government that involved contracts began to create new skepticism about the process.[29] The use of contractors in the war in Iraq and the contracting decisions related to the Katrina disaster were among the most public and intense sources of criticism. There have been a number of scholars who have written about various problems associated with contracting in Iraq. Some have emphasized programmatic and policy consequences of those decisions, others have focused on accountability issues, and still others have been concerned with legal issues related to those decisions.

In their book *The Responsible Contract Manager,* Stephen Cohen and William Eimicke provide a discussion of the US military and Iraq as an example of when not to contract. They note that "the war in Iraq is the most contracted-out war in world history. It is clear that overcontracting was one of a number of strategic errors in this war.... It is the amount of contracting that is of issue here."[30]

They raise a number of issues related to democratic accountability and emphasize the lack of coverage under military discipline in situations such as Abu Ghraib prison by contractor personnel as among the most grievous. They also note the problems that emerge when contractors try to rebuild infrastructure destroyed by the war at the same time that fighting continues. This is especially problematic in a war like that in Iraq, when the conflict is not a traditional conflict between sovereign nations. They further note that a number of contracts may have been let for political reasons; that makes management control particularly difficult.[31]

Cohen and Eimicke conclude their analysis with the hope "that the experience of cost overruns, corruption, and inadequate accountability will influence future contracting practices by the military and the government. . . . There is little question that the war in Iraq was characterized by overcontracting as well as poor contract management practices. The key lesson is that the extent of contractor effort and the management of contractor behavior must be subject to at least as high a level of strategic analysis as any other military activities."[32]

Allison Stanger's work *One Nation under Contract: The Outsourcing of American Power and the Future of Foreign Policy* uses the Iraq war to raise a series of questions about basic government accountability. She notes that GAO repeatedly warned "that the DOD is courting disaster by failing to address long-standing problems in the oversight and management of contractors. The Iraq operation only places those shortcomings in stark relief." She lists a number of problems associated with that contracting experience. She notes that the size of the contracts required five or six layers of subcontracting, which only further clouds transparency (she is particularly concerned about the ability of contractors to carry weapons). She describes the situation as one where "the ingredients for large-scale corruptions are thus firmly in place."[33]

She finds that "private actors, both for-profit and not-for-profit, increasingly played roles that were once the exclusive preserve of government. . . . A single individual can now make a significant difference in these areas without being on the U.S. government payroll. The proliferation of hybrid organizations that do not fall neatly into the government, business, or non-profit categories is the institutional manifestation of this new reality."[34]

Paul Verkuil, in *Outsourcing Sovereignty: Why Privatization of Government Functions Threatens Democracy and What We Can Do About It*, has commented that "the war in Iraq has been either an outsourcing nightmare or a bonanza, depending on whether you are the government or a private contractor. The war has posed enormous personnel and deployment challenges for the military. War requires the ability to bring services on line quickly which can be done only if the military contracts some services to the private sector. This necessity, however, brings with it management problems of the first order."[35]

Martha Minnow's *Boston College Law Review* article, "Outsourcing Power: How Privatizing Military Efforts Challenges Accountability, Professionalism, and Democracy," provides an even stronger critique of the process within the Defense Department. She writes:

> Private contractors have played key roles in recent high-profile scandals. These scandals hint at the degree to which the U.S. military has increased the scope and scale of its reliance on private security companies in recent decades. This trend offers many advantages, including nimbleness in the

deployment of expertise and geographic flexibility. But it also departs from conventional methods of accountability through both public oversight and private market discipline. The lack of transparency in the use of private contractors compounds the problem of assessing the impact of their increasing role. Failures of basic governmental oversight to ensure contract enforcement by the Department of Defense are well-documented. Departures from conventional government contracting procedures exacerbate these failures and obscure whether inherently governmental functions are in effect privatized. The large sums of money involved contribute to risks of corruption and a scale of private lobbying that can distort the legislative process. These developments jeopardize the effectiveness of military activities, the professionalism of the military, the integrity of the legislative process and foreign policy decision making, public confidence in the government, national self-interest, and the stability of the world order.[36]

The Development of Increased Skepticism about Contracting Out: The Obama Administration

The critique of the Iraq war raised a number of issues that began to find their way into the political discourse surrounding the 2008 presidential election. During the Obama campaign, one of the items mentioned in a document titled "Restoring Trust in Government and Improving Transparency" called for ending abuse of no-bid contracts. The campaign document stated:

> The current Administration has abused its power by handing out contracts without competition to its politically connected friends and supporters. These abuses cost taxpayers billions of dollars each year. According to a 2006 study by the House Government Reform Committee, federal contracting mushroomed from $203 billion in FY 2000 to $377 billion by FY 2005—an increase of 86 percent. And the value of contracts not subject to full and open competition grew from $67 billion to $145 billion during the same period—an increase of 115 percent. According to a report by the Center for American Progress, during just the last three years more than five federal officials have been convicted of crimes involving federal contracting, three others were placed under indictment, and more are under investigation. Barack Obama will end abuse of no-bid contracts. He will require that all contract orders over $25,000 be competitively awarded unless the contracting officer provides written justification that the order falls within a specified exception and that the requirements and evaluation criteria are clear for every contract.[37]

After the election and during the transition period, the Obama team released what they called "Blueprint for Change: Obama and Biden's Plan for America." That document focused on transparency changes that would have an impact on the contracting-out process. The Obama team noted, "Every American has the right to know how the government spends their tax dollars, but that information has been hidden from public view for too long." They viewed transparency as a way to track special interest spending.

> The nation's top government contractors have spent millions lobbying the government and contributing to federal candidates. Many of these companies go on to cash-in on lucrative no-bid contracts. For instance, Halliburton, the sixth-largest recipient of federal contracts, has spent more than $2.8 million on lobbying and $527,800 on political contributions since President Bush took office. As president, Obama will create a "contracts and influence" database which will disclose how much federal contractors spend on lobbying, and ensure citizens have easy access to contract details and contractor performance, such as compliance with federal regulations.[38]

A few months after taking office, the Obama administration promised to save taxpayer dollars by eliminating what doesn't work, improving oversight, and cracking down on waste. In March 2009 it asked agencies to save $40 billion in contracting annually by FY 2011 and to reduce the use of high-risk contracts. That memo stipulated that "every agency is taking steps to reduce the share of dollars obligated through new contracts in FY 2010 by 10 percent in each of the following categories: (1) contracts without competition; (2) contracts after a competition that receives only one bid; (3) contracts using time-and-materials/labor-hour; . . . and (4) contracts using cost-reimbursement."[39]

In July 2010, the White House reported that

> the President's mandate has instilled a new sense of fiscal responsibility in agencies and has slowed the costly and unsustainable contracting growth rate of the past decade. Agencies are ending ineffective contracts as well as contracts that support programs that are no longer needed, and they are increasing competition and reducing the use of high-risk contract practices that can lead to cost overruns.
>
> Between FY 2000 and FY 2008, total spending on contracts awarded without competition increased significantly from $73 billion to $173 billion. Dollars obligated under contracts that were open to competition, but generated only one bid, also increased dramatically from $14 billion in FY 2000 to $67 billion in FY 2008. Through its reform efforts, the Obama Administration has stopped this growth—and reduced it.[40]

The memo characterized the contracting reform initiative as part of a larger effort the president has undertaken to rein in wasteful spending. Other related initiatives included new rescission authority, "do not pay lists" to avoid improper payments, the curbing of earmarks, discretionary program cuts, statutory pay-as-you-go legislation, and technology reform efforts.

The Obama administration's administrator for federal procurement policy, Daniel Gordon, described what he called "the new fiscal discipline" in testimony before the Senate Budget Committee. He highlighted three interrelated efforts: agencies are focused on cutting contract costs, agencies are reducing the use of high-risk contracting practices, and agencies are building the capacity and capability of the acquisition workforce.[41]

But as the economic conditions deteriorated, the Obama administration's views on contracting were somewhat unclear. Contracts to the private sector were a form of stimulating the private-sector economy, but they also increased the federal budget.[42]

Power or Price?

Rhetoric aside, from the beginning it has not been easy for agencies to deal with the instructions that accompany the circular A-76 requirements. It did seem clear that the circular sought to define the limits of the reach of the federal government and to reinforce the commitment to capitalism and the primacy of the private sector. Along with this rhetorical commitment, many observers have believed that the policy has always seemed to assume that its motivation stemmed from a desire to limit the power and influence of the federal government. But the details that would follow over the years seemed to avoid making this argument explicit and, instead, focused on an argument that the private sector could perform at a lower price than could a government agency.

And while the policy continued to talk about "commercial activity" related to the purchase of goods and services, there was little discussion of the conceptual parameters of the task. As Phillip Cooper has noted, the differentiation between contracting out and privatization is not always understood. He argues that "real privatization involves taking the government completely out of a particular area of service delivery, where contracting continues the government's responsibility for a service but uses another organization to perform the service delivery."[43] Yet for some of the proponents of contracting out the decision to contract is closely linked to a belief that the service should not be performed by a government agency. Thus giving the responsibility to the private sector is a way of diminishing commitment to the provision of the service by the public sector even though it requires federal dollars to support the contract.

It was relatively easy to understand a situation in which the government purchased items that already existed off the shelf (one favorite example is the purchase of toilet paper for government agencies). But what about the situation in which private-sector contractors were performing services that did not actually have a market outside of government? And what does it mean to provide a service rather than a tangible product when the service is defined within the expectations and role of the public sector? Further, what occurs when the price of the services was created by the contractor rather than by the hidden hand of the market? Indeed, it seems as if the market for contracting out is determined by the groups of contractors rather than through some way of involving citizens (who are the basis for the classic economic framework of consumer control of markets). If the contract was determined because a skill set was not available inside the government service, wasn't this effectively moving a public-sector monopoly to a private-sector monopoly, especially if few private bodies responded to the request for proposals?

This is a case where the logic of the argument for contracting out is drawn directly from experience and assumptions in the private sector. As such, it seemed to gravitate to behavior based on several assumptions. First, the burden of proof should be on the agency to make a case why the work should be performed by the public sector rather than relying on the private sector. The attempts in later years to differentiate between services that are inherently governmental and those that are not indicate the confusion that surrounds the requirements.

Second, while there have been attempts over the years to acknowledge that price is not the only factor that should determine who receives a competitive contract, cost normally overpowers the other factors in the decision process. The separation of the contracting function from the program or policy function within many agencies sometimes minimizes attention to the complex details of program administration since the contract staff may not be familiar with the substance of the work performed under the contract.

Third, because funds for contracts often come from different budget categories than do funds for staff time, there has been limited ability to cost out or analyze the need for time and expertise of government staff who would be assigned to monitor the contract. Costing processes are particularly complex in situations where sole-source contracts are let (i.e., contracts are given without competition), and agencies may find themselves in a situation where they are without staff who understand the technical dimensions of the task.

These assumptions and realities illustrate the difficulty that both practitioners and scholars face when trying to find a way to examine the implementation of this set of requirements. While it is often couched in a series of technical fiscal techniques that mainly evoke the interest of accountants and financial analysts, peeling back the layers that encapsulate the activity exposes the complexity that is found in the public-private set of relationships. This initiative illustrates many of the contradictions in the US system and, as well, demonstrates the volatility of the swings back and forth between confidence in the public sector and confidence in the private sector. These swings suggest that Albert Hirschman's analysis of shifting involvements may make attempts to clearly define inherently governmental functions almost meaningless.

Contracting and Contradictions in the US System

The efforts surrounding federal management reform agendas involving contracting out illustrate a number of aspects of the three sets of contradictions found in the US system: structural dimensions, predominant values and approaches, and attributes of the public sector.

Structural Dimensions

As this chapter indicates, contracting out has been an agenda item in both the legislative and executive branches. However, the congressional role in this reform area has largely involved monitoring the activity of the executive branch and, as a result, a reliance on GAO for assessment of executive activities. There are few instances in which Congress played a more proactive role that would define its expectations about the extent and type of contracting activities unless there was some accusation of abuse of the system (which was usually attached to specific programs and was likely to trigger congressional input during either appropriations or authorization processes). Occasionally the government reform committees would express views about this reform agenda, but this did not seem to occur frequently.

Although several legal scholars have characterized the problems with A-76 as raising constitutional principles, there are few if any formal legal challenges to the process.[44] As such, the activity in this reform area can be characterized as found almost entirely in the executive branch and located within the Executive Office of the President, in OMB. The expectations are transmitted through executive orders or circulars from the president to agencies and departments.

The arguments for contracting out have also blurred the potential differences in developing contracting systems across federal, state, and local levels. If one separates administrative functions to differentiate between policy roles, fiscal roles, and service delivery roles, there are fewer and fewer examples of federal service delivery in the domestic policy area. This became more complex because of the increase in block grants and other ways of providing discretion to third parties to decide how to spend federal funds. Yet there is little acknowledgment of the impact of these differing roles in the three levels of government.

Predominant Values and Approaches

Efforts to minimize the activity of federal agencies and the role of career civil servants can be seen as an expression of Thomas Paine's belief that "that government is best which governs least." Even though contracting out does not always result in lower budgets, over the years the debates over A-76 clearly indicate that the private sector perceives that it is privileged by these efforts. Despite some rhetorical moves to argue for public-private cooperation, the debate has largely been posed as a win/lose situation. In fact, when public entities bid against private entities, that sets up an implicit conflict situation. This perception has led to the belief that when contracting grows, the public sector loses.

But the contradictions between efficiency, effectiveness, and equity values are perhaps the most important problem for the contracting-out reform efforts. As has been noted, despite irregular attempts to look beyond the public choice arguments for contracting out, the efficiency mind-set overpowers everything else.[45] Indeed, it appears that the A-76 development has made the system operate to give the burden of proof to the public sector to show why the work should not go to the private sector.

Occasionally, decisions made by agency officials about whether or not to contract include effectiveness arguments. But it is extremely rare to raise issues dealing with equity in that process. For example, such a decision would include assessment of who would be helped by the choice to move to the private sector. Creaming behaviors seem rational when private-sector groups find that they can minimize costs and increase their profits when they avoid serving difficult clients of programs. In addition, it has been suggested that elimination of lower-level jobs in the federal government has had a negative effect on the ability of lower-income people and people of color to come into the federal system. In addition, the belief that the market will self-regulate has justified limited attention to monitoring roles and failure to deal with corruption and transparency.

Attributes of the Public Sector

The experience over the life cycle of implementation of one version or another of A-76 indicates that there has been a belief that one can clearly separate policy and administration. That is, the decision to carry out a task can be made independently of the decision about who should perform it. The belief that one can sort out the differences between inherently governmental and inherently nongovernmental parallels the belief that there is a clear and consistent way to determine what is in the private sector and what is in the public sector. Just as the boundary lines between public and private have been blurred, so have the boundaries between inherently governmental and inherently nongovernmental. The persistent belief in the clarity of these boundaries seems to be a two-dimensional approach to a three-dimensional problem and has turned into a political mantra in the policy debate.

The A-76 history also indicates a failure by both political parties to acknowledge the fragmented nature of the US system. Throughout its lifetime, those who were charged with the implementation of the reform conceptualized it as a government-wide effort and searched for a one-size-fits-all strategy. Despite its limited staffing capacity, the unit within OMB charged with the implementation most frequently saw its role as based on a top-down, centralized strategy. There was little attention to the differences between program and policy sectors and the special problems attached to their cultures, the nature of their interest groups, and the structure of their implementation frameworks and policy designs. Instead of noting that some agencies had real difficulty complying with the requirements, those agencies were viewed as recalcitrant players and obstructionists.

Conclusions

It is difficult to make an argument that circular A-76 has created an approach that has improved the implementation of a significant number of programs in the federal government when the Iraqi experience is before us. The problems faced in contracting out have been discussed as an example of an attempt to simplify a very complex set of relationships. Yet there is little indication that the Iraqi experience has explored behaviors within the existing system that might improve the effectiveness and equity as well as the efficiency of programs. For example, the process has been limited to contracts between the federal government and the private or nonprofit sector. It has not explored the arrangements that have been devised through cooperative agreements; this is a mechanism that would structure substantial involvement between the grantee and government staff, requiring both parties to work together to accomplish the goals of the arrangement.

Given the contradictions found in the US system and the complexity of the system, it is important to find a way to establish collaborative arrangements that allow win-win situations to develop. The current A-76 system is not able to devise venues that can balance multiple views. Instead, the system defined actors and processes that tilted the balance to use frameworks that fail to provide an opportunity to acknowledge important aspects of the contradictions.

Notes

1. This discussion of the history of A-76 relies on a Congressional Research Service (CRS) report for Congress: Halchin, *Federal Activities Inventory Reform Act* (hereafter cited as CRS).
2. See Cooper, *Governing by Contract,* 18, 24, 31.
3. Ibid.; CRS, 2, 3.
4. Quoted in CRS, 3.
5. Since that time, the reach of the contracting relationship has extended beyond the military and has included contracts with private-sector groups in many different policy areas. See Smith and Lipsky, *Nonprofits for Hire,* for one such example.
6. Ibid., 3, 4.
7. Cooper, *Governing by Contract,* 42–43.
8. Ibid., 43.
9. CRS, 4.
10. Quoted ibid.
11. Quoted ibid.
12. Quoted ibid., 5.

13. Stanger, *One Nation under Contract*, 8.
14. CRS, 6.
15. Ibid., 7.
16. Brian Friel, "Study Promotes Fairness in A-76 Competitions," GovExec.com, December 23, 1999, www.govexec.com/dailyfed/1299/122399b1.htm. Quoted in CRS.
17. GAO, *Government Contractors*. Quoted in CRS, 2.
18. Ibid., 2.
19. See Carroll, "Rhetoric of Reform," 304.
20. CRS, 13–15.
21. *Washington Post* columnist Joe Davidson began a Federal Diary column with the following sentence: "'Inherently governmental' is one of those Washington terms that can signal a boring discussion is ahead." Joe Davidson, "Intelligence Contractors' Pay, Numbers Raise Concerns," *Washington Post*, September 20, 2011.
22. Allan V. Burman, administrator, Office of Federal Procurement Policy, to the heads of executive agencies and departments, policy letter 92-1, September 23, 1992. This letter was sent just two months before the election of Bill Clinton.
23. Quoting from the appendixes:

    The following is an illustrative list of functions considered to be inherently governmental functions:

    1. The direct conduct of criminal investigations.
    2. The control of prosecutions and performance of adjudicatory functions (other than those relating to arbitration or other methods of alternative dispute resolution).
    3. The command of military forces, especially the leadership of military personnel who are members of the combat, combat support or combat service support role.
    4. The conduct of foreign relations and the determination of foreign policy.
    5. The determination of agency policy, such as determining the content and application of regulations, among other things.
    6. The determination of Federal program priorities or budget requests.
    7. The direction and control of Federal employees.
    8. The direction and control of intelligence and counter-intelligence operations.
    9. The selection or nonselection of individuals for Federal Government employment.
    10. The approval of position descriptions and performance standards for Federal employees.
    11. The determination of what Government property is to be disposed of and on what terms (although an agency may give contractors authority to dispose of property at prices within specified ranges and subject to other reasonable conditions deemed appropriate by the agency).
    12. In Federal procurement activities with respect to prime contracts,
        (a) determining what supplies or services are to be acquired by the Government (although an agency may give contractors authority to acquire supplies at prices within specified ranges and subject to other reasonable conditions deemed appropriate by the agency);

(b) participating as a voting member on any source selection boards;

(c) approval of any contractual documents, to include documents defining requirements, incentive plans, and evaluation criteria;

(d) awarding contracts;

(e) administering contracts (including ordering changes in contract performance or contract quantities, taking action based on evaluations of contractor performance, and accepting or rejecting contractor products or services);

(f) terminating contracts; and

(g) determining whether contract costs are reasonable, allocable, and allowable.

13. The approval of agency responses to Freedom of Information Act requests (other than routine responses that, because of statute, regulation, or agency policy, do not require the exercise of judgment in determining whether documents are to be released or withheld), and the approval of agency responses to the administrative appeals of denials of Freedom of Information Act requests.

14. The conduct of administrative hearings to determine the eligibility of any person for a security clearance, or involving actions that affect matters of personal reputation or eligibility to participate in Government programs.

15. The approval of Federal licensing actions and inspections.

16. The determination of budget policy, guidance, and strategy.

17. The collection, control, and disbursement of fees, royalties, duties, fines, taxes and other public funds, unless authorized by statute, such as title 31 U.S.C. § 952 (relating to private collection contractors) and title 31 U.S.C. § 3718 (relating to private attorney collection services), but not including:

(a) collection of fees, fines, penalties, costs or other charges from visitors to or patrons of mess halls, post or base exchange concessions, national parks, and similar entities or activities, or from other persons, where the amount to be collected is easily calculated or predetermined and the funds collected can be easily controlled using standard cash management techniques, and

(b) routine voucher and invoice examination.

18. The control of the treasury accounts.

19. The administration of public trusts.

The following list is of services and actions that are not considered to be inherently governmental functions.

1. Services that involve or relate to budget preparation, including workload modeling, fact finding, efficiency studies, and should-cost analyses, etc.

2. Services that involve or relate to reorganization and planning activities.

3. Services that involve or relate to analyses, feasibility studies, and strategy options to be used by agency personnel in developing policy.

4. Services that involve or relate to the development of regulations.

5. Services that involve or relate to the evaluation of another contractor's performance.

6. Services in support of acquisition planning.

7. Contractors' providing assistance in contract management (such as where the contractor might influence official evaluations of other contractors).

8. Contractors' providing technical evaluation of contract proposals.
9. Contractors' providing assistance in the development of statements of work.
10. Contractors' providing support in preparing responses to Freedom of Information Act requests.
11. Contractors' working in any situation that permits or might permit them to gain access to confidential business information and/or any other sensitive information (other than situations covered by the Defense Industrial Security Program described in FAR 4.402(b)).
12. Contractors' providing information regarding agency policies or regulations, such as attending conferences on behalf of an agency, conducting community relations campaigns, or conducting agency training courses.
13. Contractors' participating in any situation where it might be assumed that they are agency employees or representatives.
14. Contractors' participating as technical advisors to a source selection board or participating as voting or nonvoting members of a source evaluation board.
15. Contractors' serving as arbitrators or providing alternative methods of dispute resolution.
16. Contractors' constructing buildings or structures intended to be secure from electronic eavesdropping or other penetration by foreign governments.
17. Contractors' providing inspection services.
18. Contractors' providing legal advice and interpretations of regulations and statutes to Government officials.
19. Contractors' providing special non-law enforcement, security activities that do not directly involve criminal investigations, such as prisoner detention or transport and non-military national security details.

24. Cooper, *Governing by Contract*, 72.
25. Executive Office of the President, *President's Management Agenda*, 17.
26. CRS, 20–21.
27. Ibid., 22.
28. Burman, "Inherently Governmental Functions," 1.
29. Enthusiasm about contracting out at the state and local level was also beginning to dissipate and scholars were becoming aware of some shift of decisions. See, e.g., Warner and Hebdon, "Local Government Restructuring."
30. Cohen and Eimicke, *Responsible Contract Manager*, 159.
31. Ibid., 164, 167.
32. Ibid., 168.
33. Stanger, *One Nation under Contract*, 104–5.
34. Ibid., 162.
35. Verkuil, *Outsourcing Sovereignty*, 129.
36. Minnow, "Outsourcing Power," 989.
37. "Restoring Trust in Government and Improving Transparency," Obama campaign document, 2008, unpaged.
38. "Blueprint for Change: Obama and Biden's Plan for America," Obama transition document, 2008, unpaged.
39. See "Cutting Waste and Saving Money through Contracting Reform," Office of Management and Budget, July 7, 2010, www.whitehouse.gov/sites/default/files/omb/assets/blog/Update_on_Contracting_Reforms.pdf.

40. Ibid.
41. Statement before the Committee on the Budget, United States Senate, 111th Cong. July 15, 2010 (statement of Daniel I. Gordon, Administrator for Federal Procurement Policy, Office of Management and Budget). By September 2011, Dan Gordon had announced that his office would establish a process whereby agencies could pool their purchases of office equipment to save money. Ed O'Keefe, "White House Hopes to Cut Costs by Buying in Bulk," *Washington Post,* September 19, 2011.
42. The stimulus package developed by the Obama administration clearly relied on the economic impact of contracts and subcontracts but developed opposition because it increased the federal budget.
43. Cooper, *Governing by Contract,* 71.
44. See the work of Martha Minnow.
45. In his article "Bureaucratic Theory Meets Reality," George A. Boyne writes that "public choice theory suggests that if public officials monopolize service delivery, then the result is oversupply and inefficiency" (474).

5
PERSONNEL POLICY REFORM

I believe serving as an SES would be a noble vocation, but unfortunately an all-consuming one. Challenges are great in life and certainly hard work goes with added responsibility, but there really is not much "work/life" balance as an SES (no matter how much its importance is discussed). A typical example—an SES sent me an e-mail at 11:27 PM. I responded at 7:00 AM the next day and received a response to my message by 7:15 AM. Something is wrong with this leadership model.

* * *

Although service at this level is attractive, the realities I see every day dissuade me from working towards a position at this level. Frankly, I see little quality work at the SES level, and much quality political maneuvering (which, in the end, contributes little to long term mission success). It is true the monetary rewards of SES positions are limited, but I am more concerned by what from my perspective is a limited opportunity to do quality work.

* * *

I have applied for a number of SES positions over the years and have found the process to be frustrating at best, and often demeaning. I would be interested in an SES position if there was some assurance that selection was based on knowledge, experience, and skills, rather than on favoritism. Unfortunately, the selection process in this agency in the past has been based on individual preferences and wired for specific individuals.

Quoted in Senior Executives Association and Avue
Technologies Corporation, Taking the Helm

Drip, drip, drip. Like Chinese water torture, the House Republican approach to issues affecting federal employees is a steady stream of niggling hits at their pay, benefits and now their labor organizations. There are bills to cut the number of federal workers, further extend their pay freeze, reduce their annuities and make them pay more for their health benefits.

Joe Davidson, "A Challenge to Unions' 'Official Time'"

MOST OF THE REFORM AREAS THAT ARE INCLUDED IN THIS BOOK RARELY provoke the interest of the general population, and few make the headlines of daily newspapers or coverage on nightly network news. But personnel policy reform is an exception to this pattern. It is common for Americans to link their skepticism about the role of government to the individuals who work for the government. There has been a tendency within the United States to hold those individuals—often career civil servants—responsible for the policies that they implement that may not be popular in all parts of the American society.[1] Rarely do the views of the senior career people about the reforms become a part of the reform debate.

Yet, as some personnel scholars have noted, "Well before the formation and development of the federal executive and the civil service system, there was a distinctly American approach to governance. . . . Even though, from the beginning, citizens complained about government workers, they recognized the value of a government job, and they also recognized the need to fill these jobs with people of moral standing and intellectual ability."[2]

Further, the proper nature of the federal bureaucracy is a subject of vigorous argument. "Should it reflect a particular requirement for high moral or ethical standards? Or should the 'spoils' of appointment simply belong to the victor? Should the policy and political preferences of the elected president or of Congress dictate the selection of workers? Or should selection be based on merit, that is, on fair and open competition for politically neutral competence? Should the bureaucracy be significantly 'representative' by geography, race, or interest group? Or should federal workers be especially educated in and dedicated to principles of efficient management, social sensitivity, and 'customer service'?"[3]

Given these dangling questions, it is not surprising that the relationship between personnel and other federal management agendas is uneasy. At the same time, federal personnel policy, its institutions, and—perhaps most important—its authority base are inextricably linked to broader federal management concerns.[4] Many of the issues that have surfaced over the years hark back to the influence of the Progressive movement, which called for the professionalization of the civil service. And as the welfare state expanded along with increased dependence on science and technology, more demands for expertise came from both the executive and legislative branches.

In their edited volume on public personnel management, Carolyn Ban and Norma Riccucci noted that reforms in personnel management have parallel developments in public management generally. They noted that reforms have focused on several issues—the creation of a merit system and the value of a professional public service. They comment that reforms have also focused "on two key themes: strengthening presidential control and improving management efficiency."[5]

Many of the reforms that have been advanced in this area emerged from activity at the state (and sometimes local) level. At this writing, efforts to hold public servants responsible for the policies they are charged with administering have come from a number of states, particularly from politicians in Ohio and Wisconsin.

The tendency to blame the bureaucrat for policies is not limited to the United States. In his recent memoir, former British prime minister Tony Blair described his frustration with the civil service system by characterizing civil servants' behavior as one of inertia. "They tended to surrender, whether to vested interests, to the status quo or to the safest way to manage things—which all meant: to do nothing." Blair found it useful to refer to the BBC television series *Yes, Prime Minister* to characterize the behavior of civil servants as the avoidance of risk at all costs, even though he acknowledges that the civil service is actually quite impartial.[6] And skepticism about the power of the bureaucracy (and bureaucrats) also emerged as a strong response to the demise of the Soviet Union and other countries that moved toward an increase in the role of the private sector rather than reliance on the public sector. This reaction was related to the interest in the NPM movement in a number of countries.

Attention to the role of the federal personnel system developed during the post–Civil War period in the United States as the role of government—and its size—grew. Passage of the Pendleton Civil Service Reform Act in 1883 marked the first significant activity; the act created a Civil Service Commission, eventually placed the majority of federal government employees on a merit system, and ended the reliance on what had been termed "the spoils system," where jobs went only to political supporters.

But the report of the Brownlow Committee in 1937 really marked the beginning of a concerted effort to examine the structural and policy construct of the federal government personnel system. The growth of the federal government during the New Deal was dramatic evidence of the changes that had taken place in the size and scope of the bureaucracy since the adoption of the Constitution. Indeed, by the time of the publication of the Brownlow Committee report, use of the term "the executive branch" to describe the bureaucracy seemed to suggest that this part of the system actually belonged to the White House. It was difficult to remember that Congress had been viewed as the first branch of the government when thousands of federal government staff members were thought to be accountable only to the executive branch.

For some observers, the civil service reform movement "swung between two objectives: the protection of government from politics and the promotion of government's ability to administer politics."[7] Since the Reagan administration, there has been an attempt to balance these two competing objectives with presidential proposals emphasizing the second: the promotion of the administration's ability to administer politics.

This chapter focuses on three proposals to reform the federal personnel system that pick up the concepts found in the Brownlow report and emphasize presidential efforts at change. The first proposal reviews the Civil

Service Reform Act of 1978, advanced by President Jimmy Carter and adopted by Congress. This effort made significant changes in the federal personnel system, replacing the Civil Service Commission with an Office of Personnel Management (OPM) and creating the Senior Executive Service (SES). The creation of OPM put the central control agency for personnel clearly in the executive branch.

Second is a review of the proposals that were advanced through the National Performance Review effort of the Clinton administration that reflected the concerns of advocates of NPM and proposed a set of shifts in the way that the bureaucracy would be organized. And the third example deals with the changes that were proposed by the administration of George W. Bush dealing with personnel policies in the Department of Defense (DoD) and the Department of Homeland Security (DHS). These changes were expected to be expanded to much of the federal bureaucracy.

The Civil Service Reform Act of 1978

According to Carolyn Ban and Patricia Ingraham, the Civil Service Reform Act (CSRA) "is extraordinarily complex and touches on most aspects of the federal personnel system. The changes it proposed are far-reaching and include some reforms that are radical departures from the old system. It also contains highly technical changes in personnel procedures, along with some changes that represent little more than tinkering with existing procedures."[8]

The bill that emerged sprang from two quite different definitions of the problem. The first involved the "widespread public perception that public bureaucracies were bloated and inefficient."[9] For twenty years the federal government tackled problems that were intractable, and thus the government moved into policy arenas that were controversial. The second problem emerged from the day-to-day experience dealing with the existing personnel system. Carter's creation of the Personnel Management Project provided the venue for the development of the proposals to change that system.

Ban and Ingraham highlighted several influences on the process—the recommendations that emerged from the scientific management movement in public administration as well as the "public's long infatuation with private-sector management techniques."[10] What emerged from the process were three "major inconsistencies" in the act:

1. The conflict between the desire for greater political responsiveness and the desire for greater managerial capability and independence.
2. The conflict between the concept of a management cadre with a sense of identity and esprit de corps and the concept of competition to increase productivity.
3. The conflict between the goal of increasing managers' ability to fire problem employees and the goal of protecting whistleblowers.[11]

The Civil Service Reform Act (Pub. L. No. 95-454, 92 Stat. 111) itself was more than a hundred pages in length and has been described as the first comprehensive civil service law since 1883. It did fulfill the campaign promise of President Jimmy Carter to reform the federal civil service. To do so, it abolished the bipartisan Civil Service Commission and created three new agencies to implement these reforms: the United States Merit Systems Protection Board (MSPB), OPM, and the Federal Labor Relations Authority (FLRA).

As Ban and Ingraham noted, the legislation contains themes that at times are inconsistent with one another. The act sought greater accountability of federal employees for their performance by increasing the discretion and authority of federal managers; this was a way to respond to growing public concerns about the operations of federal agencies. At the same time, the act emphasized protection of the rights of federal employees from abuses by federal managers, responding to the Watergate experience and concerns about the way that President Nixon had dealt with the civil service system.

Central personnel agencies serve as a watchdog to assure that agencies adhere to merit principles in appointments, promotions, and dismissals.[12] For staff inside departmental and agency offices, this role is overly rigid. James Fesler and Donald Kettl have described this relationship as one in which "the central and departmental personnel offices' staff members are perceived as abominable 'no'-men, people who lack understanding of the individual program and its staffing needs, people looking for something to come up that they can turn down."[13]

The classic responsibility of a central personnel agency was shared between the three units created by the CSRA. The OPM was charged with executing, administering, and enforcing the civil service laws, rules, and regulations, preparing and conducting competitive examinations for positions common to federal agencies, and delegating this responsibility if it wishes to agencies and departments. The MSPB has responsibility for adjudicating employee appeals, reviews OPM regulations for compliance with merit-system principles, and conducts studies of the civil service system. And the FLRA was charged with protecting the statutory rights of government employees to join labor unions, choose collective bargaining representatives, and be protected from unfair labor practices. It is viewed as a parallel institution to the National Labor Relations Board.

Although it was not necessarily the main focus of the policy formulation process, for some analysts of the process the creation of the Senior Executive Service (SES) was "the most significant accomplishment of the Civil Service Reform Act of 1978."[14] The idea was not new; it had been found in the Second Hoover Commission report, and the idea of an elite corps of federal senior managers was probably influenced by the British system of generalists who could be moved around the bureaucracy as skilled managers.[15]

The SES replaced the top three tiers in the federal government service system as well as noncareer positions and political positions that were filled by the president without Senate confirmation. Approximately 8,000 individuals who were in those positions were given the opportunity to join the SES, trading some of their current job security for increased opportunities for higher salaries, faster promotions, and interdepartmental job transfers.[16]

OPM describes the system as follows: "The Senior Executive Service consists of the men and women charged with leading the continuing transformation of government. These leaders possess well-honed executive skills and share a broad perspective of government and a public service commitment which is grounded in the Constitution. . . . The SES was designed to be a corps of executives selected for their leadership qualifications."[17]

The Senior Executive Service provides top officials greater authority in assignment and determination of pay. However, the way that this authority is used appears to have been variable depending on the administration that is in power. In some agencies, for example, the mobility authority has not been used, reflecting the belief that positions require specialized knowledge of policy areas. Thus the past investment in technical ability by current SES members is viewed as more important than providing new opportunities for others. During some administrations and in some agencies, the SES authority has provided an opportunity for political appointees to remove individuals from existing jobs and reassign them to other positions. It has been suggested that the creation of the SES had very little impact on the work of federal officials, despite the arguments that were used during the formulation of the program.[18] It has also been noted that the creation of the SES sets up (or reinforces) conflicts between career employees and noncareer employees.

In addition, the act authorizes merit pay and bonuses that give senior officials greater control over middle-level managers. Under the act, pay, job retention, and discipline depend on job performance. In addition, the act increases the ability of each government agency to create its own standards and procedures within the framework of the act.

Skeptics continue to be wary of the increase in the discretion and authority of top federal managers (especially political appointees), believing that it can threaten the legitimate rights of federal employees. The concept of the civil service as an impartial body justifies concern about the presence of protections for federal employees, prohibiting practices such as favoritism. The establishment of protections for "whistleblowers" (who disclose information that they reasonably believe provides evidence of violation of laws, rules, or regulations as well as other forms of mismanagement) collides with the elements of the CSRA that provide new powers for political appointees.

As the Reagan administration took power, some long-time career federal civil servants emphasized their concern about the replacement of the Civil

Service Commission with the Office of Personnel Management. Bernard Rosen wrote, "It is inevitable that an OPM director serving at the pleasure of the president will be expected to satisfy administration interests which are contrary to the principal reason for which the central personnel agency exists."[19]

Thus, overall, the Civil Service Reform Act sought to give federal managers and politically appointed officials greater control over personnel policy at the same time that it protected staff. Yet it is not clear whether the act was able to deliver on its promises. For example, James Perry and Jone Pearce found that despite the provisions in the CSRA for the establishment of performance-based merit pay for supervisors and management officials in grades 13 to 15, little actually occurred. They found that "in practice few civil servants have been denied their periodic salary increases, regardless of performance." They identified "significant contradiction" in the merit pay system and suggested "a continued delay in the computing of any of the federal comparability adjustment into the merit portion of pay increases until the new performance appraisal systems have been in place and proven themselves over several years."[20]

The National Performance Review, 1993

Just as the CSRA followed an era of Republican administration policies dealing with personnel policy and sought to correct problems identified by Democrats who took control of the White House, the National Performance Review (NPR) followed the Reagan years, which emphasized methods that provided for White House control of the bureaucracy. As an early initiative of the Clinton administration, the NPR was led by Vice President Al Gore and sought to "create a government that works better and costs less."[21] A six-month review of the federal government engaged individuals at multiple levels within the federal government; activity was organized out of the vice president's office involving individuals assigned to various teams as well as working groups in each cabinet department.

There were multiple aspects of the NPR and a number of them dealt with personnel policy. In its initial report, the NPR focused on the impact of the piling up, "layer after layer," of personnel rules. Describing this as a "personnel quagmire," the report stated that "in total, 54,000 personnel work in federal personnel positions. We spend billions of dollars for these staff to classify each employee within a highly complex system of some 459 job series, 15 grades and 10 steps within each grade."[22]

There were a number of major action recommendations of the initiative concerning personnel, including the following:

- OPM will deregulate personnel policy by phasing out the 10,000-page Federal Personnel Manual and all agency-implementing directives.

- Give all departments and agencies authority to conduct their own recruiting and examining for all positions, and abolish all central registers and standard application forms.
- Dramatically simplify the current classification system to give agencies greater flexibility in how they classify and pay their employees.
- Agencies should be allowed to design their own performance management and reward systems, with the objective of improving the performance of individuals and organizations.
- Reduce by half the time required to terminate federal managers for cause and improve the system for dealing with poor performers.[23]

Many of the ideas that became a part of the NPR agenda were drawn from private-sector experience. It was difficult to find evidence that the classic public-sector personnel scholars and practitioners had much impact on the process. While career civil servants were very involved in the effort, the language and conceptual frameworks influencing the effort did not include many public-sector scholars or their written work. The staff drawn from various federal agencies were assigned to functions and organizations other than their own; NPR designers believed that new ideas would not come from those familiar with the agencies' work but from individuals who would approach the agency afresh. While this may have been true in some instances, it also meant that NPR staff were not familiar with the institutions and history of specific agencies.

But, at the same time that the NPR sought to decentralize personnel authority and reduce the control role of OPM as a central agency, it also proposed actions that would affect career civil servants. It called for reductions of more than 250,000 positions in the federal workforce and changes in the way that the service was structured. Flattened organizational structures were viewed not only as achieving more effective performance but also as eliminating many midlevel jobs within the service.

The problems that framed the NPR personnel activity included inflexible appointment rules; a rigid, government-wide job classification system; a complex, arcane job classification system; formula compensation rules; and reduction-in-force rules.[24] Donald Kettl, Patricia Ingraham, Ronald Sanders, and Constance Horner characterized the problem for the NPR as one that moved beyond modifying rules. They contrasted the NPR approach with that of the CSRA:

> The Civil Service Reform Act of 1978 (CSRA) provides an object lesson. Incremental reform through better rules was its essence. The architects of the act promised—and delivered—greater delegation of authority to agencies and managers, but the delegation was still rule based, and it proved to have sharp limits. The act, for example, attempted to increase public accountability (and by implication, to decrease permanence) by making the pay of managers more contingent upon performance. This was

the beginning of a variable pay compensation strategy. But by mandating the same rating-reward formula for every manager in the executive branch, the system inadvertently induced classic bureaucratic work-to-rule behavior.[25]

Analysts who have attempted to assess the impact of the NPR have found that task daunting. Don Kettl found that "assessing the NPR is difficult; there is no such thing as *the* NPR. In practice, the NPR has been a messy and sometimes disorganized multifront war against the government's performance problems." Kettl went on to argue that there are actually three different NPRs. The first focused on how the NPR could help the Clinton administration attract voters. The second highlighted "preaching the gospel of reinvention to anyone who would listen and on coordinating the cross-cutting reform efforts." And the third relied on "reinventors throughout the executive branch" to make changes in their individual agencies.[26]

Further, Kettl (and others) argued that the NPR focused on different and often conflicting goals. Despite the rhetoric to the contrary, saving money really structured the arguments of the NPR's advocates and "became the bedrock of the movement. As a result, the ghost of deficit reduction lurked behind every promise of empowering workers or improving performance.... Because the largest single piece of the promised savings was to come from reducing the number of federal employees, the threat to their jobs became the defining element of the NPR for most federal employees."[27]

Ban and Riccucci have commented that the tension between the goals of strengthening presidential control and achieving managerial efficiency was an important element of the NPR. They point to "its emphasis on deregulation both of personnel and of other highly regulated areas of management, decentralization, and devolution of authority, participative management or shared power (including Total Quality Management), and an increased focus on giving managers more authority and holding them accountable for results." They link the NPR activity in personnel to approaches found in NPM. They further note that current and future challenges of public personnel administration must deal with a constantly changing environment and that "the field is constantly seeking to reform—and sometimes even reinvent—itself in order to keep pace with the prevailing political, social, legal and economic tides in this nation."[28] Reforms in public personnel, according to Nolan Argyle, are found at every level of government, and many approaches were developed at state and local levels and made their way to the federal agenda.[29]

An analysis of the early experience of implementing the NPR by six departments or agencies illustrated the complexity of the process. The focus on deficit reduction evoked narrow compliance responses by both career and political staff unless the top official in the organizational unit had a policy agenda that could use the NPR's rhetoric to support substantive change. Six types of activity were identified in this analysis: changing policy, reorganizing the structure, making budget reductions, empowering line managers, improving customer service, and changing decision systems.[30] The experience of the six organizations showed evidence of the separation of management and policy agendas, an emphasis on executive power, an attempt to avoid politics and the conflict that occurs when one deals with Congress and interest groups, and the absence of accountability efforts that could institutionalize the reform agenda.

Whether one looked at the NPR from the perch of the vice president's office or from the view of the diverse array of agencies throughout the federal establishment, it appeared that the effort and the broad scope of the federal government initiative "did not, in the end, limit the scope of these programs, shrink their overall budgets, change the behavior of program staff or clients, or decrease the number of government employees who were responsible for administering them."[31] The emphasis on downsizing the federal government's workforce was the main message to the career bureaucracy and "set forth a prescription that would profoundly shape the context for the other changes it espoused."[32]

The George W. Bush Administration: DoD and DHS Personnel Changes

Once again a change in the White House had an impact on the personnel reform agenda. By the time of the election of George W. Bush it appeared that several of the most visible aspects of the CSRA (such as the creation of the Senior Executive Service, OPM, and merit pay requirements) had been effectively assimilated into standard operating procedures and had not significantly changed the way that the federal system operated. Indeed, Paul Light found that the CSRA "has been a particular disappointment."[33] Similarly, very few of the recommendations of the NPR appeared to have made visible changes in the system since the NPR effort largely bypassed the role of Congress in this area. Few of the recommendations made their way to either substantive legislation or budget form.

Katherine Naff and Meredith Newman have written that one of the first acts by Bush upon assuming the presidency "was to rescind Clinton's executive order establishing the Labor Management Partnership Council, clearly signaling the extent to which he intended to heed labor's concerns." He did announce a government reform agenda in August 2001, which was described as "just a range of modest personnel management initiatives."[34] But the elimination of the Labor Management Partnership Council and the early Bush reforms were characterized by the American Federation of Government Employees as "a grab bag of changes which provides higher salaries and lower accountability for the most highly paid Federal Executives."[35]

But everything changed less than a month later. The terrorist attacks on September 11, 2001, changed the dimensions of the personnel policy debate.

Bush was able to link his existing agenda that sought to minimize the role of federal government employee trade unions to the new circumstances. The bill creating the Transportation Security Administration did maintain existing authorities, but the Bush call for the merger of twenty-two existing agencies into the Department of Homeland Security made his agenda for change more explicit. Bush's press release in July 2002 made this clear: "I'm not going to accept legislation that limits or weakens the President's well-established authorities—authorities to exempt parts of government from federal-labor management relations statute—when it serves our national interest."[36] Despite some opposition within the Senate, Bush pushed his agenda and in September 2002 accused the Senate of being "stuck." "They want to micromanage the process. Not all senators, but some senators. They want to have a thick book of rules that will tell the executive branch and this administration and future administrations how to deal with security of our homeland."[37]

Naff and Newman described the congressional process as it moved through the two chambers. The effort expanded to include other agencies that were viewed as related to the September 11 situation. By April 2003, the administration called for the creation of a National Security Personnel System (NSPS) covering 700,000 civilian employees in the Defense Department.[38] Naff and Newman concluded: "It is clear from [Secretary of Defense] Rumsfeld's remark that the notion of national security will continue to be the watchword administration officials and some members of Congress would use as leverage to seek civil service reform. It is also clear . . . that the quest for HR flexibility is not going to be satisfied by government-wide civil service reform legislation. Rather, it will take place through an unraveling of the [existing] . . . framework and its replacement by agency-unique systems."[39]

Jack Underhill and Ray Oman characterized the Bush approach as one where "the administration wanted its cabinet officers (particularly those dealing with national security issues) to have more power and flexibility like that of CEOs of private companies, without the restrictions of civil service rules and union participation. . . . The terrorist attacks and national security provided a stronger and more salable argument with Congress for changing the civil service system."[40]

The reforms that were adopted through authorities granted to the Department of Homeland Security in the Homeland Security Act of 2002 and those granted to the Defense Department in the National Security Personnel System in the 2004 National Defense Authorization Act represented both continuities from the CSRA and the NPR as well as departures from those past efforts. The decision-making process in Congress, according to Douglas Brook and Cynthia King, "took a more tortured path through the Congress" than the CSRA. The provisions were incorporated into broader legislative elements but became important political issues in the 2002 midterm elections. "When the DHS bill became bogged down in the Senate in the fall of 2002, it was the personnel provision—specifically, union opposition to the personnel provision—that made the bill an issue in the 2002 midterm elections. . . . The Bush administration campaigned heavily for key Republican candidates, emphasizing the need for senators who understood the importance of national security and the need for personnel flexibilities in fighting the global war on terrorism. This argument proved strong."[41] This argument emphasized benefits to the general public over benefits to federal employees.

A year later, changes were proposed by the Defense Department in the personnel system. The NSPS was incorporated into the defense authorization bill and created a pay-for-performance system that replaced the general schedule grade-and-step system. This was expected to provide more flexibility in pay levels. In addition, the NSPS modified policies involving tenure, hiring, reassignment, promotion, collective bargaining, pay, performance measurement, and recognition and gave new discretion to the secretary of defense to override OPM policies. Some of these provisions grew out of demonstration projects that were authorized under the CSRA, particularly the pay-for-performance and broad paybands stipulations that had been developed as demonstrations within DoD. The arguments for this legislation were also crafted around the need for national security.

Others, however, looked at a range of problems dealing with civilian defense professionals. "Since the Cold War, DOD has had difficulty attracting and retaining talented career civil servants. The problem stems from private sector opportunities that often offer superior pay and fewer bureaucratic frustrations, complex and rigid government hiring and security clearance procedures that can take months, perceptions that the Government is a plodding bureaucracy where young talent lies fallow, and a changing labor market where few workers stick with a single employer throughout their careers."[42]

At the time that both the DHS and NSPS systems went into effect, it was clear that neither the Republican-controlled White House nor the Republican Congress offered the public employee unions a welcoming venue to challenge the policies. Instead, they decided to use the third branch of government—the judiciary—as the venue for change. A press account of the June 2006 decision regarding the DHS policy by the three-judge panel of the US Court of Appeals for the District of Columbia noted:

> Using some of the most scathing language ever seen in a federal court ruling, a federal appellate court panel tossed out the Bush administration's personnel plan covering 185,000 workers at the Homeland Security Department (DHS).
>
> The June 27 decision by the 3-judge panel of the U.S. Court of Appeals for the District of Columbia left Bush 0-for-3 in federal court rulings on his schemes to virtually abolish collective bargaining, eliminate

whistleblower protections, dump workers' union rights and institute pay plans where salaries would be left up to bosses.

"These (personnel) regulations subordinate all collective bargaining agreements to the prerogatives of management," the judges wrote. Under the law establishing DHS, they added, that's illegal. The Bush rules also "defy common sense" and the definition of collective bargaining, they said.

The unions that challenged the DHS plan, led by the National Treasury Employees Union, hailed the ruling and hoped it would convince Bush to stop battling them and instead bargain in good faith over new personnel rules for the DHS workers.

Bush lost the DHS case in U.S. District Court last Aug. 12. He lost a similar case, covering 700,000 civilian Defense Department workers, in that court, too, several months ago, to a coalition led by the American Federation of Government Employees. Bush wants to extend his personnel rules to all 2 million-plus federal workers, but the court rulings may give him second thoughts.

"The ruling holding the labor relations provisions entirely illegal should effectively end DHS' effort to impose these unjust and unnecessary rules that would constrict employees' workplace rights, deny them fair treatment and further erode their morale," said NTEU President Colleen M. Kelley. "The bottom line is that working against the best interests of your employees is never a winning strategy. With this landmark victory, it should now be clear that any effort to strip a meaningful workplace voice from federal employees will fail."[43]

Several months later, the Department of Homeland Security decided not to challenge the DC Circuit Court of Appeals ruling that issued an injunction halting the implementation of the original policy. On September 28, 2006, the International Brotherhood of Electrical Workers released a statement about the decision not to appeal.

Legal challenges to the DHS personnel system, known as MaxHR, were led by the American Federation of Government Employees (AFGE), the largest federal union representing workers in DHS. "Management was in a battle they knew they couldn't win. The decision not to appeal was the right thing to do for management, and more importantly for DHS employees," said AFGE General Counsel Mark Roth.

President Edwin D. Hill praised DHS's decision not to appeal on behalf of IBEW members who are part of the work force dedicated to America's security. "Three of the four judges on the D.C. Circuit Court of Appeals were appointed by Republicans, yet they struck down DHS's rules for violating our Constitution," said President Edwin D. Hill. "It's time for rational union-management dialogue at DHS and DOD that respects our nation's legal precedent and the collective bargaining rights of workers."[44]

Similar problems were encountered with the DoD personnel shifts. However, because the Democrats assumed control of both the House and the Senate in 2008, Congress—rather than the courts—became the venue for responding to them. A Congressional Research Service report summarized the status of the NSPS:

> NSPS was beset by criticisms since it went into effect in 2006. The system faced legal and political challenges from unions and employees who claimed it was inconsistently applied and caused undeserved pay inequities, among other concerns. On October 7, 2009, House and Senate conferees reported a version of the National Defense Authorization Act for Fiscal Year 2010 that included language to terminate NSPS. On October 8, 2009, the House agreed to the conference report. The Senate agreed to the conference report on October 22, 2009. On October 28, 2009, the President signed the bill into law (P.L. 111-84). DOD must now return employees currently enrolled in NSPS to the GS or to the pay system that previously applied to them or their position. If the employee's position did not exist prior to NSPS or if the previous pay scale was abolished during NSPS's lifetime, DOD must determine an appropriate pay scale for the employee. The return to the GS or other pay system must be completed by January 1, 2012, pursuant to the law.[45]

Personnel Reform and Contradictions in the US System

Efforts at reforming the personnel system at the federal level illustrate some aspects of the three sets of contradictions found in the US system: structural dimensions, predominant values and approaches, and attributes of the public sector.

Structural Dimensions

All three of the examples involving personnel policy discussed in this chapter indicate the conflict between the perspectives of the executive branch and those of Congress. The CSRA picked up concerns that had been debated since the Brownlow Committee's efforts to increase the management capacity of the White House and, effectively, to diminish the ability of Congress to establish rules and requirements that limited presidential authority. Replacing the multimember Civil Service Commission with a presidential appointee heading OPM seemed to place the personnel responsibility in the Executive Office of the President. While Congress was a party to that decision process, the changes that were devised were incremental in nature and, as students of the process have observed, were largely marginal and were able to be absorbed into existing standard operating procedures.

The personnel policies that emerged from the NPR, by contrast, were devised as activities within the executive branch. Efforts to simplify the process and eliminate rules were developed without involvement of Congress and defined as management responsibilities that belonged to the White House. Indeed, the NPR conceptualized the power in this area as residing at 1600 Pennsylvania Avenue. Given this definition, that power could be delegated by the White House to top managers within the federal establishment without acknowledgment of the formal involvement of the House or Senate.

The Bush administration's personnel reform efforts provided evidence of the potential role of the judiciary. It did not appear that the Bush White House had worried about the emergence of the courts as players in the process until the public-sector unions filed their case in court.[46]

In addition, in this case as well as others, the reform efforts involving personnel changes in the federal government were influenced by activities that were also occurring at state and local government levels. All three levels of the US government were moving in directions that were shared by others across the globe, largely through the policy approaches associated with NPM.

Predominant Values and Approaches

The personnel reform efforts that have been discussed in this chapter all represent attempts to deal with the pervasive public tendency to blame the bureaucrats when citizens disagree with public-sector action. While other issues became the basis of the rhetorical argument for change, the skepticism within the American society about public action is clearly at play in this reform area. It is perhaps the strongest in the NPR example, which really used other arguments to cover the drive to diminish the size of the bureaucracy. The personnel reform efforts have tried to accomplish both support of the career bureaucracy (giving it flexibility and discretion) at the same time that the career bureaucracy would be controlled and limited in its autonomy.

It is also clear that efficiency values associated with the private sector served as the basis for norms and models within the public service reform areas discussed in this chapter. Debates often revolved around comparisons with the private sector, including issues such as pay levels, the autonomy of managers, and the structure of the service. In the case of the NPR, private-sector perspectives became the basis for reform ideas, and there was little if any acknowledgment that the public and private sectors might require different structures and approaches.

There was some recognition in the NPR that it was appropriate to decentralize personnel decision-making authority to agencies and departments, providing the basis for design of personnel policies that were viewed as more effective in specific situations. Equity considerations were relatively rare. Instead, equity concerns were raised by the public-sector unions, who also advocated for fairness in dealings with members of the public service. The absence of this concern was most visible in the Bush personnel reforms as they sought to avoid the legitimacy of trade unions.

Attributes of the Public Sector

The story that is told in this chapter indicates how difficult it is to separate politics and management/administration. All three of the initiatives that are examined had to live with political realities. Some of them were defined by elections. Others emerged from partisan debates and took place within congressional chambers. Still others stemmed from the convergence of partisan politics and the politics of a system of shared power (usually between Congress and the White House). The reforms often started out as specific proposals, but as they moved through the decision process ideological perspectives pushed them in particular directions.

It was difficult to convince many that it was possible to move to an abstract form of good government and to accomplish a desire to protect government from politics. While one might have defended proposals as the one-best-way to accomplish change, calculation of who would benefit and who would lose from those proposals was inevitable. This clearly was at play in decisions involving deregulation, particularly those affecting public-sector unions.

Both the CSRA and the NPR conceptualized the personnel system as one that was government-wide and, in the case of the NPR, could be delegated to departments and agencies. The Bush proposals actually began with one department, moved to another, and were expected to become the model for the entire government. The creation of OPM as a central control agency associated with the executive branch was often confusing because many personnel decisions in agencies were directly affected by the decisions of congressional committees and subcommittees in both the authorizing and appropriating functions.

Conclusions

For some students of federal personnel policy, the agenda for change has been defined by technical imperatives. Like Luther Gulick, they argue that the functions of an organization require specific actions and should follow professionally defined norms. At times these norms flowed from the experience of the private sector. At other times they emerged from political realities. Each of the three examples discussed in this chapter indicated some balancing between those professionally defined norms, the experience of the private sector, and the dynamics of politics. The CSRA represented the strongest influence of the professionally defined norms; the NPR the influence of the private sector; and the Bush efforts the president's political agenda. In all three cases, however, the emphasis was on the role of the executive branch and its desire to command control of personnel management functions.

Notes

1. In March 2011, a debate occurred in a House federal workforce subcommittee in which Representative Dennis Ross (R-FL) and other members of the subcommittee sought to eliminate pay increases (bonuses, awards, and step increases) based on longevity. See Joe Davidson, "Battle Royal over Federal Worker Pay," *Washington Post,* March 9, 2011.
2. Kettl et al., *Civil Service Reform,* 87.
3. Ibid., 87–88.
4. See Radin, "Search for the M," 37.
5. Ban and Riccucci, intro., xiv.
6. Blair, *A Journey,* 205, 206.
7. Huberty and Malone, "Senior Executive Service," 869.
8. Ban and Ingraham, "Civil Service Reform," 1.
9. Ibid.
10. Ibid., 2.
11. Listed ibid., 3.
12. Described in Fesler and Kettl, *Politics,* 143.
13. Ibid.
14. Ibid., 196.
15. The idea was also included in Hugh Heclo's book *A Government of Strangers.*
16. See Foster, "1978 Civil Service Reform Act," 81.
17. Office of Personnel Management and Jason Kay, "Special Executive Service (SES) Jobs," GovCentral, accessed September 20, 2011, http://govcentral.monster.com/benefits/articles/9774-special-executive-service-ses-jobs.
18. See, e.g., Abramson, Schmidt, and Baxter, "Evaluating." See also Yeager, "Assessing."
19. Rosen, "Crises," 207.
20. Perry and Pearce, "Initial Reactions to Federal Merit Pay," 230, 237.
21. Gore, *Creating a Government,* i.
22. Ibid., 20, 21.
23. Ibid., 20–25.
24. Listed in Kettl et al., *Civil Service Reform,* 24.
25. Ibid., 25.
26. Kettl, "Building Lasting Reform," 14.
27. Ibid., 15.
28. Ban and Riccucci, intro., xiv–xv.
29. See Argyle, "Civil Service Reform."
30. See Radin, "Varieties of Reinvention."
31. DiIulio, "Works Better and Costs Less?" 6.
32. Thompson and Radin, "Reinventing Public Personnel Management," 11.
33. Paul C. Light, "Laws Gone Astray," *Government Executive,* December 2003, 94.
34. Naff and Newman, "Symposium," 194.
35. Quoted ibid., 195.
36. Quoted ibid., 196.
37. Ibid.
38. Bush did not take a government-wide approach but used the public concern after September 11 to open a window on both DHS and the DoD that would set the model for government-wide changes.

39. Naff and Newman, "Symposium," 198.
40. Underhill and Oman, "Critical Review," 402.
41. Brook and King, "Federal Personnel Management Reform," 211.
42. Murdock and Weitz, "Beyond Goldwater-Nichols," 38.
43. Mark Gruenberg, "Judge Tosses Bush Plan for DHS Workers," *Labor World,* July 12, 2006, www.laborworld.org/documents/07-12-2006v5.pdf.
44. "Union Victory at Department of Homeland Security," IBEW website, September 28, 2006, www.ibew.org/articles/06daily/0609/060928_DHS.htm.
45. Wendy R. Ginsberg, "Conversation from the National Security Personnel System to Other Pay Schedules: Issues for Congress," CRS Report for Congress R41321, July 15, 2010, summary.
46. This is perhaps the only case in this study where the system of shared powers provided an opportunity for the courts to be directly involved in the management reform agenda.

6
REORGANIZATION AS REFORM

The myth persists that we can resolve deep-seated issues of substance by reorganizing. . . . The devils to be exorcised are overlapping and duplication, and confused or broken lines of authority and responsibility. Entry into the "nirvana of economy and efficiency" can be obtained only by strict adherence to sound principles of executive branch organization. Efficiency is thus axiom number one in the value scale of administration. This brings administration into apparent conflict with the value scale of politics, whether we use that term in its scientific or popular sense.

Harold Seidman, *Politics, Position, and Power*

YEARS AGO HAROLD SEIDMAN INTRODUCED HIS BOOK ON FEDERAL ORGANI-zation by writing: "Reorganization has become almost a religion in Wash-ington. . . . Reorganization is deemed synonymous with reform and reform with progress. Periodic reorganizations are prescribed if for no other pur-pose than to purify the bureaucratic blood and to prevent stagnation. Op-position to reorganization is evil."[1]

This chapter deals with federal government reforms involving reorgani-zation. It examines the authority provided to the president to make these moves with limited congressional controls, the ways that this authority has been used, and the arguments that have been devised to support reorganiza-tion proposals. It provides several examples of relatively recent efforts to change various parts of the organizational structure of the federal govern-ment. Finally, it examines the fit between these past and current efforts and the contradictions that are a part of the American reality.

Development of Federal Reorganization Efforts

Interestingly, the first significant concern about reorganization in the fed-eral government came from Congress. A joint resolution in 1920 created a committee of three members of the Senate and three of the House to make recommendations about the organization of the executive branch. The committee could only make recommendations to the president, and while there were some moves to transfer particular programs from one part of the government to another, nothing came of those recommenda-tions.[2] By 1928 the subject of reorganization surfaced in the platform of the Democratic Party. It called for "businesslike reorganization of all de-partments of the government; elimination of duplication, waste and overlapping; substitution of modern businesslike methods for existing obsolete and antiquated conditions."[3] When Republican Herbert Hoover assumed the presidency in 1929, he brought the subject to the attention of Congress in his annual messages, and by 1932 the House created an economy committee to develop recommendations on the organization of the government.

This resulted in draft legislation that gave the president power to reorganize; the power was granted through executive orders and it had no time limit. But since the legislation was enacted in June 1932 (just months before the November election of Franklin D. Roosevelt), after the election a resolution was adopted to reject the Hoover proposals. Laurence Schmeckebier described the congressional response to this issue as one that "both broadened and narrowed the authority of the President. . . . The most marked extension of presidential power in the act of 1933 was that authorizing the President to abolish functions of any executive agency."[4] The economic crises of the era gave Congress a sense of urgency that effectively eliminated its traditional authority to abolish functions and to omit its ability to veto presidential action. The legislation was worded so that the presidential authority would expire in two years and presidential action in this area would not become effective until sixty days after decisions were transmitted to Congress.

When the two years elapsed and the presidential authority expired, a Senate committee was established to investigate the executive agencies of the government, headed by Virginia senator Harry F. Byrd. The committee contracted with the Brookings Institution for an analysis that would include options to address the issue. While the committee held hearings, it did not approve a number of the bills introduced by Senator Byrd.[5]

At the same time that Congress was focusing on the organization of the federal government, President Franklin D. Roosevelt announced his intention to appoint a committee of his own to study the issue. In a March 1936 letter to the vice president, Roosevelt not only called for a committee (which became known as the President's Committee on Administrative Management—often called the Brownlow Committee) but also asked for the cooperation of the Senate committee and, in a letter to the Speaker of the House, suggested the creation of a similar House committee.[6]

In his detailed account of reorganization efforts from 1905 to 1996, Peri Arnold noted that the constancy of efforts would make one "infer that reorganization has been successful at its manifest purpose of increasing government's efficiency. . . . But behind reorganization planning's façade of increasing administrative efficiency is a more complex story in which reorganization's effects are more profound but less predictable than they first appear. Within the development of reorganization planning as a presidential tool during this century is embedded a change in the definition of efficiency that guided reorganization planning."[7]

The More Things Change the More They Stay the Same?

Both the Brownlow and the congressional committees dealt with issues that would continue to surface in subsequent years.[8] The agenda for change involved efforts to reduce overlapping, duplication, and lack of coordination but the two branches of government did not always define these elements in the same ways. Not surprisingly, Congress sought to limit the authority of the White House through its ability to abolish functions, to limit the life of the presidential authority, and to create new units. At the same time, it was clear that Congress knew it had limited ability to deal with day-to-day issues involving supervision of staff and other forms of management control.

Following Brownlow in the post–World War II years Congress created a Commission on Organization of the Executive Branch of the Government (known as the first Hoover Commission) and also gave President Truman authority to initiate reorganization plans. In 1953 President Eisenhower appointed a President's Advisory Committee on Government Organization. The parallel activity in the two branches echoed the themes of the past. The Hoover Commission report not only focused on the authority to be given to the president but also on presidential staff resources and the structure of specific agencies (i.e., creating a Department of Health, Education, and Welfare).

Harold Seidman has commented that "the organizational commandments laid down by the first Hoover Commission constitute the hard core of the fundamentalist dogma. . . . The commission's report on 'General Management of the Executive Branch' represents the most categorical formulation of the orthodox or classic organization doctrine derived largely from business administration and identified with the scientific management movement during the early decades of the century."[9]

The back-and-forth between the White House and Congress involving reorganization did not move in a predictable direction. Some of the arguments that were used focused on the location of the authority or agenda for change, particularly if there were policy differences based on political partisanship. It was as easy for Congress to criticize the executive branch for inefficiencies and waste through proposals for reorganization as it was for the executive branch to argue that it was not able to respond to these problems because it did not have adequate power to make the changes. Yet the various versions of the reorganization acts (e.g., those of 1939 and 1945) did result in more than 120 changes in organization. Twenty-four independent agencies were eliminated, transferred, or consolidated and three major agencies were created.[10] And between 1949 and 1973, presidents used reorganization authority seventy-four times to make changes in bureaucratic structures, although Congress rejected these proposals nineteen times. Lyndon Johnson was successful in getting two new departments created but was stymied in his effort to consolidate Commerce and Labor into a single department.

And Nixon's proposals for superdepartments were completely rejected by Congress.[11]

Enactment of the Reorganization Act of 1949 formalized the expectations in this area. The president was directed to examine the organization of agencies from time to time and determine what changes would be necessary to meet six objectives:

1. promote better execution of the laws and more effective management of the executive branch
2. reduce expenditures and promote economy
3. increase efficiency of government operations
4. group, consolidate, and coordinate agencies and functions
5. reduce the number of agencies by consolidating them
6. eliminate overlapping and duplication of effort[12]

The creation of the Department of Education highlighted the relationship between congressional reluctance to accept reorganization plans and the organization of Congress itself. Beryl Radin and Willis Hawley have written that "although congressional committee organization is independent of any changes in executive branch organization, a number of members believed that reorganization in the executive branch would be followed by reorganization of the congressional committee system—a shift that would potentially create changes in committee and subcommittee leadership positions. Interest groups also feared this kind of change, believing that it would undermine coalitions and their bases of support."[13]

By 1975, then OMB staffer Clifford Berg wrote a commentary about the situation: "The course of reorganization plan authority has been erratic over the years, marked by lapses, outcries of constitutionality or at least improper delegation of authority to the executive, increasing restrictions on use of plans, and an undercurrent of suspicion that reorganization was often being employed not to improve management but rather to further some sinister presidential objective."[14] Berg was commenting on the situation of the time; as a result of fears of the "Imperial Presidency" the reorganization authority was allowed to expire in 1973.

When Jimmy Carter assumed the presidency in 1977, he sought the same authority that had been given to Nixon. The legislation that was actually passed did give him authority but clearly specified that a reorganization plan could not be used to create a new executive department. That was particularly relevant for Carter since he had campaigned on a promise to create a separate Department of Education. Although Carter emphasized the consolidation of governmental units with overlapping functions and reduction of the number of department and agency heads, he faced a different set of arguments and promises attached to reorganization proposals—those promising budget savings and greater economy. Berg observed that of the ninety-three plans submitted since 1949, only four were supported by a precise estimate of savings (and one of them was not approved by Congress). Further, Berg noted that chief executives have historically been loath to claim savings through reorganization.[15]

Despite this record, the goals of the 1949 act continued to frame a reorganization agenda. The 2003 report of the National Commission on the Public Service (the Volcker Commission report) emphasized similar recommendations. It sought the following:

1. The federal government should be reorganized into a limited number of mission-related executive departments.
2. The operating agencies in the new departments should be run by competent managers who had been given adequate authority.
3. The President should be given expedited authority to recommend structural reorganization.
4. The House and Senate should realign their committee oversight to match the mission-driven reorganization of the federal branch.[16]

Similar arguments came from GAO Comptroller General David Walker in testimony to the House Committee on Government Reform in April 2003. He viewed reorganization as a part of the broader management strategy articulated by the Bush administration and emphasized the past congressional approach of adopting fast-track approaches for specific areas. He noted that "depending on the nature of future legislative proposals that will be submitted, they could have profound implications for the relative role the Congress plays in developing legislation and conducting oversight to enhance the performance and ensure the accountability of the executive branch." Walker called for "a comprehensive review, reassessment, and reprioritization of what the government does and how it does it."[17]

Further, Walker reminded the committee that "many departments and agencies were created in a different time and in response to problems and priorities very different from today's challenges. Some have achieved their one-time missions and yet they are still in business. Many have accumulated responsibilities beyond their original purposes. Others have not been able to demonstrate how they are making a difference in real and concrete terms. Still others have overlapping or conflicting roles and responsibilities. Redundant, unfocused, and uncoordinated programs waste scarce funds, confuse and frustrate program customers, and limit overall program effectiveness."[18]

Walker called for the creation of "an effective working relationship on restructuring initiatives," and noted that "only the Congress can decide whether it wishes to limit its powers and role in government reorganizations."[19] At the same time, Walker clearly defined the role of the president as the manager of the government. He did not deal with the fragmented structure of Congress and its inability to look at the government as a whole.

Arguments for Reorganization

Although the rhetoric that surrounds the traditional arguments for reorganization has been embedded in what Harold Seidman called the "orthodox theory," the story behind the case often goes beyond that orthodoxy. As Seidman noted, the orthodox theory is "concerned primarily with arrangements to ensure that (1) each function is assigned to its appropriate niche within the government structure; (2) component parts of the executive branch are properly related and articulated; and (3) authorities and responsibilities are clearly assigned."[20] In addition, this orthodoxy has been closely entwined with efforts to reduce expenditures and deal with budget issues (at least at the rhetorical level). Although there are instances of congressional attention to reorganization, it is usually discussed in terms of specific policy approaches (rather than managerial norms) and can emerge from different sources within Congress.[21]

Usually missing from this set of arguments is anything that suggests that public organizations often exist in a complex and changing environment that makes it difficult to establish the kind of clarity and predictability that is frequently the goal of reorganization efforts. The story behind the reorganization drives often employs other arguments that emerge from a different and quite diverse set of sources. While some emerge from the management literature, where proponents believe that there are general rules that should be applied across the board to address shared problems found in most (if not all) organizations, others emerge from specific programs, policies, and problems that must be addressed and often seek to improve effectiveness as well as equity along with increasing efficiency. Although these arguments can be discussed as separate explanations, in reality many of these reasons are interrelated. Indeed, it is probably the convergence of these different reasons that explains the power and perceived saliency of the reorganization movement at particular points in time.

Herbert Kaufman described the approaches used to justify reorganization as a "frustrating quest." He wrote: "The standard reorganization strategies for rationalizing and simplifying the executive branch often clash with one another. Many consequences of reorganization, it must be admitted, cannot be tracked; some claims made for specific strategies, and some of the charges against them, rest on nothing more than faith or prejudice or self-interest. Logically and empirically, however, various strategies appear to contribute as much to exacerbation of the problems of executive organization as to their solution. The probabilities of net gains, if any, seem very small."[22]

While the standard arguments for reorganization usually focus on efficiency issues, at least seven other views about the motivation for reorganization are available.[23]

Reorganization as a Surrogate for Policy Change

Reorganization often takes place during middle stages of the policy implementation process; that is, at a time when the first blush of implementation
is completed and it becomes obvious that the expectations and goals associated with the policy adoption are not easily achieved. Reorganization efforts
offer themselves as an alternative path.

Reorganization as a Response to Public Demands for Change

Many reorganization efforts are a response to public expectations that something within the policy sector will be changed. Reorganization efforts that
attempt to meet a public demand for action require policy actors to make a
move that will be visible. When reorganization is used as the vehicle to satisfy
these demands, the action taken to create or reform an organizational unit is
highly symbolic and often appears to be a magical incantation or prayer offered by the responsible parties. Frequently this motivation arises in response
to a crisis situation, and changing the structure of the organizational unit
responsible for meeting the crisis is a way of buying time.

Reorganization That Imprints the Agenda of New Actors

Most of the reorganizations that have taken place at all levels of government
are coincident in time with the advent of new political leadership. These
actors know what many public administrators forget: Reorganizations and
shifts in organizational structures are political choices, not a mechanistic
shifting of boxes. At the same time, the decision process around changes in
structure is often less politically open and volatile than other forms of decision making.

Reorganization Based on Private-Sector Values

Arguments that emphasize increased efficiency (e.g., assertions of reduced
costs and more expeditious action) are the most common positions taken
to justify administrative reorganization. More frequently, these arguments
are based on the need for reorganization because of overlap and duplication
of functions, which result in complex and slow decision procedures that, in
turn, produce costly and inadequate services. Many reorganization efforts
have emphasized the traditional efficiency model of the private sector. Most
of them have taken place in a political climate that devalues equity and effectiveness goals and, instead, perceives that programs are expensive, inef-
ficiently operated, and less than effective in addressing the problems of their
client populations.

Reorganization as a Form of Diffused Innovation

A number of writers have described the interest in reorganization efforts as
a form of innovation that diffuses among governmental units. The diffusion
can take place in several forms of intergovernmental contact; for example,

it may show that state activity is influenced by and influences federal activity and that states are dramatically affected by what other states are doing. Our knowledge of both the formal and informal contacts between governments indicates that it is not difficult to show how information about a new practice is transmitted across state boundary lines. Individuals who are engaged in similar kinds of activities find themselves attending the same meetings, reading the same journals, and attempting to solve similar problems.

Reorganization as a Way of Improving the Policy Technology

A number of reorganizations can be seen as evidence of that aesthetic maxim, "Form follows function." That is, changes in organization structure occur because of shifts in the policy itself. These shifts can be made in a formal fashion or through new conceptualizations of the ways in which the policy is implemented; they can be seen as new ways of organizing the policy technology. This form of reorganization is driven by the substance of the policy itself. The advocates of this approach, unlike those of many of the other reasons for reorganization, begin with the demands of the policy and argue for organizational forms that make the policy implementation work most effectively.

Reorganization as a Drive for Stability and Conflict Avoidance

Interest in reorganization appears to occur during periods of time in which political leaders (and others) perceive that the public sector contains elements that are out of control. During these times, policy issues are often unsettled, with diverse sets of actors and forces demanding conflicting agendas and employing incompatible strategies. For those who value stability, times like this appear to hinge on anarchy and evoke serious fear about the future. If we see reorganization as a response to a basic need to take control, then we can see why it is a favorite technique in a number of fields where the pace of change is rapid, making policy actors feel as if they were continually reacting to externally imposed changes.

Recent Reorganization Efforts

Recent reorganization and management reform initiatives continue to use the language of the orthodox approaches (highlighting efficiency, consolidation, and eliminating overlap and duplication). This is illustrated by the elements within the Clinton administration's National Performance Review that focused on what the administration called "transforming organizational structures." The principles for change emphasized four elements that were drawn from private-sector experience: (1) organize work around customers, (2) shift accountability to markets and competition, (3) create partnerships between agencies, and (4) empower employees and redefine managers' roles. Further, they emphasized four strategies for change: streamline structures, reengineer work processes, create boundary-spanning partnerships, and create self-managing work teams.[24]

But a more complex picture emerges when one moves beyond the rhetoric used in advocating reorganization. Three relatively recent efforts illustrate both elements of the seven attributes just described as well as issues that are unique to the particular policy or program area. They involve both the creation of a new cabinet department and reorganization within a unit inside a department. These efforts are (1) reorganization in the Centers for Disease Control and Prevention (CDC) of the Department of Health and Human Services (HHS) in 2005, (2) creation of the Department of Homeland Security in 2003, and (3) proposals to establish a Department of Food Safety.

Centers for Disease Control and Prevention, Department of Health and Human Services

In April 2005, then director of CDC Julie Gerberding announced a broad reorganization of the CDC organization within HHS. She described the new structure as one that marked the agency's "readiness to confront the challenges of 21st century health threats."[25] According to the director, when the agency started the process that resulted in this reorganization, it had been more than twenty-five years since the last modernization effort. She noted that twenty-five years ago CDC had 4,000 employees and a budget of approximately $300 million. By 2003, CDC's combined workforce of both employees and contractors totaled 15,000, with a budget of approximately $8 billion.

The strategy was called the Futures Initiative and followed a number of the principles that were enumerated in the 1949 Reorganization Act. Creation of a new layer of officials provided the agency with a way to group, consolidate, and coordinate units and as a result allowed it to reduce the number of units that reported to the director. Gerberding's letter to the CDC community defined agency-wide goals and described the situation as one in which the "new structure better aligns CDC to achieve these goals." She wrote, "Our new coordinating centers will help CDC's scientists collaborate and innovate across organizational boundaries, improve efficiency so that more money can be redirected to science, and programs in our divisions, and improve the internal services that support and develop CDC staff."[26] See figure 6.1 for the organizational structure of CDC.

Working with a private-sector consultant and involving more than 500 individuals and organizations from outside of CDC, the strategy was designed to allow the organization to define its business, establish priorities, and define its customers' needs. The process sought to rationalize the work of a large organization composed largely of various types of scientists with specializations in both diseases and skill areas. These were individuals who brought deep expertise to their work and valued their ability to continue

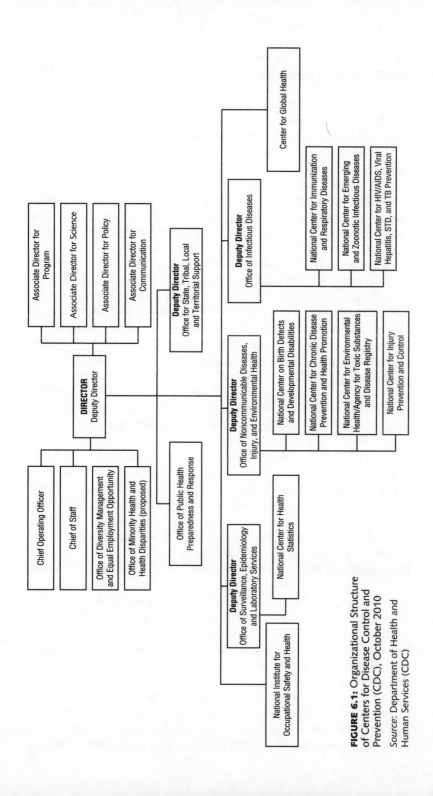

FIGURE 6.1: Organizational Structure of Centers for Disease Control and Prevention (CDC), October 2010

Source: Department of Health and Human Services (CDC)

their research and employ their expertise in a public organization setting. Decentralization of authority to individual centers provided them with the autonomy they believed they needed to do their work.

Just three months after the reorganization announcement, the *Atlanta-Journal Constitution,* the main newspaper in Atlanta (where the CDC head-quarters is located), reported the results of an anonymous online survey of almost 40 percent of CDC employees. The survey found that almost two-thirds of CDC employees opposed the reorganization, citing "an 'inappro-priate' business focus to the public health mission of CDC, low employee morale, increased bureaucracy, loss of trust, loss of important staff members and damage to the reputation of the agency."[27] The response of the CDC employees was not surprising, but the CDC experience indicated that public views can be shaped by the response of employees.

Although Gerberding's spokespeople questioned the way that the survey was conducted, by December 2005 five former CDC directors wrote a letter to Gerberding noting that they were "concerned about the previous and impending losses of highly qualified and motivated staff" at the agency. They stated, "We are concerned that so many of the staff have come to us to express their concerns about the low morale in the agency. We are concerned about the inability of many of the partners to understand the direction in which CDC is headed."[28]

While it was not unusual for staff to oppose the changes that come from reorganization, there were two other pieces to the story that brought Con-gress into the picture. One piece of the puzzle involved CDC's research on chronic fatigue syndrome (CFS). Some scientists in CDC believed that the funds could be expended more effectively if they used the resources for re-search on measles, polio, and other disease areas. However, the agency pro-vided inaccurate information to Congress regarding the use of the funds. A whistleblower on the staff alleged that officials in the agency did not support the program to the extent recommended and encouraged by Congress. When the diversion of the funds was uncovered, the HHS inspector general conducted an audit and documented the pattern. Meetings were held be-tween leaders in the CFS community and top CDC officials; CFS leaders described the situation as one resulting from scientific bias. They pointed to what they termed disparaging claims in scientific journals that the disease was not legitimate. Further investigations were undertaken by the Govern-ment Accountability Office and others.[29] This resulted in an apology to CFS leaders for the diversion of CDC funds away from CFS research and in more extensive oversight of the entire CDC program by Congress as well as the office of the secretary of HHS.

The other congressional involvement that affected the CDC reorga-nization stemmed from the diversity of programs found within the CDC portfolio. Over the years the agency was given a range of responsibilities in quite different areas. As a result, programs were accountable to different congressional committees and subcommittees. For example, the Senate Finance Committee conducted an investigation to determine whether problems resulting from CDC's reorganization harmed the agency's effectiveness. At the same time, different committees and subcommittees in both houses were concerned about the impact of the reorganization on specific programs. Two programs that illustrated this concern were the Agency for Toxic Substances and Disease Registry (ATSDR) and the National Institute for Occupational Safety and Health (NIOSH). ATSDR is effectively an environmental program and has close relationships with the Environmental Protection Agency; as a result, it is responsible to different congressional committees and subcommittees than most other parts of CDC. When ATSDR was placed under the Coordinating Center for Environmental Health and Injury Prevention (in the new structure) there was concern in some parts of Congress that the programs in that unit would not receive adequate attention.[30] NIOSH was actually created by the Mine Safety and Health Act of 1977 and worked closely with the Occupational Safety and Health Administration in the Department of Labor. While housed in CDC it operated quite independently and was not included in the CDC reorganization.

The CDC reorganization strategy did use the orthodox rhetoric to make its case, but it appeared that Gerberding used it as a way to signal her agenda. Her use of private-sector consultants was also a way to pose the conversation in generic management terms (such as concepts of "customers" and the programs as a "business") rather than focusing on specific policy or program elements. The descriptions of the process suggest that these management issues were raised without serious discussion with congressional actors who were concerned about specific policies and were knowledgeable about the historical backdrop of the programs.

Creation of the Department of Homeland Security

The story behind the creation of the Department of Homeland Security is strong evidence of the political dimensions of reorganization decisions, particularly as a response to a crisis situation.[31] The destruction of New York City's twin towers, the damage to the Pentagon, and the airplane crash in Pennsylvania on September 11, 2001, raised the question of what the federal government could do to assure that such a disaster would not happen again. For at least some members of Congress, the creation of a cabinet-level department was viewed as a way to respond to that public desire. The idea for a separate department started in Congress, while the White House originally argued that an office in the Executive Office of the President was adequate to respond to the need. The Office of Homeland Security in the White House was established less than a month after September 11.

Those concerned about the possibility of creating a department focused on the behaviors that allowed terrorists to create and execute their plans. These early analyses highlighted problems related to the relationships between criminal justice agencies, intelligence agencies, and other federal government organizations. Because he was committed to keeping responsibility for these issues within the White House, President George W. Bush did not concentrate on the details of the congressional proposals. But a month after Congress introduced DHS legislation, the president changed direction and proposed a new department.

At that point, both Congress and the White House focused on the elements that would be included in a department, the authority that would be given it, and the structure of the new organization. Once a proposal was enacted, the president was required to submit a reorganization plan to Congress within sixty days. A plan was presented on November 25, 2002, to go into effect in January 2003. The twenty-two program elements that were contained in the reorganization plan were clustered into coordinating offices, and a range of implementation activities were planned and undertaken. Absent reorganization authority (the existing authority did not allow the president to create new agencies), the legislation would travel through the regular legislative process. An agency created by executive order would require approval by the relevant congressional committees and subcommittees for either appropriations or authorization decisions.[32]

For the next few years, the focus within DHS was to find a way to organize its operations. During this period shifts in departmental leadership occurred. All of this changed in September 2005 when Hurricane Katrina struck. The Federal Emergency Management Agency (FEMA)—one of the program elements within DHS—was widely criticized for its role in responding to the hurricane. Attention was drawn to the impact of the reorganization on FEMA's ability to meet the needs of the citizens of the Louisiana and Mississippi Gulf region. Concern was raised about the relationship between activities related to terrorism and those focused on natural disasters. Soon after, the Immigration and Customs Enforcement agency—also a part of DHS—received attention as the immigration policy issue surfaced in both the White House and in Congress. The Katrina experience made some observers less sanguine about the possibilities of structural change.

There continue to be questions raised about the construct as well as the governing process that accompanied what was largely a political decision to create the department. The twenty-two program elements were drawn from a diverse array of sources, but they did not include elements from either the CIA or the FBI. This puzzled some observers since those agencies included policies and programs that appeared to be relevant to the new department's mandates. At the beginning the president wanted to bypass congressional approval and circumvent the career bureaucracy but, as Richard Conley described it, "When Congress threatened to pursue reorganization on its own, Bush quickly preempted the legislature with his own plan that sought to maximize influence over, and impose his own managerial vision on, any new structure."[33]

The experience with Katrina raised serious questions about the ability of DHS to respond to emergency management responsibilities. It not only surfaced the difficulty for FEMA to respond to both natural disasters and national security issues but it also uncovered problems in determining whether decisions should be made at the centralized level (by the secretary of DHS) or at the program level, where staff had both the training and institutional experience with past efforts.

Proposals to Create a Department of Food Safety

As of this writing, despite attention to proposals to create a Department of Food Safety by a range of both executive-branch and congressional players, there has not been agreement on legislative proposals to create a new cabinet department that brings together programs and authority from a number of different agencies.[34] This example provides a picture of the complexity of reaching agreement on the creation of a new cabinet department. It illustrates the diverse agendas of agencies with a role in the subject area as well as their response to political and economic changes in the external environment. It also indicates the limits of the structural approach in situations where functional strategies (such as coordination and networks) might become more effective.

The possibility of pulling together the various agencies involved in food safety programs and policies has hovered around the policy agenda for nearly twenty years, and creation of a separate department has been an active proposal for a decade. The main federal agencies involved in the food safety process are the Food and Drug Administration and the Centers for Disease Control and Prevention in the US Department of Health and Human Services; the Food Safety and Inspection Service, the Cooperative State Research, Education, and Extension Service, and the National Agricultural Library in the US Department of Agriculture; the US Environmental Protection Agency; and the National Oceanic and Atmospheric Administration in the US Department of Commerce.

Each of these agencies (as well as others) has its own approach to the food safety problem, and most of them have distinct interest groups, congressional committees and subcommittees, and issue networks that support their unique positions. Proposals have emerged both from Congress and from the executive branch (e.g., from the President's Council on Food Safety during the Clinton administration) as well as from science organizations. A number of the advocates for creation of a department containing all of these players assume that reorganization and structural shifts will bring policy changes that minimize these differences. It is these very changes that some of the participants in the policy discussion fear. Others, however, argue that creation of a single department does not assure policy coordination on this issue. Rather they emphasize the very different policy frames that emerge from the separate agencies: science issues in some, food production in others, and regulation in still others.[35]

In addition to the diverse policy frames found in the separate agencies, as the issue has moved over time it has emerged in different forms. Prominent in this process of change was a series of crises that brought the food safety issue to public prominence and to the front burner of interest. The first crisis emerged after September 11, when fear of terrorism involving food was discussed; the second crisis came about when problems with spinach safety created major concerns; and the third was related to fears about safety of imports from China.

Despite this and the introduction of proposed legislation in Congress, as of this writing there has not been an agreement on this issue. Over this twenty-year period, the Government Accountability Office has issued a number of reports dealing with food safety, emphasizing issues related to reorganization such as overlapping and fragmented functions. These arguments have not been effective in moving the policy debate to conclusion.

Obama and Reorganization

President Obama's interest in reorganization surfaced during his State of the Union address in January 2011. He focused on the "absurdity of salmon having to deal with separate federal bureaucracies as they swim out to sea. The Interior Department is in charge of salmon while they're in fresh water, but the Commerce Department handles them when they're in saltwater."[36]

There are at least two problems that create obstacles to what seems to be an obvious argument for reorganization. The first involves the determination of the criteria that will be used as the basis for identifying elements that go into a new organizational structure. The salmon example raises a number of questions. Should we put all of the programs and policies that deal with salmon in one organization structure? But does it make more sense to think about organizations that deal with all fish together? Or should we focus on organizations that deal with organisms that live in freshwater? Often the policies that deal with salmon have conflicting priorities—some are trying to preserve fish, others trying to sell them. To take an example from another issue area, should we put all programs for the elderly together, whether they are in health, housing, income maintenance, or social services? There is not a clear best place for programs because they have their feet in multiple policy areas.

Reorganization and Contradictions in the US System

Reorganization efforts in the US federal system illustrate a number of the aspects of the three sets of contradictions that frame this volume: structural dimensions, predominant values and approaches, and attributes of the public sector.

Structural Dimensions

Since the 1930s both the legislative and executive branches have been interested in the organization of the federal government. As this chapter indicates, early efforts involving reorganization illustrated a two-way conversation between the two branches of government. Both were concerned about these issues, and action by one seemed to provoke interest and action by the other. In a sense, this dynamic provided a setting to acknowledge the legitimate interest of both parties, and the existence of reorganization acts provided the focus for this dialogue. During some periods the predominance of one branch or another led to greater or lesser restrictions on the executive branch's authority to play an active role in reorganization efforts. And as the creation of the Department of Homeland Security indicated, the presence of a crisis in the nation provoked both branches to act. Yet even a crisis did not eliminate the urge by the president to maintain as much control over the process as possible.

There are some reorganization experiences that indicate a concern about the intergovernmental system, especially the relationship between the federal government and the states. This was an issue that was a part of the debate about the creation of the Department of Education and its part in the development of the federal role in education.[37] In addition, the role of the states was also an issue in the discussion about the effectiveness of FEMA in the Department of Homeland Security.

Predominant Values and Approaches

From the Brownlow Committee onward, reorganization proposals were based on the belief that government agencies should be organized to follow the practices of the private sector and strive for clarity of function and authority. There is little in the nearly one hundred years of experience that indicates that many of the proponents of organizational change actually found that these practices were appropriate for the public sector, where multiple actors were involved with very different agendas. In a sense this belief represents both pessimism and optimism. It is pessimistic in that it clearly makes the public sector a second-class citizen vis-à-vis the private sector. But it is also optimistic in that it believes the public sector can behave like the private sector.

As a result, reorganization proposals rarely included the issues that went beyond efficiency values involving overlap, fragmentation, and clear assignment of roles, authorities, and responsibilities. Indeed, effectiveness arguments were closely linked to these attributes and it was assumed that a rational structure would produce effective programs. Concern about equity values—particularly about who would benefit from the programs that were being reorganized—were not a part of the classic management debate when it came from the Executive Office of the President. These were concerns that belonged to a different type of political actor, not to those charged with managing programs.

It was not surprising that the congressional actors who were interested in the details of specific reorganizations were those found in appropriations and authorizing committees and subcommittees responsible for programs, whereas others worried about achieving the private-sector norms of management.

Attributes of the Public Sector

By defining reorganization as a function associated only with management and not with policy, many reorganization proponents rested their strategies on a clear separation between politics and administration. They interpreted the constitutional structure of the United States as one that differentiated the roles of the legislative branch and the executive branch. When it came to the implementation of programs, they did not view Congress as the first branch. Reorganizers tried to limit the role of Congress and often criticized the legislative branch when it sought to limit the authority of the president to change the organization structure. This was in marked contrast to the way that substantive program legislation was devised; it was likely that deliberations over the formulation and adoption of policies by Congress considered implementation issues.

The structure of Congress sometimes created confused expectations about the legislative role in reorganization. The government operations committees in both houses tended to look at reorganization from a government-wide perspective, drawing on what Seidman called the orthodox approach. This was in contrast to the way that the substantive program committees and subcommittees (both authorizing and appropriating committees) analyzed the situation, focusing on specific impacts of organization structure on the program or policy at hand.

In a sense, the congressional government operations committees mirrored the mind-set of the management offices within OMB.[38] Both were actors that tended to view the system from a government-wide vantage point and both had the effect of encouraging centralization in many reorganization approaches. And many efforts to reorganize within cabinet departments also had the effect of supporting centralization and control by offices of the secretary and limiting discretion and autonomy by specialized program units.

Conclusions

While the debates surrounding reorganization strategies have often been posed as conflicts between different approaches to structure and form, in reality these arguments illustrate two underlying problems. First, they revolve around interpretations of the Constitution. Does the Constitution establish separate powers for the branches of government, or does it create shared powers that make it inevitable that Congress will be accused of meddling in administrative matters? And which parts of the complex congressional apparatus are expected to be involved?

Second, reorganization expectations have been so closely linked to management principles drawn from the private sector that it is difficult to disentangle them from the government reorganization debate. While the classic hierarchical models that developed from scientific management have been challenged in some private-sector locations, the orthodox view of public-sector reorganization continues to draw on principles that encourage command-and-control approaches. These principles emerge from experiences over the years in both Congress as well as the executive branch. Both parties frequently use the same language drawn from that orthodox view to describe problems even though they may attach different meanings to those words.

Ignoring Congress is often a way for the public administration community to justify reorganization on the basis of technical management rules and precepts. Executive power is justified by focusing on POSDCORB functions (planning, organizing, staffing, directing, coordinating, reporting, and budgeting), borrowing from private-sector experience, or looking to parliamentary systems for lessons. Thus executive power is supported by ignoring political realities expressed in the legislative branch. It means that arguments for organizational change can be made without thinking about interest groups and the policy impacts of changing organizational boundaries. Indeed, ignoring the concerns that emerge from interest groups and policies is a way of disregarding the very lifeblood of legislative realities.[39]

Ignoring Congress is frequently justified by emphasis on efficiency arguments drawn from the private sector and based on a view of a one best way to organize public agencies. This approach ignores the role of reorganization as a solution to policy problems. We worship the god of efficiency and forget other concerns—effectiveness, equity, politics, and federalism.

We forget that many federal programs and policies contain conflicting expectations. Whether attempting to craft a Department of Education or a Department of Food Safety, the multiple constituencies and values that are at play make it difficult to argue for a simple, factory-like approach to federal organizational structures. The experience of creating the Department of Education in 1979 illustrated at least five different goals: providing symbolic status for education, giving political advantage to some interest groups, making the existing programs more efficient, making them more effective, and actually changing educational policy.[40] Each of these goals leads to somewhat different organizational forms.

The trade-offs that must be made result in policies that are rarely efficient but rather indicate efforts to balance multiple and conflicting goals.

The results often produce systems that reflect the multiple players and the fragmentation of authority that characterize our political structure. Those who approach the task from experience in the private sector seem to have difficulty understanding the constraints of making structural change in the public sector, particularly at the federal level.

It is somewhat ironic that the very people who understand the complexity of living with trade-offs and multiple goals are among the ones left out of the reorganization discussion. Middle-level managers have learned how to deal with different funding streams and multiple and conflicting expectations. They understand the political realities that Congress has to deal with and know that programs often have their feet in multiple policy areas and functions. They know that sometimes program simplification brings unanticipated consequences that either create new problems or complexify existing problems.

While neither player was happy with the experience, the debates over the substance of the various reorganization acts provided one of the few venues for both sets of actors to be involved in the process. It would be timely to examine those experiences and find a way to encourage that debate to move toward more collaborative processes where both parties accepted the reality that they would have different perspectives on the topic of reorganization authority and processes.

Notes

1. This paragraph is found in all of the editions of this book. See Seidman, *Politics, Position, and Power,* 3.
2. Schmeckebier, "Brief History," 185.
3. Quoted ibid., 187.
4. Ibid., 191, 198–99.
5. Ibid., 217–18.
6. Ibid., 218–19.
7. Arnold, *Making the Managerial Presidency,* 3.
8. See the special issues of *Public Administration Review* on the fiftieth and seventieth anniversaries of the issuance of the Brownlow report. And reorganization issues also surfaced in the Clinton administration's National Performance Review.
9. Seidman, *Politics, Position, and Power,* 4.
10. Berg, "Lapse of Reorganization Authority," 196.
11. See discussion in Radin and Hawley, *Politics of Federal Reorganization,* 53.
12. Described in Seidman, *Politics, Position, and Power,* 11.
13. Radin and Hawley, *Politics of Federal Reorganization,* 53.
14. Berg, "Lapse of Reorganization Authority," 197.
15. Ibid.
16. National Commission on the Public Service (the Volcker Commission), *Urgent Business for America: Revitalizing the Federal Government for the 21st Century* (January 2003), summary of recommendations.

17. GAO, *Executive Reorganization Authority*, 2, 1.
18. Ibid., 4.
19. Ibid., 7.
20. Seidman, *Politics, Position, and Power*, 5.
21. The authority for the executive branch to take reorganization action usually emerges from the government operations committees, while specific reorganization proposals are more likely to come from specific authorizing committees in both houses of Congress.
22. Kaufman, "Reflections on Administrative Reorganization," 392.
23. See Radin and Chanin, *Federal Government Reorganization*, chap. 1.
24. Gore, *Creating a Government*, 2–3.
25. Letter from Julie Gerberding to the CDC community, April 21, 2005.
26. Ibid.
27. "Almost Two-Thirds of CDC Employees Oppose Reorganization Plan," *Medical News Today*, July 28, 2005, accessed August 1, 2010, www.medicalnewstoday.com/releases/28184.php.
28. "Five Former CDC Directors Express Concern about Departure of Agency Leaders, Scientists," *Medical News Today*, September 13, 2006, accessed August 1, 2010, www.medicalnewstoday.com/articles/51632.php.
29. See, e.g., US Government Accountability Office, "Chronic Fatigue Syndrome: CDC and NIH Research Activities Are Diverse but Agency Coordination Is Limited," HEHS-00-98, June 2, 2000.
30. The Obama administration treated ATSDR as a separate entity.
31. This discussion draws on chap. 6 in Radin and Chanin, *Federal Government Reorganization*.
32. See Relyea, "Organizing for Homeland Security," 602. Relyea reviewed the ways that Bush pushed his agenda and managed to get the legislation he wanted through Congress.
33. Conley, "Reform, Reorganization, and the Renaissance," 304.
34. This is drawn from chap. 9 of Radin and Chanin, *Federal Government Reorganization*.
35. See discussion in Radin and Chanin, *Federal Government Reorganization*.
36. See Alan Greenblatt, "Salmon Savings May Be Tough for Obama," January 28,2011,www.npr.org/2011/01/29/133301511/salmon-savings-may-be-hard-to-come-by-for-obama.
37. See Radin and Chanin, *Federal Government Reorganization*, chap. 8.
38. There also appeared to be a similar dynamic at play when GAO focused on some reorganization questions.
39. Radin and Chanin, *Federal Government Reorganization*.
40. See Radin and Hawley, *Politics of Federal Reorganization*.

7

BUDGETING AS REFORM

Almost from the time the caterpillar of budgetary evolution became the
butterfly of budgetary reform, the line-item budget has been condemned as a
reactionary throwback to its primitive larva. Budgeting, its critics claim, has
been metamorphized in reverse, an example of retrogression instead of progress.
Over the last century, the traditional annual cash budget has been condemned as
mindless, because its lines do not match programs, irrational, because they deal
with inputs instead of outputs, short-sighted, because they cover one year instead
of many, fragmented, because as a rule only changes are reviewed, conservative,
because these changes tend to be small, and worse. Yet despite these faults, real
and alleged, the traditional budget reigns supreme virtually everywhere, in
practice if not in theory.

Aaron Wildavsky, "A Budget for All Seasons"

THERE IS PERHAPS NO OTHER REFORM AREA THAT MORE DRAMATICALLY
illustrates the difference between a parliamentary system and the US system
of shared powers than the budget process. For years I would be asked the
same question by Australian friends when the US president released his
budget: "Tell me again, what does that budget mean?" It was difficult to
explain to my friends that many presidential budgets were dead on arrival
to Congress and that observers of the American scene should not focus on
that document to determine what policies and programs would be supported with federal dollars.

For someone operating in a parliamentary system based on the Westminster system, a budget that is presented by the head of government is *the*
budget. While negotiations within the executive branch take place before the
budget is released, once it is made public that document becomes the official
document.[1] In such a system, it is clear where one looks to determine what
"the government" specifies as the official policy. In the United States not
only should one look at two very distinct branches of government operating
independently (both of which have their own internal complexities) but one
also should examine the ways that each branch has the ability to constrain
the other as the budget process unfolds. If one looked to the private sector
for ideas about the budget process, it seemed clear that President George W.
Bush (the first American president to hold an MBA) was not likely to look
beyond the executive branch.

This chapter focuses on the processes that have developed over the
years as players from the two branches have sought to modify the system.

It discusses the historical development of these relationships and how modifications in one branch created new responses in the other. It emphasizes the macro shifts that occurred within the society as federal government expenditures moved from an assumption of continual growth to a reality of scarcity and cut-back demands.[2] Three initiatives are used to illustrate these changes: the development of the Planning, Programming, and Budgeting System in the 1960s, enactment of the Budget and Impoundment Control Act in 1974, and the Budget Enforcement Act of 1990. Finally, the chapter analyzes the ways in which reforms in budgeting have dealt with the contradictions found in the US system.

Budgeting as Reform

Like several other federal management reform initiatives, the budgeting changes had their origins in state and especially local governments. The most visible example of this occurred in New York City around 1917 through the activities of the Bureau of Municipal Research. In his classic article "Emerging Conflicts in the Doctrines of Public Administration," Herbert Kaufman described this development as the spread of the executive budget in government:

> For a long time, agency requests for funds were considered individually, and there was no central point at which total expenditures were reviewed and the competing claims balanced against each other in the light of the resources available; indeed, very often, the only way government could figure out how much they were spending was to add up the appropriation bills after they had been passed. The reformers turned to the chief executives to rationalize the spending process, and out of it came the now familiar phenomena of executive review and adjustment of agency requests, and the submittal of a comprehensive budget supposed to make it possible to see the overall spending pattern.[3]

In addition, the New York City efforts reflected the values and concerns associated with the Progressive movement. Not only did they focus on rationalizing the system but they also expressed the concerns of a growing middle class about the impact of immigration on the governance system. These concerns emphasized issues of corruption that were associated with the relationship between the new immigrants and the partisan political system (often described as bossism).

This dynamic found its way to the federal government. Allen Schick focused on three distinct administrative processes involving budgets in his work on budget reform; these are planning, management, and control. He argues that "in the modern genesis of budgeting, efforts to improve planning, management, and control made common cause under the popular banner of the executive-budget concept." Further, he links reforms such as functional consolidation of agencies, elimination of independent boards and commissions, the short ballot, and strengthening of the chief executive's appointive and removal powers to the executive budget idea. He notes that "the chief executive often was likened to the general manager of a corporation, the Budget Bureau serving as his general staff."[4] According to Schick, executive budgeting emphasized the control orientation and the intention to strengthen honesty and efficiency by restricting the discretion of administrators.

As the years progressed, particularly during the New Deal era, Schick finds that there was a reorientation of budgeting to a management mission. "The rapid growth of government activities and expenditures made it more difficult and costly for central officials to keep track of the myriad objects in the budget."[5] In 1939, following criticisms by the President's Committee on Administrative Management (the Brownlow Committee), the Bureau of the Budget was transferred from the Department of the Treasury to a newly created Executive Office of the President. Subsequent reports (including that of the Hoover Commission) led to the definition of budget categories in functional terms and efforts to provide measurements attached to specific activities.

While the focus of these activities was on the executive branch, there was also parallel activity within Congress during this period. Until the Brownlow Committee deliberations, the congressional role as the first branch was clear and Congress dominated the budget formulation process from the early days of the country.[6] But the Brownlow report focused on building executive leadership and advised Congress to abandon line-item appropriations and, instead, provide broad authority to agencies. Paul Posner described these recommendations as follows: "Shifting the congressional role in executive management from ex ante to ex post would, if adopted, constitute a major shift in the congressional role and influence as well."[7] The report drew on the experiences of parliamentary systems to justify its proposals.

The Brownlow perspective was much different from that of Congress itself. A Congressional Research Service document that was prepared for members and committees of Congress provides a clear view of that difference.

> The "power of the purse" is a legislative power. The Constitution lists the power to lay and collect taxes and the power to borrow as powers of Congress; further, it provides that funds may be drawn from the Treasury only pursuant to appropriations made by law. The Constitution does not state how these legislative powers are to be exercised, nor does it expressly provide for the President to have a role in the management of the nation's finances.
>
> During the nation's early years, the House and Senate devised procedures for the enactment of spending and revenue legislation. . . . In the course of each session, Congress passed many separate appropriations bills and other measures affecting the financial condition of the federal government. Neither the Constitution nor the procedures adopted by the

House and Senate provided for a budget system—that is, for a coordinated set of actions covering all federal spending and revenues. As long as the federal government was small and its spending and revenues were stable, such a budget system was not considered necessary. . . .

The 1921 act did not directly alter the procedures by which Congress makes revenue and spending decisions. The main impact was in the executive branch. The President was required to submit his budget recommendations to Congress each year, and the Bureau of the Budget—renamed the Office of Management and Budget (OMB) in 1970—was created to assist him in carrying out his budgetary responsibilities. Congress, it was expected, would be able to coordinate its revenue and spending decisions if it received comprehensive budget recommendations from the President. In line with this expectation, the House and Senate changed their rules to consolidate the jurisdiction of the Appropriations Committees over spending.[8]

The Heritage of Budgeting Reform

A CRS staff report emphasized the way that budget decisions permeate the congressional bodies. "Because nearly every committee of the House and Senate has jurisdiction over legislation with a budgetary impact, interest in the budget process and proposals to change it radiates throughout both chambers."[9]

According to Susan Irving of the GAO, a budget process can be measured against four objectives:

- to provide information about the long-term impact of decisions while recognizing the differences between short-term forecasts, medium-term projections, and a long-term perspective;
- to provide information and be structured to focus on the important macro trade-offs, for example, between consumption and investment;
- to provide information necessary to make informed trade-offs on a variety of levels, for example, between mission areas and between different tools; and
- to be enforceable, provide for control and accountability, and be transparent.[10]

In a very useful report on past initiatives involving performance budgeting, GAO commented: "The process of budgeting is inherently an exercise in political choice—allocating scarce resources among competing needs and priorities—in which performance information can be one, but not the only, factor underlying decisions."[11] The politics of budgeting is a subject that has received significant attention.[12] However, much of the analysis focuses on partisan and interest group behavior that helps to explain the outcome of budgetary issues debates.

This analysis emphasizes another aspect of the politics of the budgetary process—the institutional differences between the demands and requirements of the executive and legislative branches. These institutional conflicts are illustrated by three initiatives advanced since the 1960s: (1) the Planning, Programming, and Budgeting System (PPBS), begun government-wide by the executive branch in 1965 following its first adoption in the Department of Defense in 1961,[13] (2) the Congressional Budget and Impoundment Control Act of 1974, which created new congressional entities that increased the legislative branch's ability to shape the federal government, and (3) the Budget Enforcement Act of 1990, which sought to respond to the budget crisis and established new congressional rules for the budget process. These initiatives focus on the two branches but also emphasize two other elements: the shifting economic environment within the country and the different functions attached to budgeting as defined by Allen Schick (planning, management, and control).[14]

The aggregate result of the action in Congress, according to the Committee for a Responsible Federal Budget, was hardly optimistic: "The congressional budget process has succumbed to an all too human tendency. When we write rules, people tend to bend and break them. When we build fences and fail to tend them, people will find ways to breach those barriers. So much has happened, so many rules and concepts have been bent or broken that the total damage to the process is greater than the sum of the parts. As a result, even well intentioned, well-informed people have difficulty understanding the budget today and our broad public policy debates suffer as a consequence."[15]

The PPBS Initiative

PPBS was adopted by Secretary of Defense Robert McNamara in 1961, at the beginning of the Kennedy administration. It attempted to provide a link between planning and budgeting functions that operated as separate entities and was devised as a management tool that would allow the secretary of defense to control and rationalize the activities in autonomous departments.[16]

The availability of new analytic approaches developed during World War II provided an intellectual stimulus to earlier proposals that linked budget processes to management and planning.[17] As already described, these proposals emerged at the turn of the twentieth century and represented agendas for rationalizing the system and controlling corruption.

In the post–World War II period, social scientists began to play a role in the decision-making process. The imperatives of war had stimulated new analytic techniques—among them systems analysis and operations research—that sought to apply principles of rationality to strategic decision making. Although still in an embryonic form, the computer technology of that period did allow individuals to manipulate what were then considered to be large data sets in ways that had been unthinkable in the past.[18]

In a sense, the techniques that were available in the late 1950s cried out for new forms of use. All of this took form in the components of PPBS, a decision allocation process that was established in the Department of Defense in 1961 and eventually extended by President Lyndon Johnson to other parts of the federal government. The analytic approach would always be closely associated with the style and interests of President John Kennedy's Secretary of Defense, Robert McNamara. A graduate of the Harvard Business School and former president of the Ford Motor Company, McNamara had great confidence in analytic skills and the rational framework that would produce data.

The process itself required an analyst to identify the objectives of the agency, to relate costs and budgetary decisions to these objectives, and to assess the cost-effectiveness of current and proposed programs. This analytic planning process was linked to the budget process (former RAND staffer Charles Hitch was actually named as comptroller of DoD with responsibility for the budget), providing a way to translate what might have been academic exercises to the actual allocation of resources. It represented the first serious effort to link strategic management processes to the budget.

The PPBS process that was put into place had at least three different goals. First, it sought to create opportunities for control by top agency officials over fragmented and diffuse organizational and program units. Despite the organization chart, the DoD was clearly a federal department that operated more like a feudal system than a tight bureaucratic hierarchy. The separate services—army, navy, and air force—were distinct and separate units with their own programs, cultures, and constituencies. The secretary of defense had limited ways of reining in the services to operate as a single department. PPBS sought to look at the DoD as a unity and to provide advice to the secretary; it represented a way for the secretary to establish control over hitherto decentralized operations. The analytical categories that were used provided a way for the secretary to identify cross-cutting programs and issues within the highly fragmented department.

Second, PPBS was an attempt to improve efficiency in the way that resources were allocated and implemented. Looking at DoD from a centralized vantage point and defining functional categories across the department, it was obvious that there were overlaps and redundancies found within the multiple units, particularly in the procurement process. For example, the system assumed that economic efficiencies were not served by processes that could not define economies of scale.

Third, the PPBS process rested on a belief that increased use of knowledge and information would produce better decisions. The experience of World War II was a heady one; advances in the availability and production of information gave PPBS proponents the sense that it was possible to differentiate the false from the true and that the conceptual models that they relied on would produce accurate and appropriate information and make those decisions within the budget process.

The office that was established in the Department of Defense to carry out McNamara's analytical agenda became the model for future analytic activity throughout the federal government. As the office developed, its goal of providing systematic, rational, and science-based counsel to decision makers included what has become the classic policy analysis litany: problem identification, development of options or alternatives, delineation of objectives and criteria, evaluation of impacts of these options, estimation of future effects, and—of course—recommendations for action. These recommendations were not only substantive directives but also recommendations for budget allocations.

In many ways, the establishment of this office represented a top-level strategy to avoid what were viewed as the pitfalls of traditional bureaucratic behavior. Rather than move through a complex chain of command, the analysts in this office—regardless of their rank—had direct access to the top officials in the department. Their loyalty was to the secretary of the department, the individual at the top of the organization who sought control and efficiencies in running the huge department. In addition to PPBS, they introduced a range of analytic methods to the federal government, including cost-benefit analysis, operations and systems research, and linear programming.

This office was viewed as an autonomous unit, made up of individuals with well-honed skills who were not likely to have detailed knowledge of the substance of the policy assignments given them. Their specializations were in the techniques of analysis, not in the details of their application. While these staff members thought of themselves as specialists, their specializations were not a part of the areas of expertise found within the traditional bureaucracy. Sometimes called the "whiz kids," this staff was highly visible; both its PPBS activity as well as its general expertise came to the attention of President Lyndon Johnson.

In October 1965, the Bureau of the Budget (later named the Office of Management and Budget) issued a directive to all federal departments and agencies, calling on them to establish central analytic offices that would apply the PPBS approach to all of their budget submissions. Staff were sent to various educational institutions to learn about PPBS's demands.

According to a report in the *New York Times,* Johnson met with the cabinet and instructed them "to immediately begin to introduce a very new and very revolutionary system of planning and programming and budgeting through the vast Federal government, so that through the tools of modern management the full promise of a finer life can be brought to each American at the lowest possible cost." Johnson argued that the use of "the most modern methods of program analysis" would "insure a much sounder judgment through more accurate information, pinpointing those things that we ought to do more, spotlighting those things that we ought to do less."[19]

The system that was mandated by Johnson was described by GAO as follows: "[It] assumed that different levels and types of performance could be arrayed, quantified and analyzed to make the best budgetary decisions. In essence, PPBS introduced a decision-making framework to the executive branch budget formulation process by presenting and analyzing choices among long-term policy objectives and alternative ways of achieving them."[20]

Even during this period, however, there were those who were skeptical about the effectiveness of the PPBS demand. In 1969 Aaron Wildavsky published an article that has become a classic—an analysis in the *Public Administration Review* that argued that PPBS has done damage to the prospects of encouraging policy analysis in American national government.[21] While the secretary of defense and the White House pushed the new system, Congress was not comfortable with it. The budget for DoD was actually presented in two forms: the PPBS form inside the executive branch and the traditional line-item budget form for Congress.

Thomas Murphy, a long-time NASA staffer who was also an academic, commented on the problems and possibilities of PPBS a few years after it went into operation in an article titled "Congress, PPBS, and Reality." He described the process as an illustration of "an administrative echo chamber which our federal system constitutes . . . and the whole process exudes a Messianic spirit." Further, "PPBS is not merely a different approach or technique for putting together a budget. Rather than merely shifting emphasis or the locus of management evaluation, it demands substantive reorganization and reshaping of analytical procedures."[22] He described the process as one that was incompatible with traditional practices of legislative oversight.

> The traditions of Congress do not enshrine efficiency as the criterion for decisions. Positions on the Appropriations Committee are sought for the specific purpose of being able to support projects and programs in which the member's district has vested interests. Such interests will not be easily dissipated in the name of general schemes of efficiency or cost-effectiveness. Budgetary decisions are still going to be made by political figures for political reasons within the context of our political system. This factor has led some to question whether any efforts to help Congress cope with PPBS would serve less to enable Congress to participate effectively in a new decision-making process than to teach it how to pervert PPBS to support the narrower interests that some congressmen are inclined to emphasize.[23]

Murphy concluded his analysis by quoting a report of the Subcommittee on National Security and International Operations of the Senate Committee on Government Operations:

> The more centralized decision making becomes in the Executive Branch, the more important some competition of this sort from Congress might be. The centralizing bias of PPBS may be more important than the anticipated technical improvements of the budgetary process, because of a lessening of competitive forces within the Executive Branch. If PPBS

develops into a contest between experts and politicians, it will not be hard to pick the winners. They will be the politicians in the Congress and the White House. It has been said, and correctly, that as interesting as observing what happens to government when confronted with PPB will be watching what happens to PPB when confronted with government.[24]

Budget and Impoundment Control Act of 1974

Like the executive branch, Congress had been considering issues related to the budget process for some time before the enactment of the Budget and Impoundment Control Act in 1974. The various legislative reorganization acts and specialized committees to review the committee structure of both the House and the Senate did not emphasize the budget, but in 1972 Congress created a Joint Study Committee on Budget Control, composed of members from the appropriations and tax committees of both chambers as well as two at-large members from the House and the Senate.

In its final report in December 1993, the joint committee provided the background for the development of the legislation:

> Increased spending for programs initiated or expanded during the "Great Society" era of President Johnson, combined with escalating expenditures to support military efforts in Vietnam, heightened concern in Congress about budget deficits and spending controls. During the 1972 election campaign, President Nixon asked Congress for authority to cut Federal spending at his own discretion so as to stay under a proposed $250 billion ceiling for FY 1973. Congress refused to go along with such an open-ended grant of authority. Congress and the White House ultimately clashed sharply over President Nixon's aggressive impoundment of (refusal to spend) appropriated monies.

Further, "In response to both the frustration generated by the fragmented nature of the congressional budget process and the perceived encroachment of the executive onto the budgetary turf of Congress, Congress passed the Congressional Budget and Impoundment Control Act of 1974."[25]

The impoundment part of the legislation reflected significant conflicts between the executive and legislative branches during the Nixon presidency. Louis Fisher has noted that "prior to 1974 several administrations had impounded funds, justified either on the basis of statutory authority or on the claim that presidents had inherent authority to withhold funds from obligation. Despite confrontations from time to time, the two branches managed to fashion political accommodations that were acceptable to both sides. Rarely was there a stalemate that required the courts to referee the dispute." According to Fisher, "This informal system fell apart during the Nixon administration. Funds were withheld in a manner, quantitatively and qualitatively, that threatened Congress's power of the purse. Budgetary priorities established by Congress through the appropriation process were quickly reshuffled by administrative officials who refused to spend funds the president did not want. As a result, the programs were severely curtailed and in some cases terminated."[26]

The law was enacted on July 12, 1974, just weeks before President Nixon resigned. It sought to

- assure effective congressional control over the budgetary process,
- provide for the congressional determination each year of the appropriate level of federal revenues and expenditures,
- provide a system of impoundment control,
- establish national budget priorities, and
- provide for the furnishing of information by the executive branch in a manner that will assist Congress in discharging its duties.

Observers have emphasized the act's contribution in providing three new entities that would increase the legislative branch's ability to shape the federal budget. It created the Senate Committee on the Budget and the House Committee on the Budget, which would coordinate the congressional consideration of the budget, as well as the Congressional Budget Office (CBO), which would be a source of nonpartisan analysis and information related to the budget and the economy. It was believed that CBO could provide a counterpoint to OMB and the Executive Office of the President. Alice Rivlin, the first director of CBO, established a process that served as the framework for subsequent staffs.

CBO's services have been grouped in four categories: helping Congress formulate a budget plan, helping it stay within that plan, helping it assess the impact of federal mandates, and helping it consider issues related to the budget and to economic policy.[27] In addition, it provided for additional committees and staff to serve as resources in the budget process. The act also created the concurrent budget resolution as a way to coordinate various elements in the budget.

According to the joint committee report, "There is general agreement that the Congressional Budget Act has led to a reassertion of the congressional role in budgeting, increased the attention of the Congress to the whole budget, and resulted in the control of impoundments. However, it is not viewed as an overwhelming success in other respects. First, it has not brought the order and timeliness to congressional budget action for which advocates had hoped. . . . Second, establishing the Budget Committees and a centralized decisionmaking process may have increased the level of budgetary conflict in the Congress."[28]

Louis Fisher, one of the major scholars on the politics of shared powers, has written that "the legislative history of the Budget Act of 1974 contains sharp disagreements about its objectives. The dominant sentiment, however, was the need to restrain the growth of federal spending." The result of the act, he argues, was mixed. "Observers and participants were reluctant to admit failure, in part because there was a felt need for a 'process.' Even members of Congress who voted consistently against budget resolutions praised the process while condemning the product."[29]

Fisher found that the budget act of 1974 "produced two consequences of immense importance for executive-legislative relations. First, under very unique circumstances the availability of a budget resolution can permit greater presidential control over the legislative process.... The second consequence, however, has been just as important and, in some ways, contradicts the first point. The willingness of Congress to adopt budget resolutions has reduced the president's incentive to submit a responsible budget. The overall effect, then, is to weaken presidential responsibility, except in highly unusual conditions."

In summary, Fisher argues that the 1974 legislation "led to a preoccupation with the internal mechanics and technicalities of the congressional budget process: authorizations, appropriations, tax bills, budget resolutions, and reconciliations. Through this process we lost sight of the need for a budget system that connects the legislative branch to the executive. To be effective, a legislative budget process must work in tandem with the White House. The total process must take advantage of the institutional strengths of Congress and the president. For the last two decades we have played on institutional weaknesses rather than institutional strengths."[30]

The Budget Enforcement Act of 1990

Between 1974 and 1990 both Congress and the American electorate increasingly focused on the growth of budget deficits. While Congress attempted to respond to the deficit problem, it was not successful in dealing with it.[31] Following the limited success of implementing the Gramm-Rudman legislation, the Budget Enforcement Act (BEA) of 1990 increased the amount of deficit reduction, continued the sequestration procedures in the earlier legislation, replaced the fixed deficit targets with adjustable ones, put adjustable limits on discretionary spending and—most notable— established a pay-as-you-go process for revenues and direct spending. The legislation established a distinction between discretionary spending (which is controlled through the annual appropriations process) and direct spending (provided outside of the annual appropriations process and largely involving entitlement programs).

According to Louis Fisher, the experience with the 1974 budget act and the Gramm-Rudman Act "convinced leaders from both branches to try another tack."[32] While the earlier budget legislation acknowledged the multiple objectives of the budget process that Irving described, at this point Congress focused almost exclusively on the short-term (and political) aspects of the deficit. Fisher has commented that three political goals were embedded in the 1990 statute: both of the branches wanted to avoid fixed deficit targets that had embarrassed them in the past; they agreed to protect the defense budget from legislative raids; and they sought to finesse the budget crisis at least through the 1992 presidential election year. As a result, the legislation was limited to a two-year life, with the possibility of extension, but that required action by Congress.

Irene Rubin described this shift as a retreat from the norms of budgeting. "Ideally, budget documents should be transparent and inclusive, and revenues should equal or exceed expenditures. The decision-making process should be predictable, and the publicly approved budget should be implemented with as few changes as possible. Public money should be spent efficiently, effectively, and honestly, and to that end, budgeters should examine and prioritize claims carefully."[33]

This picture of the congressional budget process did not match the political realities of the situation. Political partisanship at least partially explained the response to efforts both to extend the 1990 law and to agree on the substance of a budget. In 1994, the Republican Contract with America provided the basis for an attempt to pass a balanced budget constitutional amendment.[34] The Republicans had control of Congress after the 1996 elections and did agree to an extension of the BEA in 1997 with some modifications.

The Clinton administration was able to use the system to achieve reductions in the deficit and actually achieve a surplus. However, even as he announced the surplus, Clinton warned of its fragility: "I am concerned, frankly, about the size and last-minute nature of this year's congressional spending spree, where they seem to be loading up the spending bills with special projects for special interests, but can't seem to find the time to raise the minimum wage, or pass a patients' bill of rights, or drug benefits for our seniors through Medicare, or tax cuts for long-term care, child care, or college education."[35]

In its March/April 2009 issue, the *Public Administration Review* published a mini-symposium on the federal budget process. Organized by Paul Posner, the symposium focused on the article published in the journal by Irene Rubin in 2007. Rubin lamented that the budget process had become "ad hoc, fragmented, and opaque, balance has been elusive, and the failure to prioritize has become endemic."[36]

The participants in the symposium represented different perspectives on the issue at the time when there was a search for a new framework for fiscal rules.[37] Posner's introduction noted: "Crafting a budget process that can prompt embittered partisans to look beyond the political foxhole at the short- and long-term economic and social consequences of their decisions would be a triumph of political engineering. This is no easy task. As the essays in this symposium suggest, there is no consensus even among budget experts about what process reforms are desirable. Moreover, there remains substantial doubt about whether neutral reforms can be sustained absent reinforcing changes in the broader political coalition in our leadership."[38]

Budgeting and Contradictions in the US System

Viewing the budget process as one of the areas of management reform provides a somewhat different glimpse of budgeting than is usually found in both practitioner and academic perspectives. The three sets of contradictions that frame this book generate that different perspective.

Structural Dimensions

Although the founders of the US system viewed the budget process as the prerogative of "the first branch" (Congress), by the beginning of the twentieth century things changed quite dramatically. The growth of the federal government and the interest in creating a strong executive branch established strong interest in the executive budget. This would be an important element of the development of a management perspective in the Executive Office of the President. When that occurred, the traditional congressional process that was based on program and policy specialization seemed to many to be old-fashioned and unable to respond to the complexity within the American society.

The three examples discussed in this chapter illustrate the different perspectives on this situation. PPBS represented an attempt by the president to link the budget process to control, management, and planning. It sought a longer time perspective than had been put in place in the past, assuming that—as in the private sector—the demands of the country required some level of stability and rationality in the public-sector response.

The two congressional actions that have been described illustrate attempts by Congress to establish procedures that could serve as a counterpoint to the developments within the executive branch. That involved finding a way to view the budget as a whole, conceptualizing it in a top-down fashion; Congress also tried to find a way to develop an analytic capacity that might meet the abilities of the executive branch. Yet the engine that ran Congress continued the fragmentation of the system, with specialized committees and subcommittees playing both authorizing and appropriating roles as well as the inevitability that members of Congress (particularly the House) always faced two-year election cycles.

There is a tendency among the budget reformers to emphasize the potential of the details of the changes as the way to accomplish very complex and conflicting goals. Many of these reformers have romanticized the processes of the past and looked to technocratic means as a way to achieve what they view as the success of those past efforts. Because of the partisan conflict that characterizes the contemporary political scene, reformers have tried to develop systems that bypass the behavior of participants and ignore Wildavsky's argument that the process of making budgets is political and more art than science. It seems that rules without leadership and commitment do not accomplish much.

While it is rarely acknowledged, US federalism also has played a role in the budget process. Federalism explains a number of elements in the US system: the structure of the Senate, the relative weakness of the political party system, and the ways that members of both the House and the Senate attempt to represent the varied interests of their specific constituencies.

Predominant Values and Approaches

It is clear that the budget reform efforts discussed have attempted to deal with very dramatic changes in the country's economic context. However, these attempts were largely viewed as failures. Over the past fifty years, the budget process moved from allocation demands to attempts to deal with major deficit conditions. Effectively it swung from demands to balance a budget through micro decisions (in a way that is similar to that of a family's household) to great frustration about the deficits in the federal budget—the macro perspective. In a sense, it moved from an optimistic era to one of pessimism.

It is not at all obvious how the government (both the executive and legislative branches) will deal with these issues and find a way to integrate both perspectives. The systems that are in place in each of the two branches have established somewhat different pathways to the integration task. The executive branch is largely dependent on a bottom-up process where the players attached to the program level begin the conversation and the decisions move up the hierarchical structure. At the same time, the political players (in the White House and OMB) attempt to establish ground rules that constrain the bottom-up conversation. The detail and complexity of the system also provide opportunities for program officials to move some resources at the margins, allowing some discretion in the system.

By contrast, the congressional process does not follow a hierarchy. The players who attempt to articulate a macro focus (CBO and the two budget committees as well as the government operations committees) do not have the ability to demand compliance from the authorizing and appropriating committees and subcommittees. The reforms that have been adopted are not able to change that process unless the relevant players have agreed to make it work. And the election calendar also makes it difficult for Congress to commit future legislatures to the decisions. These differences obviously lead to frustration for both branches. It is not clear that it makes sense to focus on procedures and rules when the macro issues have created the current problem.

As the process has focused more and more on deficits, it is not surprising that efficiency values have overpowered the conversations. Demands for budget cuts to achieve something resembling a balanced budget make sure that the conversations are about dollars, not about program effectiveness. Budgets and conversations about dollars are very blunt instruments to determine effectiveness of programs or whether they meet equity concerns that were a part of the authorizing process.

Attributes of the Public Sector

Efforts in the executive branch to modify the budget process over the years represent a desire to clearly differentiate between policy and administration. Following the Brownlow Committee report, over the years one sees evidence that the executive branch would like to minimize the ability of Congress to get involved in what the private sector would clearly define as a management prerogative: the development of an executive budget that has the ability to look at issues beyond the annual budget process.[39] At the same time, when decisions require difficult and unpopular elements, it can be useful to the executive branch to share the problems with Congress. Conversely, it has been argued that it is useful for Congress to try to sustain whatever the executive branch is trying to do.

Unlike a parliamentary system, the US structure does not integrate partisan and institutional roles. Budget decisions can revolve around policy disputes that represent partisan political debates. As has been described, there are times when budget opposition is a function of partisan disputes when the two branches (or even two houses) live with divided government. Opposition to a presidential budget, for example, may have little to do with the specifics of the programs to be funded and more to do with a coming election cycle when the opposition party sees political payoff in opposing the president.

But there is also conflict in the system that focuses on the institutional differences between the legislative and executive branches. The White House is in power for a four-year term while Congress balances two-year terms in the House and staggered six-year terms in the Senate. And as has been noted, the fragmentation of the congressional organization makes it difficult—if not impossible—for the branch to speak with one voice. The few congressional bodies that attempt to look at the government as a whole (the budget committees, CBO, and the government operations committees) are not a comfortable fit with the dispersed authority in the rest of the legislative body.

Conclusions

The future of budget reform is hard to read. Given the dimensions of the deficit and the current economic conditions both in the United States and globally, the task is overwhelming. At the same time, one gets the sense that budget reformers are asking both branches of government to dramatically change their behavior. Like Henry Higgins in *My Fair Lady*, we seem to be asking the question, "Why can't a woman be more like a man?" We want both branches to move closer to one another but we have not given them a way to accept the different cultures and realities found in each of them. It appears that the framework offered by Charles Lindblom's "muddling through" and disjointed incrementalism continues. This is despite the fact that the reform efforts dealing with budgeting have attempted to avoid acknowledging the complexity of the US system and have not achieved ways to manage the conflict that emerges from that system.[40]

Notes

1. One can also see the impact of the structural differences in policy discussions. White papers are released by the government in power that become the blueprint for change in a parliamentary system. In the United States, similar documents released by the White House often become the beginning rather than the end of the discussion.
2. Like some of the other reform efforts, the professionalization of the budget process began at the state and local levels following the demands for professionalization that were a part of the Progressive movement.
3. Kaufman, "Emerging Conflicts," 1064.
4. Schick, "Road to PPB," 246.
5. Ibid., 249.
6. See Posner, "Continuity of Change," 1019.
7. Ibid., 1020.
8. Keith, *CRS Report for Congress*, CRS-2.
9. Heniff and Keith, *Federal Budget Process Reform*, CRS-2.
10. GAO, *Budget Process*, 5.
11. GAO, *Performance Budgeting* (1997), 4.
12. See, e.g., Wildavsky, *Politics of the Budgetary Process*.
13. PPBS is usually defined as Planning, Programming, and Budgeting System, but is also defined as Program, Performance, and Budgeting System. Both, however, are the same thing.
14. These three initiatives do have somewhat different units of analysis and goals and vary in the extent they are congressional/fiscal or executive/performance based.
15. The Committee for a Responsible Federal Budget, "Federal Budget Process: Recommendations for Reform," March 1, 2000, 2.
16. I am indebted to William West for the insights in his book *Program Budgeting and the Performance Movement*.
17. Most descriptions of PPBS call Charles Hitch of the RAND Corporation the father of PPBS.
18. This discussion is drawn from Radin, *Beyond Machiavelli*, 13–17.
19. Quoted in Williams, *Honest Numbers and Democracy*, 61.
20. GAO, *Performance Budgeting* (1997), 5. When the administration changed, the system eventually disappeared except in the Defense Department. See West, *Program Budgeting*, for a description of its current status.

21. Wildavsky, "Rescuing Policy Analysis." See also Schick, "Death in the Bureaucracy."
22. Murphy, "Congress, PPBS, and Reality," 462, 465.
23. Ibid., 467.
24. Committee on Government Operations, Subcommittee on National Security and International Operations, S. Rep., at 7–8 (1967).
25. Joint Committee on the Organization of Congress, *Organization of the Congress: Final Report,* unpaged (1993).
26. Fisher, *Politics of Shared Power,* 83.
27. Described in CRS, *Congressional Oversight Manual,* CRS-125.
28. Ibid.
29. Fisher, *Politics of Shared Power,* 227, 230.
30. Ibid., 231–32, 250. It has been noted that Fisher has also argued that the 1974 legislation weakens congressional responsibility by encouraging appropriators to become claimants rather than guardians. There are very diverse and extensive assessments of that legislation and some found that it did curb impoundments and created reconciliation bills to reduce entitlements and increase taxes.
31. The main measure was the Balanced Budget and Emergency Deficit Control Act of 1985 (known as the Gramm-Rudman-Hollings Act), which, according to Fisher, represented a recognition that "the political stalemate between President Reagan and Congress required a statutory framework with strong sanctions" (ibid., 237).
32. Ibid., 239.
33. Rubin, "Great Unraveling," 608.
34. See discussion in Fisher, *Politics of Shared Power,* 240–42, and in Joyce and Meyers, "Budgeting during the Clinton Administration."
35. Bill Clinton, press conference, September 27, 2000.
36. See Rubin, "Great Unraveling," 210n39, 608.
37. During the George W. Bush administration there was an attempt to link performance information to the formal budget process. The president's budget included performance measures in the executive budget documents. As George Frederickson noted in a communication to the author, while this did not make much difference in terms of final policy approaches, it was an interesting attempt at performance budgeting.
38. Posner, "Introduction to the Mini-Symposium," 210.
39. The Grace Commission's concern about congressional micromanaging illustrates this perspective.
40. See, e.g., Good, "Still Budgeting by Muddling Through."

8

REFORM IN FEDERALISM AND INTERGOVERNMENTAL RELATIONS

If there are truly unique aspects in the American political system, it may well be said that they lie imbedded in the ways and means of American federalism. Indeed, the creation of a viable and lasting federal system of government is probably the most unique American contribution to the political art. Throughout the history of human society, the problem of reconciling the virtues of local control with the need for centralized powers has troubled politicians and philosophers. . . . American federalism has been able to combine strength at the center with local control and reasonably uniform national progress with opportunities for local diversity. Herein lies the system's greatness. Unfortunately the values of federalism, like all values, are difficult to measure.

Daniel J. Elazar, *The American Partnership*

IT IS SOMEWHAT UNUSUAL TO FIND A DISCUSSION OF FEDERALISM AND intergovernmental relations (IGR) included as one of the topics in the management reform portfolio. But the debate over these issues illustrates a number of the elements that are found in other reform issues and discussed in this book. Many of the scholars who focus on federalism and IGR tend to downplay the management aspects of federalism and intergovernmental relations and, instead, emphasize such topics as fiscal patterns, structure of government, and constitutional requirements and legal limitations.[1] While all of these topics clearly influence management behaviors and expectations, efforts to change existing patterns have been included only on the periphery of the management reform agenda. Indeed, discussion about federalism is most often posed in normative terms that emphasize politics and policy. The addition of the concept of IGR—and intergovernmental management—does create a bridge to the management literature as it emphasizes description and management concerns.

This chapter reviews a number of initiatives since the 1950s that sought to change the way that the United States conceptualized the role of the federal government in the intergovernmental system. During this period, states have become more direct players in the federal system as they became the implementers of national policy and had authority to exert varying levels of discretion over the national requirements.[2] The US structure of federalism, combined with the national structure of shared powers between executive, legislative, and judicial institutions, provides a unique setting for the United

States. This chapter discusses the mechanisms that have been devised both as stand-alone strategies and included in broader efforts such as the National Performance Review. It gives attention to the roles of both the White House (especially OMB) and Congress in this area and the techniques that have been used to deal with issues involving conflict between levels of government.

An Area of Constant Debate

Few concepts involving federal management are clear, as has been illustrated in earlier chapters. But the debate over federalism and IGR is, perhaps, the least clear of all. It is conducted using different vocabularies and disciplines and directly confronts divisive issues such as those involving race that have emerged from the US Civil War experience. Economists and public choice advocates join constitutional scholars to frame the discussion and are not particularly interested in the details of management systems and behaviors beyond the transfer of money or formal legal requirements. And because ideological differences are close to the surface in discussions about the US federal system (dealing with race and states' rights as well as the appropriate role of the public sector writ large), many of the scholars in the field have been attracted to analyses that focus on the system as a single entity.

As a result, the academic literature exhibits a tendency to look at the system as a whole and to characterize approaches in a government-wide and broad-brush fashion. And both analysts and policymakers have been attracted to efficiency arguments and clarity about sorting out the roles of the multiple jurisdictional levels. In that sense, the federalism reform efforts mirror a number of the other initiatives already described in this book. For example, efforts to sort out the appropriate roles of the levels of government are analogous to the differentiation between the public and private sectors. Like that debate, that approach doesn't get very far. Rhetoric abounds and efforts to determine what is the proper role of each level of government rarely result in the kind of action envisioned by their proponents.

This occurs largely because of the fragmented nature of the US system, which limits the ability of reform advocates to follow through on promises and plans. In reality, debates about the proper role of the federal government are conducted program by program, policy by policy. Often ideology trumps detailed proposals, and the programs and policies that emerge seek to balance efficiency and clarity concerns with issues involving redistribution of power and resources and issues involving race.

Despite the rhetoric to the contrary, it is much more common to see diversity in the way that roles of levels of government vary by program and over time. At the same time that presidents call for clarity, the dynamics of the interplay between interest groups, Congress, and the White House result in configurations that do not illustrate a single approach to the definition of the national role in a federal system. Programs are enacted with very different designs; as a result they produce categorical programs, formula grants, block grants, and regulatory processes that create different patterns of intergovernmental relationships.

In contrast to the formal academic literature on federalism and IGR, federal reform efforts involving intergovernmental relations often operate at the margins, combining great promises with narrow and incremental changes that seek to find a way to deal with the conflict that is a normal response to the multiple levels of government. While promises such as those represented by the unfunded mandate legislation continue to emerge, coordination schemes are also advanced as ways to deal with the conflict between levels of government over the years.[3] Efforts are made to find ways to circumvent requirements through waiver processes and other processes that will involve additional players in the decision-making process.

As far back as 1981, Deil Wright commented on the difficulty of analyzing the dimensions of the IGR field. He wrote, "A combination of constraints forced me to attempt a bare-bones outline rather than a thorough and probing analysis. This sketch may, regrettably, suffer from the criticism made of a gadfly legislator who was said to be 'solid on the surface, but deep down he's shallow.'"[4] Wright sought to analyze the IGR field through two dimensions: the unit or level of analysis and the intent of the user of the analysis.

Given this, it is extremely difficult to describe the US federal system as a single system with predominant values. Wright's oft-used depiction of seven phases of intergovernmental relations indicates the shifts over time, but the chronology minimizes the reality that even within an era there are diverse IGR strategies employed that emerge in specific policies and programs.[5] In addition, programs and policies that are established in one era often continue into another. David Walker described the result as a system of "contrasting characteristics."[6] He described six sets of contrasts:

1. Overloaded and undernourished
2. Top heavy and bottom heavy
3. Overregulated and underregulated
4. Activist and passive
5. Co-optive and cooperative
6. Competitive and collaborative[7]

IGR Meets Federalism

In 1953 Congress (with the support of President Eisenhower) created the Commission on Intergovernmental Relations (known as the Kestnbaum

Commission), described by Deil Wright as "the first official broad-ranging review of national, state and local relationships since adoption of the Constitution."[8] The twenty-five members of the commission included fifteen members appointed by the president, five members of the House of Representatives, and five members of the Senate. The creation of the commission, according to Bruce McDowell, reflected Eisenhower's belief "that the federal government had been expanding into too many functions of government that belonged to the state and local governments."[9]

In the letter accompanying its report, the commission wrote:

> Many of the problems to which we have addressed ourselves have been with us since the founding of the Republic. They are likely to concern us for many years to come. No inquiry of this kind could possibly provide universally satisfactory answers to all of the difficult questions that are under discussion at any particular moment. We are hopeful that this Report will be regarded as the beginning rather than the end of a contemporary study of the subject of intergovernmental relations, and that it will stimulate all levels of government to examine their respective responsibilities in a properly balanced federal system.[10]

The themes that emerged from the Kestnbaum report have continued to preoccupy both scholars and practitioners since that time. The 1955 report emphasized problems of duplication and waste, conflict between levels of government, clearer definition of authority, and the need for efficiency in programs. It emphasized the importance of stipulating what it called "the proper division of labor and authority between the Nation and the States."[11] At the same time, the commission found that

> the lines of division are not static. They have been controversial from the beginning of our life as an independent country. They remain so today. The American federal system began as an experiment. It was the third try for a solution on this continent to the age-old problem of striking a satisfactory balance between the needs for central strength and central regulation on the one hand and the values of local freedom of action on the other. The framers of our Constitution had joined in a revolution that cut them loose from the old British imperial system, because that system imposed unwelcome controls from a remote center. . . . The federal system devised by the framers of the Constitution was the product of necessity rather than doctrine. There was no dictionary definition of federal government to apply nor any working model to copy.[12]

The search for "the proper division of labor and authority" has been the most constant theme among both scholars and practitioners since the issuance of the Kestnbaum report. The quest has involved both ideological and pragmatic arguments but it has centered around the belief, as Alice Rivlin wrote in *Reviving the American Dream*, that "both federal and state governments would function better if a clearer distinction were made between the responsibilities of the federal government and those of the states."[13]

The Life and Death of ACIR

The Kestnbaum Commission's desire to start a dialogue on issues of intergovernmental relations was fulfilled soon after its report was issued. A Joint Federal-State Action Committee in which cabinet officials worked with state governors attempted to sort out authorities between the two levels of government but was unable to gain support for its recommendations in Congress. However, Congress was willing to enact legislation creating a permanent body—the Advisory Commission on Intergovernmental Relations (ACIR)—in 1959.[14]

The structure of ACIR represented the multiple players involved in the intergovernmental policy domain. The twenty-six members of the bipartisan body included three members from each house of Congress, four governors, four mayors, three state legislators, three elected county officials, three members of the president's cabinet, and three private citizens.[15]

Both the title of ACIR and the diverse composition of its membership indicated that the commission was not to be a decision-making body but rather a group that would (or could) advise decision makers. The enabling legislation gave it authority to define common problems and focus on administrative issues, coordination, technical assistance, fiscal questions, and other problems faced by players in the intergovernmental network.[16] McDowell noted that in its thirty-seven-year life it published 130 reports with recommendations and 194 information reports, conducted twenty-three public opinion polls, issued twenty-two staff reports, and circulated about eighty issues of its quarterly magazine.

While there are a number of interpretations of why ACIR was terminated in 1996, several explanations have been given that appear to be especially relevant. First, there had been attempts to close its doors over several years but the effort to reduce the federal debt provided an opening for its opponents to argue that the funds used to support the commission were not an effective use of federal tax dollars. And the supporters of the commission were not highly visible nor did they seem to make the survival of ACIR a priority item. The second explanation, according to McDowell, focused on the partisanship that increasingly surrounded the commission over its lifetime. The conflict over its work was not only based on traditional political partisanship (Democrats versus Republicans), but it was also based on conflict between advocates of the various levels of government. As a result, ACIR found itself caught up with a political agenda that generated some supporters but also generated strong opposition. It was increasingly difficult to speak about the intergovernmental community as one with a single voice. Other explanations for the demise included the availability of other sources of information, alternative forums for negotiations, and failure of high-level commission appointees to become engaged in its deliberations.[17] At this writing, there is no federal venue that provides a setting for the exchange of views and perspectives by the various players in the intergovernmental network.

Intergovernmental Management Initiatives in the Executive Office of the President

All of the presidents since Johnson have devised some strategy to deal with intergovernmental issues. Timothy Conlan has described three types of reform. The first is grant simplification, what he notes is "the most modest reform approach. This strategy left existing categorical program structures essentially unchanged but attempted to develop new administrative processes and organizational structures to help coordinate them."[18] This reform approach yielded regional planning efforts, forms of intergovernmental consultation, and the Model Cities Program, among other initiatives. Conlan notes that Nixon built on this effort and created standardized federal regions and simplification and standardization efforts involving the federal grant process.

The second approach to reform involved the consolidation of programs into a few large grants, usually known as block grants. These grants provide state and local governments with discretion as to how the funds will be used within broadly defined policy areas. Conlan argues that the origins of this strategy began in the Hoover Commission and continued through the Eisenhower administration, but Congress was not willing to support presidential proposals.[19] The first significant block grant was approved by Congress during the Johnson administration with its creation of the Law Enforcement Assistance program.

The third approach to reform discussed by Conlan involved general revenue sharing. This was a fairly straightforward fiscal transfer effort from the federal government to states and localities. It would replace existing categorical grants and would give state and local governments no-strings funds to be spent in whatever way they considered to be appropriate. General revenue sharing was adopted during the end of the Johnson administration, a time of financial health in the federal budget, but it was eliminated soon after.

While all of these three reform strategies appeared on one or another presidential priority list, coordination and block grants surfaced more often than the revenue sharing strategy. This is not surprising since much of the period experienced serious shortfalls in the federal budget, and both Congress and the executive branch were not willing to hand over no-strings funds to other levels of government.

As it turns out, however, there are many different approaches to coordination and a number of different emphases in the design of block grants. As such, several dynamics that are found in other management issues emerged. What would be the role of the Executive Office of the President, especially the management side of OMB, in the effort? What would be the role of the relevant agencies and departments? How would Congress be involved? Would the strategy for change be government-wide or created in a cluster or program-by-program approach? Would there be new venues for coordination or would the strategy rely on existing structures and programs? How much would the federal government define expectations for programs even if the funds to states and localities were transferred via block grants?

There are not clear answers to these questions largely because there is so much controversy within the federalism/IGR field about the dimensions of the relationships between the federal government and states and localities. Deil Wright described these relationships through the depiction of three models. The first is the *inclusive authority* model, which assumes that the national government plays the superior role vis-à-vis states and localities and thus will control dealings with those levels of government. The second is the *coordinate authority* model, which emphasizes the autonomy of states; local governments are viewed as creatures of the states, and the national government's dealings with the states assume that both parties are separate and distinct. The third model is the *overlapping authority* model, which indicates that many areas of policy require all three levels, that areas of autonomy and discretion for any single jurisdiction are limited, and that levels of governments require bargaining and negotiation to obtain adequate power and influence to carry out programs.[20]

IGR Reform Efforts in OMB and in Congress: Sorting Out Roles and Responsibilities

Beginning with the Johnson administration era, both branches of government took a visible interest in intergovernmental relations and sought to confront the complexity that emerged as the federal program portfolio expanded both in numbers and scope. While there were a range of issues attached to this interest in both branches of government, the urge to sort out and clarify responsibilities of each level of government seemed to be the predominant topic that surfaced over the years. At the same time, it was not always easy to differentiate between the management arguments related to IGR and the skepticism within the American society about the reach of public-sector responsibility and authority.

In 1979, a special task force on intergovernmental management of the American Society for Public Administration issued a report that (while mentioning the legislative role) emphasized the role of the executive branch in this area. It called for "redefining and integrating the roles and functions of each level and branch of government."[21] The report noted: "The Federal system today is an 'intergovernmentalized,' confusing mix of functions and activities carried out at the federal, state, and local levels. When essential functions must be carried out by government, the appropriate roles and responsibilities of each level of government for those functions should be defined more clearly in order to improve services and to focus accountability for performance on public officials."[22]

In 1983, the Congressional Budget Office issued a report titled *The Federal Government in a Federal System: Current Intergovernmental Programs and Options for Change.* The CBO report noted that efforts to realign responsibilities between the federal government and the states had not been successful in terms of legislative action. However,

> It did help to focus attention on the need for some reorganization of the intergovernmental structure. Under the federal system, states and localities are primarily responsible for the provision of local public services—police protection, for example. The primary role of the federal government is to coordinate activities between states and to provide services with more-than-local benefits, such as national defense. In general, federal participation is necessary only if there is an important national purpose that would not be served without federal involvement.[23]

Nearly a decade later, Alice Rivlin, who had been the director of CBO when the report was issued, wrote a highly influential book that continued the debate. In *Reviving the American Dream: The Economy, the States, and the Federal Government,* she called for rethinking the current intergovernmental system. She argued that the problems that had been described by CBO had increased in magnitude because of international issues and serious financial crises. She wrote:

> Incomprehensible policies and procedures breed cynicism and distrust of government. Citizens who are mystified often suspect something nefarious is going on behind closed doors. Taxpayers who have no clear idea what their money is buying resent having to pay the bill. Hence every effort to make government work better must include the instructions: simplify, clarify, demystify. This book focuses particular attention on one aspect of those efforts: sharpening the distinction between federal responsibilities and those of state and local government.

Further, "both federal and state governments would function better—and the policies needed to energize the economy could be carried out more effectively—if a cleaner distinction were made between the responsibilities of the federal government and those of the states."[24]

During the Clinton administration there was some attention to the sorting-out agenda. John DiIulio and Donald Kettl issued a report through the Brookings Institution's Center for Public Management that used the Rivlin book as the point of departure and attempted to provide some guidelines for thinking about sorting federal responsibilities. They differentiated between three governmental functions—setting policy, financing policy, and administering policy—and noted that the argument for sorting out federal responsibilities was one where "devolution is in the details."[25]

A Presidential Responsibility?

Programs and policies that deal with relationships between the federal government and the states (and sometimes localities) are common components of domestic policy throughout both the twentieth and twenty-first centuries. President Eisenhower's creation of an Office of Deputy Assistant to the President for Intergovernmental Relations began the effort. It was followed by Johnson's Great Society, Nixon's New Federalism, and Reagan's New Federalism—all examples of policy approaches that had (or attempted to have) a dramatic impact on intergovernmental relationships.

But the management side of those initiatives was not as visible as the policy approaches. Beginning in the 1950s, there were efforts to establish an intergovernmental management agenda first in the Bureau of the Budget and then in its successor, the Office of Management and Budget. As David Walker writes, the "first and most modest reform approach was grant simplification. This strategy left existing categorical program structures essentially unchanged but attempted to develop new administrative processes and organizational structures to help coordinate them."[26]

Coordination, thus, was the IGR strategy used extensively during the Johnson administration and was found in the War on Poverty, multistate regional planning efforts, the A-95 process of intergovernmental consultation, and programs involving community development, social services, and manpower planning. One of the classic examples of the coordination strategy was found in the creation of the Appalachian Regional Commission (ARC). The ARC is a regional economic development agency that represents a partnership of federal, state, and local government. Established by an act of Congress in 1965, the ARC is composed of the governors of the thirteen Appalachian states and a federal cochair, who is appointed by the president. Local participation is provided through multicounty local development districts. Projects are funded dealing with jobs, economic and community development, education, infrastructure, and transportation. While there have been attempts to eliminate the ARC, it has continued to operate quite independently for more than forty years. Coordination occurs on a project-by-project basis and often involves other federal agencies.

At the very end of the Johnson administration in 1968 Congress enacted the Intergovernmental Cooperation Act, building on earlier efforts. And in 1969, just a few months after Nixon assumed office, circular A-95 was issued by OMB. According to OMB, that circular "is fundamentally a statement of national policy which asserts the cooperative, intergovernmental nature of

Federalism and directs the close coordination of Federal and federally assisted plans and programs . . . with State, areawide, and local plans and programs."[27] It rested not only on the Intergovernmental Cooperation Act but also the Model Cities Program established in 1966.

By the mid-1970s, there was an active Intergovernmental Relations and Regional Operations Division within OMB. It set forth procedures for federal agencies and applicants for federal assistance that would provide opportunities for states and area-wide clearinghouses to assess the impact of the federal activity on their own plans and programs. According to OMB in 1976, A-95 is based on the following premises:

- Fundamental to coordination is communication; therefore,
- If people who *should* be talking to each other are put in a position of *having* to talk to each other, then
- They *may* come to identify and understand their communities of interest and areas of conflict; and, if they do, then
- They *may* cooperate in pursuit of their common interests and try to negotiate their differences;
- To the extent that they do, federally assisted programs and projects are more likely to be better coordinated, resulting in dollar savings, better projects, and more value for public investment.[28]

The mechanisms that would provide the basis for this form of communication were found in the clearinghouses established through state and area-wide relationships. Amendments to A-95 also gave responsibility for day-to-day operational oversight of the circular to the federal regional councils. These were the bodies created in 1969 in each of the ten federal regions and were composed of representatives of a range of federal departments and agencies who were located in these regions. While seeming to move authority away from Washington, that approach also bypassed the states and localities (and their elected officials) and, instead, gave the responsibility to federal officials around the country.

Around the same time in 1974, a report was commissioned by OMB through a Study Committee on Policy Management Assistance. The report, titled *Strengthening Public Management in the Intergovernmental System*, was the result of a group of federal career executives experienced in working with state and local governments whose agencies were interested in using federal technical assistance to strengthen the core management capabilities of state and local general-purpose governments.[29]

The 1975 report defined three different elements of management dealing with assistance to state and local government by the federal government:

1. *Policy management*—the identification of needs, analysis of options, selection of programs, and allocation of resources on a jurisdiction-wide basis.

2. *Resource management*—the establishment of basic administrative support systems such as budgeting, financial management, procurement and supply, and personnel administration.
3. *Program management*—the implementation of policy or daily operation of agencies carrying out policy along functional lines (education, law enforcement, etc.).[30]

The report envisioned a process that would utilize existing bodies both in the Executive Office of the President and in each federal domestic agency to play the implementing role. It specified the use of the Domestic Council, OMB, the Undersecretaries Group for Regional Operations, and the regional councils within the White House. It noted that "strengthening public management at all levels of the Federal system is not a task susceptible to standardized, across-the-board solutions."[31]

Despite the presidential attention to intergovernmental issues in the 1970s, there continued to be dissatisfaction with the situation. In 1977, the National Governors' Conference issued a report titled *Federal Roadblocks to Efficient State Government* which argued that "the report illustrates a lack of sensitivity to the impact of management decisions on States and a lack of commitment to resolve questions raised by those responsible for implementing federal programs." The NGA acknowledged that there was attention to intergovernmental issues in the White House, but "intergovernmental management is not a high enough priority within the Office of Management and Budget to ensure that sufficient resources are applied to the detailed work of policing departments and agencies."[32]

In 1978, GAO issued a report titled *Intergovernmental Policy and Fiscal Relations* that highlighted OMB's role in the process. The report noted: "The primary responsibility for managing the Federal Government's efforts to improve intergovernmental relations rests with OMB. GAO has made numerous recommendations to OMB directed at improving various aspects of intergovernmental relations. OMB, however, has not been as successful in obtaining improvements as GAO would like. While OMB believes that emphasis in the area should be increased, it does not have the resources to insure improvements."[33]

During the Reagan years, attention to intergovernmental issues came in the form of proposals to cut the number of domestic programs found in the federal portfolio both through consolidation (creating a number of block grants) and through diminished budget outlays to the consolidated programs. Reagan did issue an executive order on federalism that was meant "to restore the division of governmental responsibilities between the national government and the States."[34] That order, according to Brian Bailey, was part of Reagan's plan to deregulate federal agencies and effort "to treat federalism issues carefully." It effectively moved waiver authority away from the agencies to OMB.[35]

While there had been subcommittees with responsibility for federalism and IGR in both the Senate and House Governmental Affairs Committees in the past, there was very little attention to the general issue of intergovernmental relations and management in Congress from that point on. This was despite the Republican control of Congress during much of the Reagan era. However, the Reagan administration highlighted the development of block grants to the states during this period, providing more discretion to the states in a number of domestic policy areas.

Attention to these issues did resurface to some degree during the Clinton administration's National Performance Review (NPR). A report that was part of the NPR titled "Strengthening the Partnership in Intergovernmental Service Delivery" echoed some of the earlier concerns. It focused on the issue of unfunded mandates, highlighted the flexibility that could be given to state and local officials through the waiver process, emphasized the use of bottom-up processes that allowed states and localities to define their needs, and tried to reach out to state and local government officials.[36] The NPR's focus on customers provided an opportunity to include attention to state and local actors as customers of the federal activity.

In addition, Clinton issued Executive Order 13083 on federalism during the last months of his administration. The original order did require that federal agencies consult with state and local officials and also designate an official within each agency who would have responsibility for the implementation of the order.[37] According to Bailey, Clinton's action defined conditions that permitted federal agencies to formulate and implement federal policy while limiting state policymaking authority.[38]

> The resulting outcry from state and local governmental organizations prompted a swift congressional response. Both Houses of Congress moved to block implementation of the order that would have given federal agencies almost unlimited power to regulate. Reasons such as a need for uniform national standards; the increased cost of decentralization; or even the reluctance of states to regulate, fearing the flight of businesses to more commercially amenable jurisdictions, would have justified federal agency regulation under E.O. 13083. Congress, sensing a clear threat both to state autonomy and its own lawmaking power, acted to quell the executive intrusion. Under fire from Congress and state and local governmental organizations, the President quickly relented by suspending the executive order. From the ashes of E.O. 13083's suspension arose a new executive order on federalism.[39]

But by the second Clinton administration, according to Conlan, efforts to establish "executive leadership, clear lines of authority, improved coordination" faded and offices and committees that had been advocates of these reforms and had formal intergovernmental responsibility were abolished in OMB, GAO, and in Congress.[40] The elimination of ACIR was, thus, just another example of the lack of interest in dealing with federalism and inter-governmental relations as a free-standing management issue.

Developments since 2000

The eight years of the Bush administration were viewed by students of feder-alism and IGR as departing from traditional debates. In a special issue of *Publius: The Journal of Federalism* titled "U.S. Federalism and the Bush Ad-ministration," several scholars noted that Bush did not focus on either limited government or devolution to the states.[41] Sidney Milkis and Jesse H. Rhodes commented that "Bush's principal legacy for federalism is centralization of power in the federal government and the executive branch."[42] Similarly, Tim Conlan and John Dinan wrote that "what emerges from this analysis is an administration that has been surprisingly dismissive of federalism concerns and frequently an agent of centralization. In one sense, Bush is merely the latest in a string of presidents who have sacrificed federalism considerations to specific policy goals when the two have come in conflict."[43]

As of this writing, it appears that the Obama administration has also avoided discussion about "principles" of federalism and IGR and, instead, has emphasized collaborative efforts that give OMB and other centralized officials responsibility.[44] The management staff capacity in both the Bush and Obama administrations was very limited following staff reorganiza-tions during the Clinton years.

Federalism and Contradictions in the US System

The efforts surrounding federal management reform agendas involving fed-eralism and intergovernmental relations illustrate a number of aspects of the three sets of contradictions found in the US system: structural dimen-sions, predominant values and approaches, and attributes of the public sector.

Structural Dimensions

As this chapter indicates, the reform efforts involving federalism and IGR have largely focused on the executive branch. While there have been some discussions and actions within the legislative branch dealing with the general areas included in this chapter, Congress has been much more responsive to these issues on a case-by-case, policy-by-policy basis, reflecting the decision-making structure of the legislative branch. It is rare that Congress acts to define relationships between levels of government in aggregate and consis-tent patterns, and it rarely looks to characterize those relationships in over-arching terms that assume that the American political system produces uniform approaches and policies.

Solutions such as executive orders on federalism from the White House or even federalism reforms from Congress assume that a consistent federalism strategy will produce a more homogeneous intergovernmental system from the array of specific policies and management regimes operating in the complex US system. While such reforms can be important in some situations, we have learned over time that highly specific programmatic interactions across governments often have more to do with determining who gets what, when, where, why, and how.[45] There are also occasions when the judiciary gets involved in the process but the courts rule on specific situations rather than general principles.[46]

It is clear that this dimension of management reform provides quite a dramatic illustration of the inevitable conflict between the players in the intergovernmental system, most often conflict between states and the federal government. Tension between the federal government's responsibility to hold grant recipients accountable to national goals and priorities and state and local governments' drive to meet self-determined needs and priorities is a basic characteristic of US intergovernmental relations. This tension exists even when the federal role is perceived to be diminished (as in an era of expanded block grants). Such tension, a factor of the mutual dependence in the system, produces an unavoidable conflict in the process and structure of a variety of federally mandated and state or locally administered activities. As such, conflict is inevitable; it neither can nor should be avoided; it therefore must be actively managed.[47]

This summary of reform efforts involving federalism indicates that conflict is highly misunderstood by both practitioners and students of public management, and, as a result, systematic attention to conflict management is lacking. In fact, many of the changes in the field have actually produced new and significant conflicts that must be managed.

The realities of federalism in a complex society such as ours mean that conflict is inevitable. The nature of intergovernmental conflict is not likely to change even through different varieties of federalism. Conflicting parties will still be linked by mutual dependence, their interactions will still be conditioned by environmental factors, and they will still oppose one another in attempts to change their relative positions. This is likely to occur even when the key actors change and the policy issues involved are modified or added to.

Predominant Values and Approaches

The conflict between the federal role and the state/local role that underlies this reform area sets the scene for the expression of the contradictions involved in values and approaches. One of the players seeks flexibility and discretion while the other seeks accountability and control. One player looks at the total system (assuming a macro approach) while the other focuses on the micro level and the way that details of requirements affect its day-to-day work. What is optimistic to one player is likely to be pessimistic to another. What is inefficient to one player is efficient to another. Similarly, the players differ in terms of their definitions of both effectiveness and equity. Equity for some players means the equal distribution of resources to all states, while for others it involves a response to individuals and communities that have suffered from the history of racism. These conflicts are found not only in direct contacts between federal and state/local players but also in the way that members of Congress are concerned about how proposed policies and programs will affect their specific constituencies.

As a result, the rules and requirements involved must be constructed on the acknowledgment of conflict and search for ways to manage that conflict rather than focus on only one perspective.

Attributes of the Public Sector

Both the conflict between politics and administration and the tension between government-wide versus program- or policy-specific activities are illustrated in this reform area. Despite efforts to separate politics and management involving IGR by clearly defining and separating functions, this chapter has indicated that the two perspectives are inevitably intertwined. While there were attempts in the 1970s to separate politics and management, this chapter has discussed how difficult it has been to sustain a separate management perspective on issues involving federalism and the transfer of funds along with requirements involving the use of those funds to states and localities. The overlapping authority model described by Deil Wright seems to be predominant in the current environment.

The other aspect of this topic area involves the level of centralization within the executive branch. This includes both conceptual and managerial approaches. As has been discussed, there has been a strong tendency for the occupants of the White House (both Republicans and Democrats) to approach federalism and IGR on a government-wide basis, seeking to devise approaches that are one-size-fits-all and consistent across the wide range of programs and policies that have IGR aspects to them, ignoring differences in types of policies, differences among jurisdictions in history and population, and areas of need. Decentralization of authority to departments and agencies is more likely to pick up those differences than approaches that look to a small staff within OMB to make those decisions.

Conclusions

Students and practitioners of federalism and IGR have had difficulty working out an approach to this area of reform that is convincing to the American citizenry. It is not a highly visible area and it frequently evokes an "eyes glaze over" response from the public when its issues are aired.[48] It often builds on the skepticism within American history about the role of government, especially the federal government. Given that history, it is not an area that can easily borrow ideas from either the private sector or from a nonfederal parliamentary system. It is challenging to find a way to discuss the balance between federal and state/local responsibilities in a large and diverse country that, as Albert Hirschman described in terms of public-private relationships, is constantly changing and redefining what level of government is appropriate for change.

Notes

1. Robert Agranoff's work is one of the main exceptions to this pattern. See, e.g., "Intergovernmental Policy Management."
2. The interrelationship between levels of government has increased quite dramatically over the years, and states (and often localities) are dependent on federal government contributions for significant portions of their total budgets. The funds do not end at the political jurisdiction receiving the federal dollars but are passed through to other third parties via contracts to do federally funded work. In other cases, the federal role is defined through requirements and mandates without specific federal funds available to carry out those requirements.
3. The Unfunded Mandates Reform Act of 1995 called for Congress to develop processes that restrict the enactment of legislation that creates unfunded costs for state and local governments. Despite this legislation, the approach does not seem to have yielded the results that its proponents envisioned. See Posner, "Unfunded Mandates Reform Act."
4. Wright, "Concept of Intergovernmental Relations," 1.
5. Wright, *Understanding Intergovernmental Relations.*
6. Walker, *Rebirth of Federalism,* 15. Walker's analysis appears to suggest that despite the contrasts, the US system is moving toward the executive federalism system found in Canada, Australia, and Germany (24).
7. Ibid.,16.
8. Ibid.
9. McDowell, "Advisory Commission," 111.
10. The Commission on Intergovernmental Relations, *A Report to the President for Transmittal to the Congress,* June 28, 1955.
11. Ibid., 9.
12. Ibid.
13. Rivlin, *Reviving the American Dream,* 7.
14. See McDowell, "Advisory Commission," for discussion of these developments.
15. Ibid., 112.
16. See ibid. for details.
17. This draws on McDowell.
18. Conlan, *From New Federalism to Devolution,* 22.
19. Ibid., 24.
20. Wright, *Understanding Intergovernmental Relations,* 40.

21. American Society for Public Administration, *Strengthening Intergovernmental Management*, iii.
22. Ibid.
23. Congressional Budget Office, *Federal Government*, xi.
24. Rivlin, *Reviving the American Dream*, 3, 7.
25. DiIulio and Kettl, *Fine Print*, 12.
26. Walker, *Rebirth of Federalism*, 22.
27. OMB, *What It Is*, 2–3.
28. Ibid., 4.
29. Executive Office of the President, *Strengthening Public Management*, vii.
30. Ibid., vii–viii.
31. Ibid., xii.
32. National Governors' Conference, *Federal Roadblocks*, viii, 45.
33. GAO, *Intergovernmental Policy*, ii.
34. Exec. Order No. 12,612, 52 Fed. Reg. 41685 (Oct. 26, 1987).
35. Bailey, "Federalism," 337.
36. See Galston and Tibbetts, "Reinventing Federalism."
37. See, e.g., Donna E. Shalala, Secretary of the Department of Health and Human Services, to Heads of Operating Divisions and Staff Divisions, memorandum, "Executive Order on Federalism," November 22, 1999.
38. Bailey, "Federalism," 332.
39. Ibid., 332–33.
40. Conlan, *From New Federalism to Devolution*, 301.
41. *Publius* 37, no. 3 (2007).
42. Milkis and Rhodes, "George W. Bush," 478.
43. Conlan and Dinan, "Federalism," 279.
44. See, e.g., Jeffrey D. Zients, Deputy Director for Management, to the Heads of Departments and Agencies, OMB, memorandum, "Pilot Projects for the Partnership Fund for Program Integrity Innovation," October 19, 2010.
45. See Radin and Posner, "Policy Tools."
46. This chapter does not focus on the cases in which courts have limited both executive-branch and legislative-branch action involving federalism issues.
47. See Buntz and Radin, "Managing Intergovernmental Conflict."
48. Some observers believe that many management reform efforts generate an "eyes glaze over" response. But federalism and IGR scholars tend to highlight the lack of interest in the general public about their issues.

9

PERFORMANCE MEASUREMENT

Everything that can be counted does not necessarily count; everything that counts cannot necessarily be counted.

Attributed to Albert Einstein

Administration leaders have little choice but to frame guidance in a way that makes it applicable to hundreds, if not thousands, of managers tackling varied challenges. But perhaps it is time to admit there is no one formula for managing for results. There is no checklist of actions a manager can take to ensure his or her program succeeds.

Elizabeth Newell, "Management Matters"

If Congress or OMB wants to see outcomes, they need to realize that we don't have real-time data and we might not see results immediately. Outcomes cannot be measured on a daily basis. As a result, we tend to measure activity rather than results.

Performance improvement officer, quoted in Partnership
for Public Service and Grant Thornton, A Critical Role

EFFORTS TO INTRODUCE PERFORMANCE MEASUREMENT PROCESSES INTO the federal government can be viewed both as ends in themselves as well as means to other management reform goals. Performance measurement activities have been linked in one way or another to other reform efforts discussed in this volume. In large part they are a way of answering the "so what" question. They have been initiated as ways to assess impacts of contracts, to determine how personnel changes meet their goals, to reveal whether reorganization efforts achieve what has been proposed, to determine whether budget proposals are made on the basis of performance information, and to ascertain whether there are differences in the way that government deals with the private sector or with state or local governments.

Yet, much of the literature on performance measurement focuses on the technical demands of the assessment process.[1] At the beginning of the work on this topic, what seemed to many to be a fairly clear-cut task of assessing the outcomes produced by programs funded with federal tax dollars turned out to be much more complex than the advocates of performance measurement had assumed.[2] While a concern about the performance of federal agencies can be found in a range of initiatives throughout the latter part of the twentieth century, the passage of the Government Performance and Results Act of 1993 (GPRA) was the effort that began the contemporary interest in performance measurement. The most visible example of the early efforts was found in the Planning, Programming, and Budgeting System (PPBS) that was begun in the Department of Defense during the Kennedy administration and expanded throughout the federal government during the Johnson era.[3]

GPRA was originally crafted in Congress and was one of the few management efforts that had roots in legislation, not simply in executive orders. It required all federal agencies to develop strategic plans, annual performance plans, and annual performance reports. These requirements were linked to the annual budget process and asked agencies to focus on the outcomes that emerged in the use of the federal dollars that were appropriated to them.[4]

Although the initiative emerged from Congress, it actually came from the Senate Committee on Governmental Affairs (largely the Republican members and staff), a body that did not have a well-institutionalized role in the process of developing and funding federal programs. John Mercer, often described as the father of GPRA, brought his local government experience in Sunnyvale, California, to Washington and sought to create a budgeting process that was driven by performance data.[5]

Some of the most influential players in the public administration community hailed the passage of GPRA as evidence that federal decision making would lead to more precisely defined program goals and that the decisions themselves would be based on program performance information.[6] The Senate committee made a number of assumptions about the requirements. It argued that past efforts at performance measurement and reporting had been successful. It reflected a belief that GPRA would not impose a major additional cost or paperwork burden on federal programs. And it assumed that some federal agencies were already moving in the same direction.[7]

The Senate committee report also drew on the experience of other countries with performance measures. It cited the work of the Paris-based Organisation for Economic Cooperation and Development (OECD) that "suggests that several countries may be 5 to 10 years ahead of the U.S. in this effort, and that their performance measurement efforts are a key part of broader efforts to better manage for results."[8]

Despite the optimism that surrounded the passage of GPRA in 1993, at the early stages of the Clinton administration, the major elements of the legislation were not to go into effect until 1997. This reflected some acknowledgment that despite the rhetorical optimism, the requirements would confront a complex implementation process. Thus 1997 was the year when the first strategic plan and the first performance plan were developed. In subsequent years, agencies also provided reports on their ability to meet their performance measures. These requirements were completed by the agencies and delivered to both Congress and to the White House alongside the normal budget documents, paying at least lip service to the system of shared powers in the US structure.

However, it was not easy to operate in the shared powers system. Partisan political differences colored much of the early GPRA implementation. Indeed, the Republicans in Congress called the effort the "Results Act," highlighting the outcomes of the federal programs and avoiding discussion of processes for attaining those outcomes. The Republican leadership (not the members of specific committees and subcommittees) devised its own assessment of the strategic plans developed by departments and agencies.[9] By contrast, the Democrats continued to use the full name of the bill or to call it GPRA, reflecting a more complex view of the process.

To some extent the conflicts were fanned by institutional differences between the executive and legislative branches but they were also fed by partisan political differences. On top of this complexity, many federal agencies charged with domestic policies did not actually carry out the implementation of policies but relied on others to move to service delivery. David G. Frederickson and H. George Frederickson's study of performance measurement activity in five health programs dramatically illustrated the difficulties involved in using performance measurement as a policy and management tool in third-party government.[10]

The George W. Bush administration's Program Assessment Rating Tool (PART) was put in place early in that administration as a part of the President's Management Agenda.[11] While PART shared some attributes with GPRA, it differed from the bipartisan legislative approach in several ways. It was located only in the executive branch. The role of OMB in the process was much clearer than it had been in GPRA and required agencies to seek agreement from OMB before they could define their performance measures and determine what data they would use to report their actual performance. Unlike GPRA (which focused on offices and organization units), PART was designed around specific programs. PART did not require an annual program assessment; rather approximately 20 percent of all programs were assessed each fiscal year.

Each of the programs was rated along four dimensions: program purpose and design, strategic planning, program management, and program results. The last category received 50 percent of the weight of the assessment. Programs were also rated as effective, moderately effective, adequate, ineffective, and results not demonstrated. When the Bush administration developed its own requirements through PART, the status of GPRA was not at all clear. Yet the two approaches did have quite different perspectives on the performance assessment process.

It is difficult to argue against the goals of these two efforts. Determining whether public funds are actually accomplishing the outcomes expected of the programs and policies those dollars support is both important and commendable. The issue is not whether one supports performance measurement in general but whether the policies that have been put in place to carry out those goals have been effective or adequate.

Given the size and scope of the US federal government, it is not easy to characterize the experience with federal government performance requirements. That experience produced a highly complex situation that is variable and often idiosyncratic to a particular program or policy. The experience with both GPRA and PART at the point that the Obama administration took office can be summarized as follows:

1. *The limits of a one-size-fits-all approach.* While there are a number of reasons that explain the limited ability of efforts such as PART to influence decision making, one of the most important explanations lies in the inability of OMB to effectively acknowledge the diversity in structures of federal programs. The one-size-fits-all approach of OMB attached to PART flies in the face of that diversity. It ignores that diversity (and the typology offered in James Q. Wilson's classic book, *Bureaucracy,* that describes the differences between programs in terms of their ability to measure outputs and outcomes). Wilson notes that agencies with the ability to define and measure both outputs and outcomes, because of the nature of their work (he calls them production agencies), have the easiest time with performance measurement requirements. By contrast, agencies that have great difficulty devising information systems and agreements over the definition of outputs and outcomes (he calls them coping agencies) have significant problems meeting the OMB requirements because they live with disagreement about goals of programs, the means of achieving even conflicting goals, and availability of data to measure either outputs or outcomes.

There are some types of programs that have particular problems meeting the performance measurement stipulations. Two are particularly problematic: block grant programs and research and development programs. Both of these examples indicate how important it is for advocates of performance measurement and management to tailor specific requirements to meet the realities of each agency and program. Block grants are the most problematic form of program design that touches on the difficulty of defining accountability for program outcomes in a federal system. Efforts to hold federal agencies accountable for the way that programs are implemented often assume that the agencies themselves have authority to enforce such requirements.[12] Performance measures that are effective must make sense to officials within a particular agency; when requirements are devised government-wide they often evoke perverse responses that don't lead to increased attention to performance.

2. *A government-wide approach.* The very structure of the US system makes it extremely difficult to devise detailed performance requirements that are appropriate for the entire federal government. Unlike a parliamentary system that provides a structure that allows the executive function to look at the government as a whole, the federal US system is devised to minimize the exertion of concentrated power. As a result, power and authority are separated and shared across all aspects of the political landscape. This

occurs through the delineation of separate institutions charged with executive, legislative, and judicial functions as well as through the assumption of shared as well as separate powers among the national, state, and sometimes local levels of government.

This creates conflict between the legislative and executive branches, fragmentation of responsibilities within the legislative branch through separate appropriations and authorizing bodies, and differentiated responsibilities and roles inside agencies and departments. Variations in the resources and authority available to achieve programmatic results as well as variations in the level of complexity of tasks and outcome expectations emerge from this structure.

The result—as many have described—is a crazy quilt of program and policy design that reflects policy prescriptions at different points in time, inconsistencies of goals and expectations even across similar programs, and overlapping and conflicting strategies. When one examines the diversity of programs to be implemented in a single agency, it is rare to find consistency across those programs, making it difficult to apply a standardized framework to all elements. While in a perfectly rational and efficient world one might want to eliminate some of these attributes, it would be necessary to change the structure of the US government in order to do this.

3. *The diversity of approaches found in programs.* Very few federal programs are designed to accomplish a single goal.[13] Embedded in most programs is a combination of efficiency, effectiveness, and equity goals. These are expressed in programs that actually contain multiple and often conflicting goals, reflecting the political process of achieving coalitions of support within Congress. It becomes difficult for program managers to achieve such goals. They are often asked to serve specific client groups who had been previously unserved, maintain existing service systems, deliver quality services, and spend the lowest possible amount of money doing so. Yet much of the literature on performance measurement ignores this complexity and, instead, calls only for the achievement of efficiency goals. As Luther Gulick commented, "This brings administration into apparent conflict with certain elements of the value scale of politics."[14]

Both GPRA and PART effectively ignored equity values in the way that they implemented the performance measurement activities. Since many of their approaches were borrowed from the private sector, it is not surprising that efficiency became the prevailing value and there was very little attention to social equity questions.[15]

4. *The role of OMB in the process.* One of the strongest complaints lodged against the implementation of the PART requirements involved the role of OMB in the process. This is an area in which PART implementation was significantly different from the GPRA process. GPRA attempted to involve both the executive branch and Congress in the process and did not give OMB the crucial decision-making role.

The focus on OMB (particularly in PART) essentially ignored the role of Congress and operated as if the executive branch (through OMB budget examiners) had the major authority to make the determinations about relevant goals in each program. The result was that PART assessments at times have actually preempted congressional decisions because they did not accord with the views of the White House. While Congress had the ability to ignore the recommendations of the White House, that process involved the expenditure of significant energy and time. That sometimes created problems for the career bureaucracy.

As the role of OMB increased, the specialized perspectives of experts in a program area often became lost in the debate. Focusing on programs through a budget lens is important but does not always allow for an appreciation of the nuances of program realities that are necessary to understand both the constraints and opportunities found in devising and carrying out performance assessments. Experience shows that centralization of authority supports a situation in which politics almost always trumps science and professional technical advice. Because OMB operates mostly out of public view, it narrows the access of the public to important information. It was difficult to determine the reasons why and how the PART assessments were considered.

The centralization of these requirements demoralizes the career public service. Careerists often believe that these are decisions that should be made by individuals familiar with the details of programs and policies. One understated and underappreciated story is that of the dedication and intelligence that reside in many parts of the civil service.

5. *The use of the performance information.* Both PART and GPRA share a confused set of expectations about the users of performance assessment. When GPRA was put into operation it never differentiated between the expectations of a range of potential users of the reports that were issued by agencies and departments in compliance with GPRA requirements. It assumed that a single type of report would meet the needs of program managers, political appointees within agencies, controllers of budgets both inside agencies and in OMB, policy designers in the White House, the range of actors within Congress, interest groups, and the general public. The required documents—strategic plans, performance plans, and performance reports—were assumed to provide information that all of these players could use to determine whether programs (or agencies) were meeting expected outcomes.

There was very little evidence that many of these players actually considered the GPRA documents as they performed their roles. Rarely were these documents cited in appropriations committee hearings, and it was difficult to determine whether either career or political staff within agencies did use them to either modify programs or policies or to justify budget requests. Although there were a few exceptions to this pattern, overall the use of GPRA documents was minimal anywhere in the decision-making process. Given the fragmented nature of the decision-making process in Congress, this is not surprising. And there was very little evidence that the public (or even the constituency communities) gave them much attention.

A similar pattern was found in the PART process. Although PART did focus exclusively on the executive branch and not on Congress, the situation was not much better. It was not surprising that PART assessments were basically invisible in either the appropriations or the authorizing processes in Congress. The fragmented nature of congressional decision making meant that it was up to a particular committee or subcommittee if it would even consider the performance measurement information.

But it was also very difficult to determine how OMB and the White House themselves used the findings in the process of constructing a budget. There have been several attempts to study this process but the lack of transparency within the White House makes it difficult to determine how the PART assessments were considered (if at all).[16] There was great variability in the way that OMB budget examiners approached their task, and arguments that were made in some program areas that led to budget decreases actually seem to have justified budget increases in other situations. Indeed, the basis for ratings that were given to programs was difficult to figure out.

What is clear is that use of performance information through PART or GPRA by program managers is rare. Indeed, the legitimate need for program managers to think about program outcomes seems to have been largely ignored by the press and critics of specific policy areas. Low ratings have been used to accuse career managers of incompetency and not as diagnostic information that could help them make changes to improve the way they implement programs. Although OMB developed a website that made the PART ratings available to the public, the rationale for these ratings was hard to determine and most of the assessments have been attentive solely to efficiency measures (ignoring effectiveness and equity program goals).

6. *Resources for performance measurement activities.* Both the GPRA experience as well as that in PART have indicated that the current public service does not have adequate expertise to identify appropriate performance measures for specific programs and determine what information sources are available and required. Despite more than a decade of experience with these two sets of performance requirements, training has not been available to improve the ability of agency staff to meet performance measurement requirements.[17] Performance measurement requires a combination of knowledge of specific programs as well as familiarity with the technical aspects of performance measurement. Too often agencies depend on outside consultants to perform this work and while they may be of assistance, at least part of the process could be viewed as an intrinsically governmental function that should not be contracted out.[18]

In addition to failures to provide training, other resource limitations are clear. It is rare for an agency to have an opportunity to make a case for the creation of data systems that could produce appropriate information to assess performance. Not only are these systems expensive but the requirements of the Paperwork Reduction Act have provided obstacles to agencies that try to argue for them. And it is usually assumed that agencies will take existing resources from their budgets to pay for the cost of addressing performance requirements.

7. *Attaching performance measurement information to the budget process.* Both GPRA and PART follow the tradition of some past federal reform efforts that link assessment of performance to the budget process (especially PPBS). The GPRA requirements were linked directly to agency submission of budget requests, and responsibility for PART was given to the OMB budget examiners who put together program budgets. PPBS, Managing by Objectives (MBO), and zero-based budgeting (ZBB) were past efforts to link some form of evaluation of programs to budget decisions. The budget process has its own regularity and is one of the most automatic of decision processes. But, as GAO has noted, some of these past efforts failed because they developed performance plans and measures in isolation from congressional processes.

There was little evidence that either GPRA or PART played much of a role in congressional processes. There is an argument to be made that the annual budget calendar does not provide a venue that allows for a consideration of the details of program implementation. When the conversation is around the size of budgets, it is difficult to raise substantive policy issues. Much of the performance rhetoric that emerges from the press (or from the OMB staff) speaks of the budget process as if it were a simple, well-defined set of activities that produces rational allocation patterns. This approach removes issues of values and political choices from the process and also ignores the multiple functions of budgeting (which include both budget execution and budget creation).

There are, however, other ways to use performance information outside of a direct link to the budget process. The system that was put in place in the United Kingdom to rate the performance of local government through the Audit Commission was not linked to the budget process. Instead the information that was developed was released to "name and shame" the government unit that had been examined.

Congress Returns to the Table

These (and other issues) seemed to be responsible for congressional action during the lame duck session at the very end of the 111th Congress in December 2010. Up to that point, Congress had minimal interest in performance measurement policies and the Obama administration had not developed a clear approach to those issues. The passage of the GPRA Modernization Act of 2010 occurred without much public attention to the issue and—once again—the Senate Government Affairs Committee took the lead.[19]

In its committee report attached to the legislation, the Senate reviewed the GPRA experience:

> During the 103rd Congress, this Committee acted on concerns—among its members as well as the public—that the federal government was not working as well as it should. Sharing the public's frustration and following its previous legislative and oversight work to address waste, inefficiency, and ineffectiveness in federal programs, . . . the Committee believed that the regular and systemic measurement and reporting of program performance, compared to pre-established goals, would be valuable to the federal government (including Congress) and provide a beneficial supplement to the Committee's previous work in the area of management improvement. . . . GPRA was intended to improve congressional decision making by providing objective information on the relative efficiency and effectiveness of federal programs and spending.[20]

The 2010 legislation was built around the original GPRA construct but also reflected the experience of both the GPRA and PART implementation. However, the congressional action did not focus on the process that was put in place under PART. Indeed, neither the committee report nor the legislation itself even acknowledged the effort that had been emphasized by the George W. Bush administration.

The 2010 legislation included the following elements:

- It called on the agencies and OMB to reach out to congressional committees in the process of not only devising strategic plans but also in establishing government-wide priority goals and agency priority goals. These priority goals are to be the main focus of the GPRA activity.[21] However, it was not clear which congressional committees would be contacted. Would it be authorizing committees, appropriations committees, or overview committees such as the government operations committees? The mechanism for establishing priorities was also unclear. Would the priorities require joint agreement between the executive and legislative actors and include the range of actors involved in a policy issue?
- It highlighted the need to focus on cross-cutting issues and called on OMB to orchestrate that process.[22] It was hard to know whether the cross-cutting issues would be defined only by the executive branch and how the congressional actors would be involved in this process. It appeared that the responsibility in OMB would be given to the small management staff, and the role of the budget side of OMB was not clear.
- It timed requirements to synchronize with new administrations (e.g., strategic plans would be timed to the change of administration).[23]

- It required agencies to update their performance reports rather than devising new reports. All of the reports were to be available on a single OMB website and would not be available in printed form but online.
- It was more explicit about the roles of agencies, OMB, and GAO. Agencies were expected to have a chief operating officer and a performance improvement officer. Although the performance improvement officers were defined as coming from agencies, in reality they were conceived as department-wide officials.[24] OMB was expected to create a Performance Improvement Council. GAO was tasked with conducting evaluations of the implementation process.
- OMB was asked to identify skills and competencies that were needed by agency staff to conduct this work.
- Congress made it clear that "nothing in this Act shall be construed as limiting the ability of Congress to establish, amend, suspend, or annul a goal of the Federal Government or an agency."[25]

Despite the reappearance of Congress in this area, there continue to be questions that remain unanswered about the balance between the role of the executive branch and that of Congress in the performance measurement activity.

1. Is performance measurement an inherently executive-branch concern? The congressional interest in this area comes from the few sectors of the legislative branch that are most likely to focus on management issues rather than substantive policy areas or the politics of budgeting.[26]
2. If the responsibility for performance measurement is to be shared with Congress (and sometimes the judiciary), how do we define the specific roles and processes in each branch? There is a need to be clear about the relationship between the two branches as well as the relationship between players within each branch.
3. How do we deal with federalism and the role of the states? Does the executive branch have the authority to impose performance requirements on states when Congress has enacted programs that give discretion to states (and sometimes localities)?
4. What is the relationship between performance measurement information and the budget process? Should questions related to efficiency values be the only measure of success?

Can the United States Learn from Other Countries?

As noted earlier, the earliest interest in performance measurement in the Senate drew on experience in other countries. Not only did the senate report in 1997 cite the OECD data but several years later GAO issued a report titled

*Managing for Results: Experiences Abroad Suggest Insights for Federal Man-
agement Reforms.*

A subsequent report, *Results-Oriented Cultures: Insights for U.S. Agencies
from Other Countries' Performance Management Initiatives,* described performance management systems in Australia, Canada, New Zealand, and the
United Kingdom. It was based on staff visits to those countries and conversations with officials from national audit offices; central management and
human capital agencies; agencies responsible for a range of functions including policy development, regulation, and service delivery; representatives
of employee associations; and academics.

In its report, GAO found that "the experiences of these four countries
may prove valuable to federal agencies in the United States as they develop
their own initiatives to integrate individual performance with the achievement of organizational goals."[27] None of these reports noted that the US
political structure is very different from the international examples that
were located in parliamentary systems.

Unlike many other management initiatives, drawing on experience in
other countries has been a relatively constant theme in the federal performance measurement area. Two organizations with very different political
agendas have had spokespeople in Washington working in this area who have
had experience in other countries. The two organizations—the Mercatus Institute at George Mason University and the Center for American Progress—
have continued the international comparative interest. Like GAO, neither of
these organizations focuses on the differences between the US shared powers
structure and that of parliamentary systems.

The Mercatus Center at George Mason University

The director of the Government Accountability Project at Mercatus, Mau-
rice P. McTigue, came to the Virginia center after completing his term as
New Zealand's ambassador to Canada. He had been a cabinet minister and
a member of Parliament in New Zealand who led an effort to restructure
New Zealand's public sector. McTigue is quite visible in Washington and
draws on his New Zealand experience to offer analysis of the performance
measurement activities within the US federal government. The center is
generally associated with the Republican Party and its agenda. It issues annual performance report scorecards that seek to answer the question,
"Which federal agencies best inform the public?" These reports emphasize
authority and responsibility within the agencies, and they tend to focus on
executive-branch powers and generally ignore the role of Congress in the
implementation of performance measurement programs.

The Center for American Progress

Jitinder Kohli is a senior fellow with the Doing What Works project at the
Center for American Progress (CAP). CAP is an organization

that is associated with the Democratic Party and deals with a range of both domestic and international issues. Kohli's work at the center focuses on government efficiency, regulatory reform, and economic issues. Prior to joining CAP, Kohli spent fifteen years in the British government. Most recently, he served as the director general of strategy and communications for the British Department for Business, Innovation and Skills, where he worked on the merger of two government departments. Previous positions involved regulatory reform issues and issues involving public agency productivity. He has also worked on social policy, leading the British government directorate responsible for the relationship with the nonprofit sector. As of this writing, Kohli has produced a number of op-ed pieces that deal with US performance measurement, drawing on his experience in Britain to offer recommendations to the Obama administration. Like McTigue, Kohli focuses on executive branch power and emphasizes relationships between the agencies and OMB. In one report, Kohli suggested that the US president model his behavior on the strategy used by British Prime Minister Tony Blair.[28]

It is interesting that these organizations in the United States continue to rely on the personal experience of individuals who were involved in performance measurement activities in other countries and yet do not look to the international literature that has been developed in this area that raises concern about a single, universal model. For example, Christopher Pollitt, then of Erasmus University of Holland, published an article in 2005 titled "Performance Management in Practice: A Comparative Study of Executive Agencies" that raised issues dealing with significant differences among countries as well as differences among different policy sectors. This is particularly interesting because Pollitt's study was exclusively focused on parliamentary systems.

In contrast, however, much of the literature on this topic in the United States continued to reflect an advocacy position on performance measurement rather than an analytic posture that provided some acknowledgment of the limitations of both GPRA and PART. There appeared to be more interest in the technical demands of doing performance measurement rather than the failure of the process to be linked to the nuances and structures of US decision making.

Performance Measurement and Contradictions in the US System

Efforts at developing a federal government performance measurement system illustrate a number of aspects of the three sets of contradictions found in the US system: structural dimensions, predominant values and approaches, and attributes of the public sector.

Structural Dimensions

Both the development of GPRA and that of PART illustrate the conflict between the executive branch and Congress that occurs in a shared-powers system. The original GPRA legislation of 1993 as well as the GPRA Modernization Act of 2010 were crafted in Congress and devised to provide a role for both congressional players as well as the executive branch. However, the congressional players in the process—the government operations committees and GAO—were not the main participants in either the appropriations or authorizing processes, the lifeblood of the congressional role. Neither the original GPRA legislation nor the 2010 version really conceptualized a way for the performance measurement information to find its way to those two processes. As a result, the legislation often seemed to stay at an abstract, even rhetorical level and had minimal ability to be used in decision making. There seemed to be the illusion that Congress had the ability to agree on priorities that cut across program areas and could be defined as government-wide goals.

PART did not even attempt to acknowledge the role of Congress in the process. Not only was it structured to respond only to the White House and OMB, but it didn't really take into account the tension between the White House and the departments and agencies. In fact, even though it relied on OMB budget examiners to agree to performance measures and information sources submitted by the agencies, it often failed to acknowledge the differences between budget examiners or the culture of discretion provided to them.

In the end, both branches of government seemed to approach performance measurement as if they were operating in the structure of a parliamentary system. That meant that there was a clear set of government policies that could emerge from both branches with a level of consistency, continuity, and clarity. They were not willing to concede that the US system created both institutional conflict between the branches and also partisan political conflict that was expressed in decision making. Given divided government, that was always a relevant issue.

The second structural issue revolves around the intergovernmental relationships that flow from the US federal system. This is an issue that has never been seriously considered in the performance measurement area in the United States. In part this occurred because most of the countries that were touted as leaders in the field were not only parliamentary systems but were also unified and centralized systems. The GPRA effort actually began with the assumption that what was effective at the local level of government could be easily transferred to the federal government. And there was never attention to the programs that were designed to provide discretion to states (and sometimes localities). Perhaps the most dramatic evidence of this was found in the way that the PART program attempted to define the specific goals of the Community Development Block Grant program. That program was designed to allow localities (and states) to determine and define what goals would be established for that jurisdiction for the use of the federal funds for community development. Over the years there was a range of definitions including economic development, infrastructure, housing, environment, and other approaches. Through the PART effort OMB attempted to constrain those choices and define the program as focused only on economic development goals. Pressure from localities and states provoked resistance from Congress to overturn the OMB effort.

Predominant Values and Approaches

Performance measurement efforts encompass both optimistic and pessimistic views about the federal government. Some of the advocates of the efforts believe that the information that is provided through the process will actually serve to support the programs that are a part of the government portfolio.[29] Others, however, have used the performance requirements as a vehicle to cut back on government and to blame the bureaucrats. Neither group is explicit about their objectives for supporting the measurement programs. And both are convinced that criticism of the means built into both PART and GPRA is actually a critique of the goals of performance measurement. Despite the rhetoric about performance information as neutral and simply "the facts," there was often a political hidden agenda at play in this reform area.

As has been noted, the performance measurement efforts rarely moved beyond attention to efficiency goals. Even though many programs contain a mixture of goals that represent all of the 3 *e*'s (efficiency, equity, and effectiveness), efficiency goals drove the process. This was particularly true in the PART effort. But even the GPRA effort rarely accentuated the equity values even when programs were specifically designed to serve underserved groups within the population. Most of the data that was used to measure performance was collected at an aggregate level and did not provide information about groups within the population (e.g., disaggregated by race, gender, or ethnicity) that were expected to benefit from the program.

Attributes of the Public Sector

One of the underlying beliefs attached to the performance management initiatives was an assumption that the information that could be used in the process was neutral and that it was possible to separate politics and administration in the process. From the earliest days of GPRA, its advocates sought to find a way to eliminate politics from the budget process and, instead, to devise a budget approach that was completely technocratic and based on neutral information. This was a dramatic departure from the literatures (from Aaron Wildavsky on) that examined budgeting as a political process.

Ironically, however, when one viewed the actual use of both GPRA and PART information, it appeared to be limited only to instances when participants in the process found a way to use that information to further their political goals. Rather than being neutral information, the performance information was used in a form similar to legal briefs: as a way to make a case for a preferred position.

As has been described, one of the major concerns with both GPRA and PART has been about its government-wide approach rather than a program/policy- or agency-specific strategy. The different policy designs of programs in the federal repertoire were largely ignored in the implementation of the performance measurement requirements. As noted, it was very difficult to expect the same response from agencies administering programs that were based on different policy instruments.[30] Not only did these programs have different types of constituents, interest groups, and congressional actors but they also delivered their services in very different forms.

During the period when both GPRA and PART were developed, the capacity of the staff in OMB charged with this responsibility was very thin. While it could promulgate requirements across the government, it had very limited capacity to follow through on the implementation of those requirements. And of course a one-size-fits-all approach did not fit with the fragmentation of Congress or indeed with the structure of the budget side of OMB itself. Budget examiners dealt with specific program areas in a way that paralleled the jurisdiction of appropriations subcommittees in both the House and Senate.

In addition, the centralized approach tended to accentuate the role of policy generalists rather than individuals who were conversant with specialized issues, particularly in science-related programs. All of this meant that the process did not really touch the heart of program management because managers charged with carrying out the programs were rarely involved in the process.

Conclusions

Although performance measurement efforts were related to other management reform issues, these efforts did not usually meet the expectations that others had of their contribution. Both GPRA and PART were cast in an environment that constantly faced conflict between the White House and Congress. It was hard to find significant examples of programs and policies in which the performance information appeared to have made a difference in either budget allocations or program substance.[31] The reliance on processes that were created in parliamentary and centralized systems did not allow the United States to deliver on the expectations that were attached to the initiatives. Those expectations assumed that the executive branch had control over the processes that were developed.

Notes

1. Much of the literature dealing with the technical aspects of performance measurement is found in the IBM Endowment for the Business of Government

portfolio. That organization has sponsored and published a number of reports and books on this set of issues.

2. Colin Talbot has written about this problem across the globe. "The kinds of interventions carried out by performance regime actors have likewise been the subject of a great deal of research and analysis, but again of a very unintegrated nature. We know quite a bit about certain types of interventions (league tables, targets, internal markets, specific capability interventions, and so on), but this has rarely been pulled together into any understanding of the range of interventions or their interactions." Talbot, *Theories of Performance,* 216.

3. GAO observed that GPRA melded the "best features of its predecessors." GAO, *Performance Budgeting* (1997), 7.

4. This discussion draws on Radin, *Challenging the Performance Movement,* esp. 118–21.

5. Ibid., 119.

6. This was particularly the case in the National Academy of Public Administration (NAPA) as well as other groups. When GPRA was considered and eventually adopted, NAPA provided support for its approach. See Senate Committee on Governmental Affairs, *Report to Provide for the Establishment, Testing, and Evaluation of Strategic Planning and Performance Measurement in the Federal Government,* 1997, quoted in Radin, *Challenging the Performance Movement,* 120.

7. Radin, *Challenging the Performance Movement,* 120; see discussion in chap. 3 of the present book.

8. Senate Committee, 11.

9. The difference in language suggested that the Republicans believed that a focus on results was doable and could be viewed as the equivalent of the private sector's bottom line of profit.

10. See Frederickson and Frederickson, *Measuring the Performance of the Hollow State.*

11. See Radin, *Challenging the Performance Movement,* 122–25, for a description of the process.

12. See Radin, "Performance Management," 244.

13. See Radin, *Challenging the Performance Movement,* chap. 5, "Competing Values: Can the Performance Movement Deal with Equity?"

14. Gulick, "Science," 100.

15. Radin, *Challenging the Performance Movement,* chap. 5.

16. One example of this literature is found in Gilmour and Lewis, "Assessing Performance Budgeting."

17. There was some discussion with the Office of Personnel Management and Congress about supporting performance measurement training programs for managers, but fiscal limitations appear to have stood in the way of developing such proposals.

18. See chapter 4 of this volume.

19. The committee was actually renamed the Senate Committee on Homeland Security and Government Affairs.

20. Committee on Homeland Security and Governmental Affairs, GPRA Modernization Act of 2010: Report to Accompany H.R. 2142, S. Rep. No. , at 2 (2010).

21. Ibid., 4–5. "H.R. 2142 strengthens the Congressional consultation process by encouraging agencies to describe how agency goals and objectives incorporate

the views and suggestions obtained through consultations with Congress. This legislation clarifies that the agency shall periodically consult with and obtain majority and minority views from its authorizing, appropriations, and oversight committees when developing or making adjustments to its strategic plan. It also requires Congressional consultations occur at least once every two years; this is to ensure that each Congress has input on the goals, objectives, strategies, and performance measures of the agency. Moreover, it allows the agency to have an opportunity to provide a progress report on its performance and ensures that various committees are getting the types of performance information they need."

22. Ibid., 2–3. "Across the federal government, various agencies operate similar or related programs. GAO has found that mission fragmentation and program overlap are widespread across the government and that addressing this challenge is essential to the success of national strategies in areas such as homeland security, drug control, and the environment. Without appropriate coordination, such programs may be implemented in a fragmented manner which wastes scarce resources, confuses citizens, and limits the overall effectiveness of the federal effort. H.R. 2142 requires an agency to describe how it is working with other agencies to achieve its own goals and objectives, as well as the crosscutting priority goals of the federal government. GAO found that agencies were not coordinating their efforts in order to address common challenges and achieve common objectives. GAO noted that such mission fragmentation and overlap among agencies makes it particularly difficult to address cross-cutting national issues, such as homeland security, drug control, and the environment."

23. Ibid., 2–3. "Finally, GAO also found that timing issues may hinder the development of useful agency strategic plans. Specifically, agencies are often required to update strategic plans just before a presidential election and without input from a new Congress. If a new president is elected, the updated plan is essentially moot and does not have the commitment and sustained attention of top leadership within the agency."

24. In large departments, this often means that the department-wide official is not familiar with the details of the specific programs and policies implemented by agency-level officials.

25. GPRA Modernization Act of 2010, H. R. 2142, 111th Cong. (2010), § 15 (a).

26. Interest in performance in Congress has come from the government operations committees in both chambers as well as GAO.

27. GAO, *Results-Oriented Cultures,* 3.

28. See Kohli, *From Setting Goals to Achieving Them.*

29. For example, this is an argument that has been made by Joseph Wholey and his colleagues in Harry P. Hatry, Elaine Morley, Shelli B. Rossman, and Joseph S. Wholey, "How Federal Programs Use Outcome Information Opportunities for Federal Managers," pamphlet, IBM Endowment for the Business of Government, May 1, 2003.

30. See Salamon, *Tools of Government.*

31. At a presentation sponsored by the Georgetown University Public Policy Institute during the Bush administration, former OMB official Robert Shea (the major figure involved with the PART effort) was asked to give an example of a program where PART information played a role in the decisions involving the budget process. He could not name such a program.

10

LIVING WITH CONTRADICTIONS

The world is a perpetual caricature of itself; at every moment it is the mockery and the contradiction of what it is pretending to be.

George Santayana

I learned to make my mind large, as the universe is large, so that there is room for contradictions.

Maxine Hong Kingston

Life is never free of contradictions.

Manmohan Singh

THIS DISCUSSION OF SIX DIFFERENT MANAGEMENT REFORM EFFORTS IN THE US federal system indicates that there is a variety of approaches that make up the management reform portfolio. Each of the efforts discussed in this book—budgeting, reorganization, personnel management, contracting, federalism, and performance measurement—represents a specialized community within the public management field, defined by experts, theories, and explicit agendas for change. Many of these efforts emerged from attempts to make government more like a business, highlighting competition, entrepreneurism, markets, and efficiency. Several of the efforts were accompanied by support of interest groups that could advocate for them within the political environment. Others, however, lacked advocates who could operate within that environment.

But at the same time that these efforts differ from one another in some important ways, all of them operate within the three sets of contradictions that have been defined in this volume. As first discussed in the introduction, these three contradictions are the structural dimensions of the US system (both the system of shared powers between branches of government as well as federalism); the predominant values and approaches found in the system (conflict between pessimism and optimism about the role of government as well as the conflict between the classic values of efficiency, effectiveness, and equity); and attributes of the US public sector (the tension between politics and administration as well as strain between government-wide approaches versus program/policy-specific approaches).

As the following discussion indicates, the response to these contradictions by the six reform efforts does not follow a single pathway. Yet each of those efforts did have to respond to the contradictions in one way or another. Some changed their approaches depending on the environment and the pressures on them. Others, by contrast, had a set of approaches that remained fairly consistent over time. Few of the examples indicated that the contradictions were taken seriously; the response was largely to ignore them. It is this pattern of ignoring the contradictions that has been challenged in these pages because it often did not produce effective results.

Structural Dimensions

It is clear that all six of the management reform efforts found it difficult to deal with the shared-power structure of the US system. This largely centered on the competition between the executive and legislative branches of government. This competitive environment created conflict that frustrated many efforts at change. Indeed, it is the very centerpiece of the US system—the system of shared powers between the branches of government as defined in the Constitution—that seems to have produced major problems for those who have advocated management reform.

Until the New Deal, it was relatively easy to think about Congress as the first branch of government. Urbanization, industrialization, and the development of a private management field all contributed to new attention to the expectations of the executive branch's behavior. It gave new meaning to Alexander Hamilton's observation that "the true test of a good government is its aptitude and tendency to produce a good administration."[1]

While Hamilton did not think about defining "good administration" in terms of either a parliamentary system or the private sector, by the World War II era public administration reformers started to look to both of those sources for management reform ideas. That seemed appropriate as the executive branch grew in size and function. But both the parliamentary experience as well as the private-sector experience emphasized behaviors that rested on clear powers and authority. Reformers seem to have created an image of an American executive branch that rested on those attributes.

The drive for executive-branch control is expressed in all six of the management reform efforts discussed in this book. The budget reform efforts, for example, represented competition between the two branches, with the executive branch attempting to develop procedures that would allow it to play the ascent role in the system. Or, in effect, the executive branch wanted to go it alone in the way that is possible in a parliamentary system. The budget efforts also indicate the response by Congress to the executive drive for control. Yet when Congress tried to respond, the fragmentation of the system (separate committees and subcommittees and two legislative bodies) made it difficult to create a common framework. As fiscal problems became more and more important, the budget process became increasingly volatile and it was easier to deal with budget numbers than with the complexity of program details.

A similar dynamic occurred in terms of reorganization efforts. Reorganization reform went back and forth between the two branches. Congress was unwilling to give the White House sole control over reorganization deci-sions (giving the executive this authority would be obvious in the private sector or in a parliamentary system), and over time the pendulum moved back and forth between the two ends of Pennsylvania Avenue. Personnel reform efforts also became increasingly associated with the power of the executive branch, but at various points congressional actors found ways to thwart those agendas. And the tension between the two branches was clearly expressed in efforts to develop and require performance measurement activities.

Efforts to rationalize the federal system in management faced a some-what different dynamic because of the structure of Congress. When the White House tried to establish clear perspectives sorting out the roles of the national government and of states (and local governments), members of Congress were more likely to deal with the impact of changes on their geo-graphic constituencies and not highlight consistent approaches.

Indeed, federalism often stood in the way of other reform efforts when members of Congress were concerned about the impact of budget decisions, contracts, and reorganization on other levels of government. In addition, it was often difficult to get members of Congress to focus on management issues unless the substantive consequences of those decisions (e.g., who would benefit from the programs or policies) were raised by interest groups and other players.

Reformers could draw on parliamentary and private-sector experience to design efforts that would increase the control of the executive branch. But it was more difficult to find models for the congressional role. The Grace Commission did create an analogy between Congress and a private-sector board of directors but that argument evoked serious criticism. Should the congressional role be limited to an oversight or monitoring role? That would place Congress in a reactive and not a proactive role. What does it mean to share powers, be it with Congress or with the states? Should there be something created that was akin to the advise-and-consent powers in the Senate, where the president nominates top officials but the Senate has to approve the nominations?

There seem to be three different responses to this issue that would char-acterize the impact of structure on the six reform efforts discussed. They are (1) the executive branch goes it alone, (2) Congress focuses on playing a monitoring/oversight role, and (3) the two branches develop a shared-power relationship. Table 10.1 indicates that all six reform efforts attempted to focus on the power of the executive branch as their strategy, two involved Congress through a monitoring role, and three made some attempt to work toward a shared-power strategy.

This pattern suggests that much of the management reform agenda has sought to simplify and clarify the roles of the three branches. Emphasizing the role of the executive branch alone ignores the explicit constitutional

TABLE 10.1: Structural Dimensions

Reform	Executive: go it alone	Congress: monitoring	Shared power
Budget	X		X?
Federalism	X		
Contracting	X	X	
Performance	X		X?
Personnel	X	X	
Reorganization	X		X?

limits on the ability of the president and seeks to establish separate rather than shared powers. Similarly, the management reform agenda has often ignored the demands of a federal system and—like the response to shared powers between branches of government—does not effectively deal with overlapping responsibilities between the federal level, states, and localities.

Predominant Values and Approaches

From its earliest days, the US government sought to differentiate itself from the European systems that provided its cultural and institutional framework. The oft-quoted statement by Thomas Paine, "That government is best which governs least," captured the skepticism articulated by the founders that led to both the Declaration of Independence and the Constitution. Strong centralized governments were associated with religious control and the power of royalty. And neither was accepted as the model for the US system.

At the same time, when public administration began to develop as an independent field, it wrapped itself in the optimism of change from the Enlightenment. As noted earlier, as a part of the Progressive movement it established a position around good-government values and argued for the potential of government action based on generic principles of management.

Actually the public management field attempted to reconcile these two competing values by attaching itself to models of change that were directly borrowed from the private sector. From the Brownlow Committee onward, one can see this link. Not only were the reform initiatives drawn from private-sector experience, but the worship of the market that was found in the NPM agenda provided the intellectual framework for this posture. Reform advocates could argue that the public sector was clearly secondary in status and effectiveness to the private sector. Implicit in this process of borrowing from the private sector was a way of rationalizing public-sector behavior in private-sector terms.

Despite the arguments of some economists that government should not only think about efficiency values as it sought to improve its work (but also to consider effectiveness and equity), concern about efficiency continues to drive the management reform efforts that were discussed in this book.[2] Each of the six reform efforts had to find a way to cast its contribution around efficiency values. Contracting efforts were characterized as clear win-or-lose situations. Minimizing the size of the government workforce expressed the pessimism found in Thomas Paine's quote about the role of government. The more that the decisions about a public-sector contract involved the same issues as those related to private-sector contracts, the more effective it was thought to be. The criteria that were used to choose between proposals sometimes moved beyond price issues, but those elements were secondary to price considerations. At times effectiveness questions appeared in the criteria, but equity issues were extremely rare.

Highlighting efficiency approaches that are borrowed from industrial staffing in the private sector, federal personnel reform efforts are sometimes difficult to disentangle from blame-the-bureaucrat arguments. Thinking about federal bureaucrats in the same way that one would approach a factory worker both demeans the professionalization and expertise of the staff as well as ignores differences between the tasks and functions performed. What is effective in the private sector (based on profit maximization) is incorrectly assumed to be the same as what is effective for public action.

Similarly, reorganization reforms were based on private-sector practices. As noted earlier, one could move to optimism about government if it behaved like the private sector. Avoiding overlap and fragmentation and making clear assignment of roles and responsibilities were ways to achieve greater efficiency. But these are not issues usually raised in authorizing or appropriations committees or subcommittees. Only the generalist government operations committees, which had limited authority over the system, found these issues central.

Budget reformers were most likely to express pessimism about the public-sector role. But when crises and major problems occurred, then there might be a tendency to look at the role of the public sector to deal with those crises. Budget reform in the White House attempts to see the budget process as a whole. But there is limited ability to achieve this in Congress, with the exception of CBO, GAO, and the budget committees. Budget reform is also conducted in a way that avoids substantive program and policy impacts.

Reforms dealing with federalism have to cope with conflicting imperatives: states and localities want flexibility and discretion while the federal government highlights accountability and control. And it is difficult to define the way that efficiency values are expressed because of the differences in the level of analysis employed. Something can be viewed as efficient at a federal, macro level but not at a state or local micro level.

Performance measurement reforms can both be used to improve programs as well as become methods of killing programs and policies. But advocates for these efforts rarely make these arguments explicit. Rather, they

TABLE 10.2: Predominant Values and Approaches

Reform	Model on private sector	Efficiency values predominant	Minimize attention to program substance	Deal with problems and crises
Budget	X	X	X	X
Federalism	X	X	X	
Contracting	X	X	X	
Performance	X	X	X	
Personnel	X	X	X	
Reorganization	X	X	X	X

base their case for reform on good-government arguments rather than revealing the substantive goals of the reform programs. Yet they focus on specific programs and encourage the use of specific information sources to achieve their agenda.[3]

The pattern that emerges from this analysis indicates that all of the six reform efforts modeled their approaches on private-sector practice, emphasized efficiency values, and minimized attention to program or policy substance. Two of the efforts did seem to deal with problems and crises that stimulated more active roles for public action (see table 10.2).

This pattern does not suggest that most reformers looked beyond the private sector for their strategies and proposals. Yet this is difficult to understand since the US tradition has been to experience both optimistic and pessimistic views about the role of government. Similarly the tradition does include some views that there are differences between public- and private-sector action and roles. Reliance on the market and efficiency values is, in itself, a way of expressing pessimism about government action. It also avoids discussion of who makes decisions (political representatives or experts) and on what grounds.

Attributes of the Public Sector

There are two issues that are relevant to federal management reformers that deal with attributes of the public sector in the United States. The first is the classic public administration dichotomy: Can administration be separated from politics? The second relates to the strategic decision concerning the focus of reform efforts: Should activity be government-wide or should it be tailored to specific programs, policies, or agencies?

All six of the reform efforts that were studied had to deal with both of these issues. There is a strong tendency in all of them to emphasize the potential of centralized power of the executive branch and to move toward a one-size-fits-all strategy. This approach is difficult to implement in a system in which the sharing of powers puts obstacles in the way of untethered executive-branch power. As the discussion of structure indicated, the president is limited in terms of discretion and ability to make decisions unilaterally without some form of involvement of Congress. And the structure of Congress itself establishes fragmentation of decision making, with separate processes in both chambers and separate approaches in the authorizing and appropriations committees and subcommittees. Thus there is no single body that has clear authority to rely on technical determinations as a way of establishing decisions.

These efforts also seem inappropriate in a system that is as large and diverse as the US federal government. Programs, departments, and agencies are very different from one another; they reflect different strategies of change, operate in different cultures, and utilize multiple modes and policy instruments.

Contracting reform, for example, has tried to rely on a definition of what is inherently governmental to establish the parameters of contracting reach. But there is no single body in the government (in any of the branches) that has the authority to make such a definition. Yet the contracting reform advocates have attempted to establish that pathway and, in fact, to define the federal contracting role in a way that reaches across the entire federal government. They have sought technical fixes to what is essentially a political problem. And the determination of who will get the contract often involves dealing with potential grantees who have political clout in the system.

The personnel reform efforts indicate that proponents of change have attempted to establish a system that allows federal executive-branch officials to make decisions without considering a variety of political realities. While their preferred state may have been based on political values or ideologies, they devised their most recent strategy largely ignoring Congress and relevant interest groups that have a legitimate interest in the management proposals. Like contracting reform efforts, these proposals sought government-wide changes and emphasized the role of the central agencies (the Office of Personnel Management as well as OMB).

Many of the reorganization efforts were based on an assumption that one could clearly differentiate between policy and administration and that there were strong administrative arguments that would lead to specific organizational structural recommendations. Those arguments were drawn from private-sector sources and supported a belief that a consistent set of arguments would appropriately apply to all parts of the federal government. While this set of arguments was relatively constant inside the executive branch, there was little attention to the appropriate criteria that would be acceptable to members of Congress.

Efforts to reform the federal system illustrated some of the same dynamics as other reform efforts. Attempts to devise a government-wide approach did not mesh with the views of at least some of the multiple actors with authority to stop if not to start change. These attempts did not give adequate attention to the differences between programs in the federal portfolio or to the significant variation in the perceptions of states and localities.

Budget efforts were largely driven by a belief drawn from the Progressive era that the executive branch should have control over an executive budget and that the congressional role should be secondary to the activity in the White House. This idea did not correspond to structural realities. It did not mesh with the partisan and institutional differences between the two branches of government. But perhaps most importantly, it was difficult to fit into an election cycle where all members of the House stood for reelection every two years.

Performance measurement activities were linked to the budget process and were constructed on a single approach to all programs and structures within the federal government. Many of the performance measurement advocates assumed that performance information was neutral and that it was possible to take politics out of the process. Use of that information was quite rare, and when it was used often took the form of briefs for preexisting positions. Those efforts were based on one-size-fits-all approaches and did not reflect the variety of programs and approaches in the federal establishment. That led to centralization of implementation processes within OMB and little attention to the details of specialized programs that were not familiar to OMB generalists.

Table 10.3 represents the pattern of the six reforms dealing with attributes of the public sector. All six reforms moved toward executive-branch strategies that emphasized one-size-fits-all approaches and highlighted technical rather than political realities. Four of the reforms moved toward centralization in the executive branch.

There appears to be a strong sentiment among federal management reformers that politics (however it is defined) should be avoided and that politics and administration should be viewed as two separate and independent worlds.[4] Politics encompasses a range of actors and issues. It can involve Congress, elections, interest groups, campaign funding, conflicting values, and other issues and players that are a part of the external world of

TABLE 10.3: Attributes of the Public Sector

Reform	Executive branch: One size fits all	Centralization	Highlight technical rather than political realities
Budget	X		X
Federalism	X	X	X
Contracting	X	X	X
Performance	X	X	X
Personnel	X	X	X
Reorganization	X		X

public organizations. The other attribute of the public sector that is relevant involves the tendency to conceptualize management reform in one-size-fits-all terms. It ignores differences among program structures and designs, historical experience that varies by program and policy areas, and diverse accountability relationships between agencies, congressional bodies, and external groups. And it moves toward an increase in the centralized role of OMB and other parts of the White House. Centralization means a strong tendency to look for strategies that rely on a one-size-fits-all approach, that locate management concerns in OMB (rather than in the agencies and departments), and that look to GAO as the congressional location for management questions.

Ignoring the Contradictions?

Given the pattern that emerges when one looks at this collection of federal management reform efforts, it is not surprising that so little seems to have been accomplished as a result of these attempts. Like Sisyphus, reformers seem to have repeated many of the same strategies over and over again. Yet they have not been able to accomplish the changes they desired from the reforms. And if one acknowledges that the US system is composed of a number of contradictions, it appears that these reform efforts do not provide a way for decision makers to balance those conflicting imperatives but rather have constructed strategies that move in a single direction. It seems that the reformers actually have ignored the contradictions.

But the message from this analysis is not to swing to a completely different approach. Given the nature of the US society, it does make sense to look to the private sector for reform ideas. But it is extremely important to acknowledge that there are differences between public and private-sector environments, especially in the political structure of shared powers that is a part of the American heritage.

This volume has attempted to show how federal management reform initiatives as designed over the past fifty years have not made the federal system operate more efficiently, effectively, or equitably. As efforts have been defined and implemented they have actually created new problems that obstruct the achievement of the goals of the reform proponents.

This analysis of the six reform efforts does not lead one toward a grand scheme that serves as an alternative to the strategies of the past. Rather it leads one to emphasize an approach that is modest, ever changing, and constantly searching for ways to balance conflicting imperatives. Several principles are important to emphasize, as outlined in the following sections.

Acknowledge the Size, Diversity, and Complexity of the US System

Whether the result of technology, population shifts, economic globalization, or climate change, we can expect the US society to be constantly changing.

What seems relevant today may seem peripheral tomorrow. This leads to the dynamic so effectively described by Albert Hirschman in *Shifting Involvements*. The balance between conflicting perspectives is not cast in stone, but we can expect the US society to continue to experience constant tensions between the elements discussed in this volume.

We have glimpses of the issues that exacerbate the tension built into the US political system. Globalization often leads to further uncertainty and a sense that the United States cannot control the aspects of its social and economic conditions that it may have once believed it could control. The demise of the Soviet Union and political shifts around the globe have led many to question the traditional beliefs that led societies to define and structure their traditional roles of government.

Not only do these developments change patterns of international relationships but they also have led to different expectations about how decisions are made and who is involved in them. The great interest in networks has made many in the public management community question the appropriateness of ideas such as the principal-agent theory when there are multiple principals and multiple agents, each of which has different (and legitimate) expectations about their and others' roles.

The experience with contracting in Iraq has sensitized some observers to the differences between those with formal authority and ability to apply sanctions (usually public-sector officials) and those in the private sector who have a legitimate role in some aspects of the process but do not worry about formal authority. Yet the economic crises of the past few years have shown how private-sector players can have massive impacts on public issues.

It is fascinating that the concept of American exceptionalism has been revived in the second decade of the twenty-first century. The term itself has been used by conservative Republicans who are comfortable using the concept as a way of justifying American tendencies to go it alone. At the same time, President Obama has not used the word itself but has used the concept to highlight the values in the Constitution that are found in American democratic practices. Use of this term indicates how the concept has "become a litmus test for patriotism."[5]

Be Wary of Worshipping the Gods of Efficiency

Given the reality of fiscal limitations and budget deficits it is not surprising that actors throughout the political and management systems constantly emphasize the importance of what they call efficiency. Yet it is not always clear what is meant by this term. Does it mean that the public sector, by definition, is less efficient than the private sector because it does not have a measure of success analogous to the profit margin? Is it ever possible to compare public and private definitions of effectiveness when the private sector only focuses on efficiency? Is the goal of the effort really cutting spending so that taxes can be reduced? What is the counterpart in the public sector to the hidden hand of the market as the mechanism for defining efficiency? Can we think about shared and separated power as analogous to the political market? Does efficiency need the designation of clear authority in order to be accomplished? If so, isn't the federal structure intrinsically inefficient because it does not have clear designation of authority and power but, instead, establishes complexity and gridlock between players? For some, efficiency in the public sector is really a mystery. It does seem that efficiency needs clear authority yet that is something that, by design, the American system lacks. This does not mean that one values inefficiency. Rather it calls for ways to balance and trade off competing values, though that does limit the ability of the system to devise the most efficient approaches.

One is tempted to designate the god of efficiency as a false god, not dissimilar to the god Ba'al, who was worshipped by the ancient Semitic people.

Acknowledge the Limits of Institutions

It is tempting to look at the institutions charged with implementing federal management reform as suboptimizing organizations: making sure that what they are interested in is taken care of at the expense of everything else. Both the executive branch and congressional bodies that have been major players in the management reform agendas seem to have displayed suboptimizing behavior. They have ignored the larger context and environment in which they work and have focused on their specific reform plan.

The management side of OMB exhibits this behavior. The small staff charged with the management reform agendas focuses on its tasks in a way that blindly moves toward centralization through the one-size-fits-all approach. This staff, particularly when some individuals within it are drawn from only private-sector experience, has tended to focus on the task and search for comparabilities with the private sector without defining possible differences between the public and private sectors.[6] Drawing on private-sector terms (e.g., efficiency, customer, publicness, business) without clearly defining them makes for confusion.

This staff has operated alone, often failing to draw on the program and policy expertise within the OMB budget examiner staff. And it certainly has been limited in its ability to develop information and advice from the program staff in departments and agencies. The limited size of the staff and its lack of technical knowledge about specific programs and agencies has pushed away sources of information that are relevant to the task.

The congressional institutions that have played the most visible role in management reform exhibit some of the same problems. The two sets of government reform committees in the Senate and the House have limited authority to play a role in the actual authorizing and appropriating processes that are the core of congressional power. These committees do look at the government as a whole, but they actually have quite limited ability to craft both budgets and programs that meet the aspirations of the management reform agenda. The congressional structure, thus, constrains the ability of these committees to tie together the general approaches with specific programs and policies through joint efforts between congressional committees and subcommittees. It is sometimes amusing to hear advocates of federal management reform call for major changes in the structure of Congress without acknowledging the constitutional basis for many of the behaviors they want to change.

Much of the staff work that has been attached to management reform initiatives in Congress has been performed by GAO. While there are important and useful studies and reports that have been developed by this agency, there is great variability among the perspectives of the staff charged with these analytic tasks. Some of the staff focus on generic management approaches (some of these approaches were drawn from the experience of private-sector consulting firms) while others have developed policy and program specializations that allow them to think about general issues in specific program frameworks. For example, the reports on federal reorganization efforts exhibit both tendencies. If staff have experience in a policy field, they understand the political consequences of reorganization efforts. If they do not, they fall back on private-sector principles of management.

Be Skeptical about One-Size-Fits-All Approaches

Given the structure, size, and complexity of the US political system, one should be very skeptical about devising one-size-fits-all strategies. Yet, as noted earlier, that seems to be a very common tendency among advocates of various management reform efforts. Not only does that approach fly in the face of most congressional processes but it also generates a series of conflicts that are not consistent with expectations of both state and local governments. In addition, it avoids acknowledging the differences among programs and policies and the diverse cultures of the organizations in the federal government portfolio.

While it is tempting to think about a process that is more like that found in a parliamentary system, it seems obvious that that assumption doesn't get us very far in the US system. It may be time to devise alternative approaches to the one-size-fits-all strategy that provide legitimate options to a single choice between centralized or decentralized approaches. A repertoire of possibilities that are defined by the executive branch—giving choices to others—would indicate that it is willing to respond to differences between programs and policies in terms of their design, constraints, and congressional expectations.

"Politics" Is Not a Curse Word

It is difficult to identify many management reform efforts that do not generate controversy in one element or another in the political environment surrounding the reform agenda. While reformers may seek autonomy and control over decisions, it is extremely unlikely that they can do this. It is the political system that legitimizes the authority and power of the management structure. We might seek neutral information to justify reform activity but rarely does information escape from the determination of who benefits and who loses from decisions. And since the US political system is designed to stimulate conflict between branches of government, politics is here to stay. Ignoring the actors, issues, and venues involved does not get reform advocates very far.

Conflict Is Natural; It Cannot Be Avoided

Each of the six reform areas indicated a reluctance to deal with the conflicts that emerge from the contradictions discussed. The structure, the values, and the attributes of the public service in general all generate conflicts and tensions. Efforts to sort out clear lines of demarcation between public and private, definitions of "inherently governmental," and even attempts to define "efficiency" all breed differences and conflict. It is not helpful when groups such as the Grace Commission call the congressional role "congressional meddling." It suggests that they have failed to read the Constitution. While it is clear that the various actors in the system are challenged to find ways to work together, that seems far from what has been defined as co-management. This is an area that requires time, commitment, and patience. Management reform challenges us all.

So What Is a Management Reformer to Do?
A Dozen Questions to Be Asked

As I noted in the introduction, I do not expect the readers of this book to agree with all of my positions and arguments. My hope is that this analysis raises questions about the approaches that have been used in the past and allows both academics and practitioners to consider a range of less traditional methods that can serve the goals underlying federal management reform. The answers to these questions will vary but asking them is crucial. I believe that these queries are likely to open up possibilities for alternative approaches to federal management reform.

1. *Who are the actors involved or affected in the reform and what are their concerns?* The participants in reform are many and diverse. We should expect to include elected officials (members of Congress as well as the executive branch), appointed officials, careerists, both line and staff officials, and interest groups. It should also include actors involved in adopting the policy and those involved in implementing it.
2. *What are you trying to accomplish?* Are there multiple goals involved?

3. *Are there lessons that you can draw from past and similar proposals?* What can you learn from the past? Has there been disappointment from existing efforts? Have you drawn on models from other sectors or situations (the private sector, parliamentary systems) that might have limited applicability to the United States?

4. *What elements in the environment are likely to have an impact on the fate of a reform proposal?* These would include economic and political realities, crisis situations, and macro political trends.

5. *What are existing beliefs that might keep you from considering alternative approaches?* Are there alternative ways of framing the issue and crafting strategies that have been ignored in the past? Can you unlearn your attachment to past efforts?

6. *What resources do you have available at both the adoption and implementation stages?* Resources could include authority, influence, expertise, public support, and money. Who are the experts that you are drawing on; are they experts in specific programs or experts in reform?

7. *What are the contradictions in the US system that might constrain your preferred options?* Are there dangers in searching for clarity in areas such as efficiency goals?

8. *How does the system of shared powers (particularly between the legislative and executive branches) constrain your possibilities?* Are there advocates for change in both branches who have authority or influence over these decisions? What mechanisms are in place that provide assistance to both branches (e.g., OMB, GAO, congressional committees and subcommittees)?

9. *Are there mechanisms in place that provide a way to manage the conflict between perspectives?* The conflict could come from both partisan and institutional sources. Are there other reforms and processes that are likely to be affected by the proposed change?

10. *Are you dealing with an issue that involves symbolic action, or does it focus on substantive change?*

11. *Who can stop the adoption and implementation of your preferred approach?* This could include the courts, Congress, interest groups, and intergovernmental actors.

12. *Are there differences between the views of practitioners and those of academics who are giving advice to decision makers?* Are there concepts that academics believe are dead (such as the dichotomy between politics and administration and POSDCORB) that appear to be alive in the practitioner community?

Attempting to analyze a potential reform effort through these (and other) questions should provide a federal management reformer with useful information. Such an analysis is likely to produce strategies that are messy, modest, and hopefully realistic.

Notes

1. Hamilton, Jay, and Madison, *Federalist,* no. 76, 491.
2. Okun, *Equality and Efficiency.*
3. One can contrast the strategies expressed in two different maxims. "What is measured counts" is quite different from the Einstein quote, "Everything that can be counted does not necessarily count; everything that counts cannot necessarily be counted."
4. While some academics argue that the separation between politics and administration no longer exists, I have found that it is alive and well in much of the public management community.
5. Kathleen Parker, "President Obama and That 'Exceptional' Thing," *Washington Post,* January 30, 2011.
6. See Ed O'Keefe, "Zients to Lead Government Reorganization Project," *Washington Post,* January 30, 2011.

BIBLIOGRAPHY

Abramson, Mark, Richard Schmidt, and Sandra Baxter. "Evaluating the Civil Service Reform Act of 1978: The Experience of the U.S. Department of Health and Human Services." In Ingraham and Ban, *Legislating Bureaucratic Change*, 112–47.

Agranoff, Robert. "Intergovernmental Policy Management: Cooperative Practices in Federal Systems." In *The Dynamics of Federalism in National and Supranational Political Systems*, 248–83. London: Palgrave Macmillan, 2007.

Alford, John. "Defining the Client in the Public Sector: A Social-Exchange Perspective." *Public Administration Review* 62, no. 3 (2002): 337–46.

Allison, Christine Rothmayr, and Denis Saint-Martin. "Half a Century of 'Muddling': Are We There Yet?" Special issue, *Policy and Society* 30, no. 1 (2011): 1–8.

Allison, Graham T. "Public and Private Management: Are They Fundamentally Alike in All Unimportant Respects?" In *OPM Document 127-53-1*, 27–38. Washington, DC: Office of Personnel Management, 1980.

American Society for Public Administration. *Strengthening Intergovernmental Management: An Agenda for Reform.* Washington, DC: American Society for Public Administration, 1979.

Appleby, Paul H. *Big Democracy.* New York: Alfred A. Knopf, 1945.

Argyle, Nolan J. "Civil Service Reform: The State and Local Response." *Public Personnel Management* 11, no. 2 (1982): 157–64.

Arnold, Peri E. *Making the Managerial Presidency: Comprehensive Reorganization Planning, 1905–1996,* rev. 2nd ed. Lawrence: University Press of Kansas, 1998.

Bailey, Brian E. "Federalism: An Antidote to Congress's Separation of Powers Anxiety and Executive Order 13083." *Indiana Law Journal* 75: 333–51.

Ban, Carolyn, and Patricia Ingraham, eds. "Civil Service Reform: Legislating Bureaucratic Change." In Ingraham and Ban, *Legislating Bureaucratic Change*, 1–10.

Ban, Carolyn, and Norma M. Riccucci, eds. Introduction to *Public Personnel Management: Current Concerns, Future Challenges,* 2nd ed. White Plains, NY: Longman, 1991.

Berg, Clifford L. "Lapse of Reorganization Authority." *Public Administration Review* 35, no. 2 (1975): 195–99.

Bevir, Mark. "The Westminster Model, Governance and Judicial Reform." *Parliamentary Affairs* 61, no. 4 (2008): 559–77.

Blair, Tony. *A Journey: My Political Life.* New York: Alfred A. Knopf, 2010.

Box, Richard C. "Running Government Like a Business: Implications for Public Administration Theory and Practice." *American Review of Public Administration* 29, no. 1 (1999): 19–43.

Boyne, George A. "Bureaucratic Theory Meets Reality: Public Choice and Service Contracting in U.S. Local Government." *Public Administration Review* 56, no. 6 (1998): 474–84.

————. "Public and Private Management: What's the Difference?" *Journal of Management Studies* 39, no. 1 (2002): 97–122.

Bozeman, Barry. *Management and Policy Analysis.* New York: St. Martin's, 1979.

————. *Public Values and Public Interest: Counterbalancing Economic Individualism.* Washington, DC: Georgetown University Press, 2007.

Bozeman, Barry, and Stuart Bretschneider. "The 'Publicness Puzzle' in Organization Theory: A Test of Alternative Explanations of Differences between Public and Private Organizations." *Journal of Public Administration Research and Theory* 4, no. 2 (1994): 197–223.

Brook, Douglas A., and Cynthia L. King. "Federal Personnel Management Reform: From Civil Service Reform Act to National Security Reforms." *Review of Public Personnel Administration* 28 (2008): 205–21.

Buntz, C. Gregory, and Beryl A. Radin. "Managing Intergovernmental Conflict: The Case of Human Services." *Public Administration Review* 43, no. 5 (1983): 403–10.

Burke, John P. *Bureaucratic Responsibility.* Baltimore: Johns Hopkins University Press, 1986.

Burman, Alan V. "Inherently Governmental Functions: At a Tipping Point? Should the Government Rethink Its Long-Standing Policy on Contracting Out Work?" *The Public Manager,* Spring 2008. http://findarticles.com/p/articles/mi_m0HTO/is_1_37/ai_n27964143/.

Camus, Albert. *The Myth of Sisyphus and Other Essays.* New York: Penguin, 2000.

Carpenter, Daniel. "The Revolution of National Bureaucracy in the United States." In *The Institutions of American Democracy: The Executive Branch,* edited by Joel Aberbach and Mark Peterson, 41–71. Oxford: Oxford University Press, 2005.

Carroll, James D. "The Rhetoric of Reform and Political Reality in the National Performance Review." *Public Administration Review* 55, no. 3 (1995): 302–12.

Cline, Allen Wrisque. "The Modernisation of British Government in Historical Perspective." *Parliamentary Affairs* 61, no. 1 (2008): 144–59.

Clinton, Bill, and Al Gore. *Putting Customers First '95: Standards for Serving the American People.* Washington, DC: Government Printing Office, 1995.

Cohen, Steven, and William Eimicke. *The Responsible Contract Manager: Protecting the Public Interest in an Outsourced World.* Washington, DC: Georgetown University Press, 2008.

Commission on Intergovernmental Relations. *A Report to the President for Transmittal to the Congress,* June 28, 1955.

Congressional Budget Office. *The Federal Government in a Federal System: Current Intergovernmental Programs and Options for Change; A CBO Study.* Washington, DC: Government Printing Office, 1983.

Conlan, Timothy. *From New Federalism to Devolution: Twenty-Five Years of Intergovernmental Reform.* Washington, DC: Brookings Institution Press, 1998.

Conlan, Tim, and John Dinan. "Federalism, the Bush Administration, and the Transformation of American Conservatism." *Publius* 37, no. 3 (2007): 279–303.

Conley, Richard. "Reform, Reorganization, and the Renaissance of the Managerial Presidency: The Impact of 9/11 on the Executive Establishment." *Politics and Policy* 34, no. 2 (2006): 304–42.

Cooper, Phillip J. *Governing by Contract: Challenges and Opportunities for Public Managers.* Washington, DC: CQ Press, 2003.

CRS (Congressional Research Service). *Congressional Oversight Manual.* Washington, DC: CRS, 2007.

Davidson, Joe. "A Challenge to Unions' 'Official Time' on the Federal Clock." Federal Diary, *Washington Post,* June 2, 2011.

Desmarais, Celine, and Emmanuel Abord de Chatillon. "Are There Still Differences between the Roles of Private and Public Sector Managers?" *Public Management Review* 12, no. 1 (2010): 127–49.

DiIulio, John J., Jr. "Works Better and Costs Less? Sweet and Sour Perspectives on the NPR." In Kettl and DiIulio, *Inside the Reinvention Machine,* 1–13.

DiIulio, John J., Jr., and Donald F. Kettl. *Fine Print: The Contract with America, Devolution, and the Administrative Realities of American Federalism.* Washington, DC: Brookings Institution Press, 1995.

Downs, Anthony. *An Economic View of Democracy.* New York: Harper and Row, 1957.

Downs, George W., and Patrick D. Larkey. *The Search for Government Efficiency: From Hubris to Helplessness.* New York: Random House, 1986.

Elazar, Daniel J. *The American Partnership: Intergovernmental Co-operation in the Nineteenth-Century United States.* Chicago: University of Chicago Press, 1962.

Elmore, Richard F. "Graduate Education in Public Management: Working the Seams of Government." *Journal of Policy Analysis and Management* 6, no. 1 (1986): 69–83.

Executive Office of the President. *The President's Management Agenda: Fiscal Year 2002.* Washington, DC: Office of Management and Budget, 2001.

———. *Strengthening Public Management in the Intergovernmental System: A Report Prepared for the Office of Management and Budget by the Study Committee on Policy Management Assistance.* Washington, DC: Government Printing Office, 1975.

Fenwick, John, and Janice McMillan, eds. *Public Management in the Postmodern Era: Challenges and Prospects.* Northampton, MA: Edward Elgar, 2010.

Fesler, James W. "The Brownlow Committee Fifty Years Later." *Public Administration Review* 47, no. 4 (1987): 291–96.

Fesler, James W., and Donald F. Kettl. *The Politics of the Administrative Process,* 2nd ed. Chatham, NJ: Chatham House, 1996.

Fisher, Louis. *The Politics of Shared Power: Congress and the Executive,* 4th ed. College Station: Texas A&M University Press, 1998.

Foster, Gregory D. "The 1978 Civil Service Reform Act: Post-Mortem or Rebirth?" *Public Administration Review* 39, no. 1 (1979): 78–86.

Frederickson, David G., and H. George Frederickson. *Measuring the Performance of the Hollow State.* Washington, DC: Georgetown University Press, 2007.

Frederickson, H. George. "Comparing the Reinventing Government Movement with the New Public Administration." *Public Administration Review* 56, no. 3 (1996): 263–70.

Galston, William A., and Geoffrey L. Tibbetts. "Reinventing Federalism: The Clinton/Gore Program for a New Partnership among the Federal, State, Local and Tribal Governments." *Publius: The Journal of Federalism* 24, no. 3 (1994): 23–48.

GAO (US General Accounting Office or Government Accountability Office). *Budget Process: History and Future Directions; Statement of Susan J. Irving before the Subcommittee on Legislative and Budget Process and the Subcommittee on Rules and Organization, House Committee on Rules.* T-AIMD-95-214. Washington, DC: GAO, 1995.

———. *Executive Reorganization Authority: Balancing Executive and Congressional Roles in Shaping the Federal Government's Structure; Statement of David M. Walker, Comptroller General of the United States.* GAO-03-624T. Washington, DC: GAO, 2003.

———. *Government Contractors: An Overview of the Federal Contracting-Out Program.* T-GGD-95-131. Washington, DC: GAO, 1995.

———. *Intergovernmental Policy and Fiscal Relations: Program Plan.* Washington, DC: GAO, 1978.

———. *Managing for Results: Experiences Abroad Suggest Insights for Federal Management Reforms.* GAO/GGD-95-120. Washington, DC: GAO, 1995.

———. *Performance Budgeting: Observations on the Use of OMB's Program Assessment Rating Tool for the Fiscal Year 2004 Budget.* GAO-04-174. Washington, DC: GAO, 2004.

———. *Performance Budgeting: Past Initiatives Offer Insights for GPRA Implementation.* GAO/AIMD-97-46. Washington, DC: GAO, 1997.

———. *Results-Oriented Cultures: Insight for US Agencies from Other Countries' Performance Measurement Initiatives.* GAO-02-862. Washington, DC: GAO, 2002.

Gilmour, John B., and David E. Lewis. "Assessing Performance Budgeting at OMB: The Influence of Politics, Performance, and Program Size." *Journal of Public Administration Research and Theory* 16 (2006): 169–86.

Gilmour, Robert S., and Alexis A. Halley. "Co-managing Policy and Program Development." In *Who Makes Public Policy: The Struggle for Control between Congress and the Executive,* edited by Robert S. Gilmour and Alexis A. Halley. Chatham, NJ: Chatham House, 1994.

Glaser, Barney G., and Anselm L. Strauss. *The Discovery of Grounded Theory: Strategies for Qualitative Research.* Chicago: Aldine Transaction Press, 1967.

Good, David A. "Still Budgeting by Muddling Through: Why Disjointed Incrementalism Lasts." *Policy and Society* 30, no. 1 (2011): 41–51.

Goodnow, Frank J. *Politics and Administration: A Study in Government.* New York: Russal and Russell, 1967.

Gore, Al. *Creating a Government That Works Better and Costs Less: Report of the National Performance Review.* Washington, DC: Government Printing Office, 1993.

Gruber, Judith E. *Controlling Bureaucracies: Dilemmas in Democratic Governance.* Berkeley: University of California Press, 1987.

Gueorguieva, Vassia, Jean Accius, Carmen Apaza, Lamar Bennett, Clinton Brownley, Shea Cronin, and Panote Preechyanud. "The Program Assessment Rating Tool and the Government Performance and Results Act: Evaluating Conflicts and Disconnections." *American Review of Public Administration* 39 (2009): 225–45.

Gulick, Luther. "Science, Values and Public Administration." In Gulick and Urwick, *Papers on the Science of Administration,* 191–95.

Gulick, Luther, and Al Urwick, eds. *Papers on the Science of Administration.* New York: Institute of Public Administration, Columbia University, 1937.

Halchin, L. Elaine. *The Federal Activities Inventory Reform Act and Circular A-76.* Washington, DC: Congressional Research Service, 2007.

Hamilton, Alexander, John Jay, and James Madison. *The Federalist: A Commentary on the Constitution of the United States.* New York: Modern Library, 2000.

Harmon, Michael M. "The Simon/Waldo Debate: A Review and Update." *Public Administration Quarterly* 12, no. 4 (1969): 437–51.

Heclo, Hugh. *A Government of Strangers.* Washington, DC: Brookings Institution Press, 1977.

Heniff, Bill, Jr., and Robert Keith. *Federal Budget Process Reform: A Brief Overview.* Washington, DC: Congressional Research Service, 2004.

Hirschman, Albert O. *Shifting Involvements: Private Interest and Public Action.* Princeton, NJ: Princeton University Press, 1982.

Hodge, Graeme A. *Privatization: An International Review of Performance.* Boulder, CO: Westview, 2000.

Hogwood, Brian W. "The Machinery of Government, 1979–97." *Political Studies* 45 (1997): 704–15.

Hood, Christopher. "Can We? Administrative Limits Revisited." *Public Administration Review* 70, no. 4 (2010): 527–34.

———. "A Public Management for All Seasons?" *Public Administration* 69, no. 1 (1991): 3–19.

Hood, Christopher, and Guy Peters. "The Middle Aging of New Public Management: Into the Age of Paradox." *Journal of Public Administration Research and Theory* 14, no. 3 (2004): 267–82.

Huberty, Robert M., and James L. Malone. "The Senior Executive Service." In *Mandate for Leadership: Policy Management in a Conservative Administration,* 869–902. Washington, DC: Heritage Foundation, 1981.

Ingraham, Patricia, and Carolyn Ban, eds. *Legislating Bureaucratic Change: The Civil Service Reform Act of 1978.* Albany: State University of New York Press, 1984.

Joyce, Philip G., and Roy T. Meyers. "Budgeting during the Clinton Administration." *Public Budgeting and Finance* 21, no. 1 (2001): 1–21.

Kaufman, Herbert. "Emerging Conflicts in the Doctrines of Public Administration." *American Political Science Review* 50, no. 4 (1956): 1057–73.

Kaufman, Herbert, ed. "Reflections on Administrative Reorganization." In *Setting National Priorities: The 1978 Budget,* 391–418. Washington, DC: Brookings Institution, 1977.

Keith, Robert. *CRS Report for Congress: Introduction to the Federal Budget Process.* CRS 98-721. Washington, DC: Congressional Research Service, 2008.

Kettl, Donald F. "Building Lasting Reform: Enduring Questions, Missing Answers." In Kettl and DiIulio, *Inside the Reinvention Machine,* 9–83.

———. *The Next Government of the United States.* New York: W. W. Norton, 2009.

———. *Reinventing Government? Appraising the National Performance Review; A Report of the Brookings Institution's Center for Public Management.* Washington, DC: Brookings Institution Press, 1994.

Kettl, Donald F., and John J. DiIulio Jr., eds. *Inside the Reinvention Machine: Appraising Governmental Reform.* Washington, DC: Brookings Institution Press, 1995.

Kettl, Donald F., Patricia W. Ingraham, Ronald P. Sanders, and Constance Horner. *Civil Service Reform: Building a Government That Works.* Washington, DC: Brookings Institution Press, 1996.

Khojasteh, Mak. "Motivating the Private vs. Public Sector Managers." *Public Personnel Management* 22, no. 3 (1993): 391–401.

Kohli, Jitinder. *From Setting Goals to Achieving Them: The American People's Number One Strategy to Build Confidence in Government.* Washington, DC: Center for American Progress, 2010.

Kurland, Nancy B., and Terri D. Egan. "Public v. Private Perceptions of Formalization, Outcomes and Justice." *Journal of Public Administration Research and Theory* 9, no. 3 (1999): 347–458.

Lachman, Ram. "Public and Private Sector Differences: CEOs' Perceptions of Their Role Environments." *Academy of Management Journal* 28, no. 3 (1985): 671–80.

Lawrence, Paul R., and Jay W. Lorsch. *Organization and Environment.* Homewood, IL: Richard D. Irwin, 1969.

Light, Paul C. *The Tides of Reform: Making Government Work, 1945–1995.* New Haven, CT: Yale University Press, 1997.

Lijphart, Arend. *Patterns of Democracy.* New Haven, CT: Yale University Press, 1999.

Lynn, Laurence E., Jr. "The New Public Management: How to Transform a Theme into a Legacy." *Public Administration Review* 58, no. 3 (1998): 231–37.

———. *Public Management as Art, Science and Profession.* Chatham, NJ: Chatham House, 1996.

Marone, James. *The Democratic Wish: Popular Participation and the Limits of American Government.* New York: Basic Books, 1990.

McDowell, Bruce M. "Advisory Commission on Intergovernmental Relations in 1996: The End of an Era." *Publius: The Journal of Federalism* 27, no. 2 (1997): 111–27.

Milkis, Sidney M., and Jesse H. Rhodes. "George W. Bush, the Party System, and American Federalism." *Publius: The Journal of Federalism* 37, no. 3 (2007): 478–503.

Minnow, Martha. "Outsourcing Power: How Privatizing Military Efforts Challenges Accountability, Professionalism, and Democracy." *Boston College Law Review* 46, no. 5 (2005): 989–1025.

Mosher, Frederick C, ed. "The American Setting." In *American Public Administration: Past, Present and Future,* 1–10. Tuscaloosa: University of Alabama Press, 1975.

Murdock, Clark A., and Richard W. Weitz. "Beyond Goldwater-Nichols: New Proposals for Defense Reform." *Joint Force Quarterly: Military Module* 38 (2005): 34–41.

Murphy, Thomas P. "Congress, PPBS, and Reality." *Polity* 1, no. 4 (1969): 460–78.

Murray, Michael A. "Comparing Public and Private Management: An Exploratory Essay." *Public Administration Review* 35, no. 4 (1975): 364–71.

Naff, Katherine C., and Meredith A. Newman. "Symposium: Federal Civil Service Reform; Another Legacy of 9/11?" *Review of Public Personnel Administration* 24 (2004): 191–201.

National Governors' Conference. *Federal Roadblocks to Efficient State Government.* Washington, DC: National Governors' Conference, 1977.

Newell, Elizabeth. "Management Matters: The Results Game." *Government Executive,* September 22, 2010.

Nutt, Paul C., and Robert W. Backoff. "Organizational Publicness and Its Implications for Strategic Management." *Journal of Public Administration Research and Theory* 3 (1993): 209–31.

Okun, Arthur M. *Equality and Efficiency: The Big Tradeoff.* Washington, DC: Brookings Institution Press, 1975.

OMB (Office of Management and Budget). "Performance and Management Assessments." In *Budget of the United States Government: Fiscal Year 2004,* 71–92. Washington, DC: Government Printing Office, 2003.

———. *What It Is—How It Works: A Handbook.* Circular No. A-95. Washington, DC: Government Printing Office, 1976.

Osborne, David, and Ted Gaebler. *Reinventing Government: How the Entrepreneurial Spirit Is Transforming the Public Sector.* Reading, MA: Addison-Wesley, 1991.

Osborne, Stephen P. "Delivering Public Services: Time for a New Theory?" *Public Management Review* 12, no. 1 (2010): 1–10.

Partnership for Public Service and Hay Group. "Leading Innovation in Government." 2011. www.haygroup.com/downloads/us/leading_innovation_in_government_-_a_study_with_the_partnership_for_public_service_and_hay_group.pdf.

Partnership for Public Service and Grant Thornton. *A Critical Role at a Critical Time: A Survey of Performance Improvement Officers.* April 2011. www.ourpublic service.org/OPS/publications/viewcontentdetails.php?id=160

Perry, James, and Kenneth Kraemer, eds. *Public Management: Public and Private Perspectives.* Palo Alto, CA: Mayfield, 1983.

Perry, James L., and Jone L. Pearce, "Initial Reactions to Federal Merit Pay," *Personnel Journal,* March 1983, 230, 237.

Pollitt, Christopher. "Performance Management in Practice: A Comparative Study of Executive Agencies." *Journal of Public Administration Research and Theory* 16 (2005): 25–44.

Pollitt, Christopher, and Geert Bouckaert. *Public Management Reform: A Comparative Analysis.* Oxford: Oxford University Press, 2000.

———. *Public Management Reform: A Comparative Analysis,* 2nd ed. Oxford: Oxford University Press, 2004.

Posner, Paul L. "Unfunded Mandates Reform Act: 1996 and Beyond." *Publius: The Journal of Federalism* 27, no. 2 (1997): 53–72.

Posner, Paul L. "The Continuity of Change: Public Budgeting and Finance Reforms over 70 Years." *Public Administration Review* 67, no. 6 (2007): 1018–29.

———. "Introduction to the Mini-Symposium on the Federal Budget Process: The Persistence of Reform." *Public Administration Review* 69, no. 2 (2009): 207–10.

Radin, Beryl A. *Beyond Machiavelli: Policy Analysis Comes of Age.* Washington, DC: Georgetown University Press, 2000.

———. *Challenging the Performance Movement: Accountability, Complexity, and Democratic Values.* Washington, DC: Georgetown University Press, 2006.

———. "The Government Performance and Results Act (GPRA) and the Tradition of Federal Management Reform: Square Pegs in Round Holes?" *Journal of Public Administration Research and Theory* 10, no. 1 (2000): 111–35.

———. "Performance Management and Intergovernmental Relations." In *Intergovernmental Management for the 21st Century,* edited by Paul L. Posner and Timothy Conlan, 243–63. Washington, DC: Brookings Institution, 2008.

———. "The Search for the M: Federal Management and Personnel Policy." In *The Promise and Paradox of Civil Service Reform,* edited by Patricia Ingraham and David Rosenbloom, 37–62. Pittsburgh: University of Pittsburgh Press, 1993.

————. "Varieties of Reinvention." In Kettl and DiIulio, *Inside the Reinvention Machine,* 107–30.

Radin, Beryl A., and Joshua M. Chanin, eds. *Federal Government Reorganization: A Policy and Management Perspective.* Boston: Jones and Bartlett, 2009.

Radin, Beryl A., and Willis D. Hawley. *The Politics of Federal Reorganization: Creating the U.S. Department of Education.* New York: Pergamon, 1988.

Radin, Beryl A., and Paul Posner. "Policy Tools, Mandates and Intergovernmental Relations." In *The Oxford Handbook of American Bureaucracy,* edited by Robert Davant, 447–71. Oxford: Oxford University Press, 2010.

Radin, Beryl A., et al. *New Governance for Rural America: Creating Intergovernmental Partnerships.* Lawrence: University of Kansas Press, 1996.

Rainey, Hal G., Robert W. Backoff, and Charles H. Levine. "Comparing Public and Private Organizations." *Public Administration Review* 36, no. 2 (1976): 233–44.

Rainey, Hal G., and Barry Bozeman. "Comparing Public and Private Organizations: Empirical Research and the Power of the A Priori." *Journal of Public Administration Research and Theory* 10, no. 2 (2000): 447–70.

Rainey, Hal G., Sanjay Pandey, and Barry Bozeman. "Research Note: Public and Private Managers' Perceptions of Red Tape." *Public Administration Review* 55, no. 6 (1995): 567–74.

Relyea, Harold C. "Organizing for Homeland Security." *Presidential Studies Quarterly* 33, no. 3 (2003): 602–24.

Rhodes, R. A. W., John Wanna, and Patrick Weller. *Comparing Westminster.* Oxford: Oxford University Press, 2009.

Riccucci, Norma M. *How Management Matters: Street-Level Bureaucrats and Welfare Reform.* Washington, DC: Georgetown University Press, 2005.

————. *Public Administration: Traditions of Inquiry and Philosophies of Knowledge.* Washington, DC: Georgetown University Press, 2010.

Rivlin, Alice M. *Reviving the American Dream: The Economy, the States, and the Federal Government.* Washington, DC: Brookings Institution, 1992.

Robertson, Peter J., and Sonal J. Seneviratne. "Outcomes of Planned Organizational Change in the Public Sector: A Meta-analytic Comparison to the Private Sector." *Public Administration Review* 55, no. 6 (1995): 547–58.

Romzek, Barbara S., and Melvin J. Dubnick. "Accountability in the Public Sector: Lessons from the Challenger Tragedy." *Public Administration Review* 47, no. 3 (1987): 227–38.

Rosen, Bernard. "Crises in the U.S. Civil Service." *Public Administration Review* 46, no. 3 (1986): 207–14.

Rosenbloom, David H. *Building a Legislative-Centered Public Administration: Congress and the Administrative State, 1946–1999.* Tuscaloosa: University of Alabama Press, 2000.

————. "Public Administrative Theory and the Separation of Powers." *Public Administration Review* 43, no. 3 (1983): 219–27.

Rubin, Irene. "The Great Unraveling: Federal Budgeting, 1998–2006." *Public Administration Review,* 67, no. 4 (2007): 608–17.

Salamon, Lester M., ed. *The Tools of Government: A Guide to the New Governance.* New York: Oxford University Press, 2002.

Schick, Allen. "A Death in the Bureaucracy: The Demise of Federal PPB." *Public Administration Review* 33, no. 2 (1973): 146–56.

———. "The Road to PPB: The Stages of Budget Reform." *Public Administration Review* 26, no. 4 (1966): 243–58.

Schmeckebier, Laurence F., ed. "A Brief History of Reorganization Efforts." In *Reorganization of the National Government: What Does It Involve?* 181–225. Washington, DC: Brookings Institution Press, 1939.

Seidman, Harold. *Politics, Position, and Power: The Dynamics of Federal Organization,* 5th ed. New York: Oxford University Press, 1998.

Senior Executives Association and Avue Technologies Corporation. *Taking the Helm: Attracting the Generation of Federal Leaders.* 2010. www.seniorexecs.org/tiny_mce/plugins/filemanager/files/Full_Report.pdf.

Simeon, Richard, and Beryl A. Radin. "Reflections on Comparing Federalism: Canada and the United States." *Publius* 40, no. 3 (2010): 357–65.

Simon, Herbert. "The Proverbs of Administration." *Public Administration Review* 6, no. 1 (1946): 53–67.

———. "Why Public Administration?" *Journal of Public Administration Research and Theory* 8, no. 1 (1998): 1–11.

Simon, Herbert A., Peter F. Drucker, and Dwight Waldo. "Development of Theory of Democratic Administration: Replies and Comments." *American Political Science Review* 46, no. 2 (1952): 491–503.

Skowronek, Stephen. *Building a New American State.* New York: Cambridge University Press, 1982.

Smith, Geoffrey. *Westminster Reform: Learning from Congress.* London: Trade Policy Research Centre, 1979.

Smith, Stephen, and Michael Lipsky. *Nonprofits for Hire: The Welfare State in the Age of Contracting.* Cambridge, MA: Harvard University Press, 1995.

Stanger, Allison. *One Nation under Contract: The Outsourcing of American Power and the Future of Foreign Policy.* New Haven, CT: Yale University Press, 2009.

Stark, Andrew. *Drawing the Line: Public and Private in America.* Washington, DC: Brookings Institution Press, 2010.

Talbot, Colin. "Performance in Government: The Evolving System of Performance and Evaluation Measures, Monitoring and Management in the United Kingdom." ECD Working Paper Series No. 24. Washington, DC: World Bank, 2010.

———. *Theories of Performance: Organizational and Service Improvement in the Public Sector.* Oxford: Oxford University Press, 2010.

Thompson, Frank J., and Beryl A. Radin. "Reinventing Public Personnel Management: The Winter and Gore Initiatives." In Ban and Riccucci, *Public Personnel Management,* 3–20.

Tocqueville, Alexis de. *Democracy in America.* New York: Langley, 1840.

Tomkin, Shelley Lynne. *Inside OMB: Politics and Process in the President's Budget Office.* Armonk, NY: M. E. Sharpe, 1998.

Underhill, Jack, and Ray Oman. "A Critical Review of the Sweeping Federal Civil Service Changes: The Case of the Departments of Homeland Security and Defense." *Review of Public Personnel Administration* 27 (2007): 401–20.

Verkuil, Paul R. *Outsourcing Sovereignty: Why Privatization of Government Functions Threatens Democracy and What We Can Do about It.* Cambridge: Cambridge University Press, 2007.

Walker, David B. *The Rebirth of Federalism: Slouching toward Washington,* 2nd ed. New York: Chatham House, 2000.

Warner, Mildred, and Robert Hebdon. "Local Government Restructuring: Privatization and Its Alternatives." *Journal of Policy Analysis and Management* 20, no. 2 (2001): 315–36.

West, William F. *Program Budgeting and the Performance Movement: The Elusive Quest for Efficiency in Government.* Washington, DC: Georgetown University Press, 2011.

Whitaker, Richard. "Parliament and Government, 2005–06: Reforms and Reflections." *Parliamentary Affairs* 59, no. 4 (2006): 694–702.

Wildavsky, Aaron. "A Budget for All Seasons: Why the Traditional Budget Lasts." *Public Administration Review* 38, no. 6 (1978): 501–9.

———. "The Political Economy of Efficiency: Cost-Benefit Analysis, Systems Analysis, and Program Budgeting." *Public Administration Review* 27, no. 4 (1966): 292–310.

———. *The Politics of the Budgetary Process.* Glenview, IL: Scott Foresman, 1984.

———. "Rescuing Policy Analysis from PPBS." *Public Administration Review* 29 (1969): 189–202.

Williams, Walter. *Honest Numbers and Democracy.* Washington, DC: Georgetown University Press, 1998.

Wilson, James Q. *Bureaucracy: What Government Agencies Do and Why They Do It.* New York: Basic Books, 1989.

Wright, Deil S. "The Concept of Intergovernmental Relations: Assets and Liabilities." Paper presented at the annual meeting of the American Political Science Association, New York City, September 1981.

———. *Understanding Intergovernmental Relations,* 2nd ed. Monterey, CA: Brooks/Cole, 1988.

Yeager, Frank A. "Assessing the Civil Service Reform Act's Impact on Senior Manager Work Priorities." *Public Administration Review* 47, no. 5 (1987): 417–24.

ABOUT THE AUTHOR

Beryl A. Radin is a member of the faculty at the Georgetown Public Policy Institute and a fellow of the National Academy of Public Administration. Her government service includes an assignment as a special adviser to the assistant secretary for management and budget of the US Department of Health and Human Services. She calls herself a "pracademic" because she has moved back and forth between the worlds of a practitioner and an academic.

Professor Radin has written a number of books and articles on public policy and public management issues, including *Beyond Machiavelli: Policy Analysis Comes of Age* (Georgetown University Press); *The Accountable Juggler: The Art of Leadership in a Federal Agency* (CQ Press); and *Challenging the Performance Movement: Accountability, Complexity, and Democratic Values* (Georgetown University Press). She is a past president of the Association for Public Policy Analysis and Management, former head of the public administration section of the American Political Science Association, and was editor of the *Journal of Public Administration Research and Theory* from 2000 to 2005. She received the 2009 H. George Frederickson Award for career achievement in scholarship from the Public Management Research Association and was the recipient of the 2002 Donald Stone Award given by the American Society for Public Administration's section on intergovernmental management.

INDEX